The Psychology of Wine

The Psychology of Wine

Truth and Beauty by the Glass

Evan Mitchell and Brian Mitchell

PRAEGER
An Imprint of ABC-CLIO, LLC

A B C · C L I O

Santa Barbara, California • Denver, Colorado • Oxford, England

Library of Congress Cataloging-in-Publication Data
Mitchell, Evan.
   The psychology of wine : truth and beauty by the glass / Evan Mitchell and Brian Mitchell.
      p. cm.
   Includes bibliographical references and index.
   ISBN 978-0-313-37650-4 (hard copy : alk. paper) — ISBN 978-0-313-37651-1 (ebook)
   1. Wine and wine making—Popular works. 2. Wine—Psychological aspects. I. Mitchell, Brian, 1938– II. Title.
   TP548.M665   2009
   641.2′2019—dc22
                              2009009733

13   12   11   10   9   1   2   3   4   5

This book is also available on the World Wide Web as an eBook.
Visit www.abc-clio.com for details.

ABC-CLIO, LLC
130 Cremona Drive, P.O. Box 1911
Santa Barbara, California 93116-1911

This book is printed on acid-free paper ∞

Manufactured in the United States of America

Contents

Prologue

It's white, or it's red—what more's to be said?
Well, plenty.
"A bottle of wine,"
Louis Pasteur observed,
"contains more philosophy than all the books in the world."
But how to pry into the wine and tease its insights out?
How to say what they're about?
And then . . . what does the wine tell about us?

PART I

Wine, Mind and Soul

One

Drinking Antiquity

A white to start. I asked the waiter to bring what he considered the island's best. He brought an assyrtiko, luscious mouth-filling medley of stone fruits with a finish that seemed never to end—or maybe that was just how I was feeling about the evening.

At sunset on Santorini the buildings seem impossibly white. It can leave you almost snow-blind. Only the aquamarine of distant cupolas provides a distraction of color and a kind of relief to your eyes. Looking out over the caldera, at the fire-crested waves and the inky indistinctness of the "burned islands"—this is perfection in setting. It was just such a view that was laid out before us at our chosen cliff-top restaurant. It was end of season, and we had the place, and the waiter's attentions, pretty much to ourselves.

I'd spent the day walking all over, around the fractured coastline, through ruins and into numerous vineyards I'm not sure I should have been walking through. I had a mind to drink the island's own wine, this island considered by some to be what's left of Atlantis. And, while a born skeptic, I found myself pining for the kind of wine that might encourage such mythic musings.

As we finished the first bottle our waiter returned with another, a red this time. Not a Santorini wine, this instead came from the mainland's North. He wanted to give this wine, his favorite, to us. To sit and share it with us and so share in our mood. It was a xinomavro, literally "sour black," mellow with bottle age, soft but deep, an enveloping wine. The waiter talked his passion for his country, its myths and history and its wines. Wine, he said, is a divine gift of the gods, a bounty to man, a sacred blessing and remedy for all ills.

Plato, in his *Laws*, declares wine to be "a medicine given for the purposes of securing modesty of soul and health and strength of body." Horace, that greatest of lyric poets, sees illumination in it, "Wine brings to light the hidden secrets of the soul," and instruction towards our deepest desires, for wine "teaches new means for the accomplishment of our wishes." And that canniest of heroes Odysseus, perhaps the most notable Greek of epic and legend, reflects on heartfelt fellowship, "I myself feel there is nothing more delightful than when the festive mood reigns in the hearts of people ... while the tables before them are laden with bread and meat, and a steward carries round the wine ... this, to my way of thinking, is perfection." Perfection indeed.

Wine and its drinking in company, then—truly a promoter of friendship and good will, a fosterer of hospitality, of custom and civilization itself as it has come to us. These were the things we talked of as we looked out over Homer's "wine-dark sea." It seemed as though we were drinking antiquity.

(Only one of the authors was present on this evening in Santorini. The other sincerely wishes he had been.)

Two

The God of Wine

You'd expect the god of wine to be set apart by the manner of his birth. And so he is.

His mortal mother, Semele, was daughter of Cadmus, the founder of Thebes. Robert Callasso, in his magical encapsulation of classical myth, *The Marriage of Cadmus and Harmony*, renders Semele's seduction thus:

> Zeus stretched out on Semele's bed ... a young man with vine shoots in his curls. Finally he settled into that most perfect of shapes: the serpent. Zeus prolonged their union like some story without end, a rehearsal of the life of the god about to be generated ... Now the snake was pressing his mouth against Semele's mouth, a dribble of nectar trickling down onto her lips intoxicated her, and all the while the vine leaves were sprouting up on the bed ... The earth laughed. Dionysus was conceived.

The ever-jealous Hera, wife of Zeus, deceived Semele into demanding that her immortal lover reveal himself to her in all his Olympian glory—a sight that extinguished her life. Zeus plucked the child from the dead mother's womb, and took the fetus into his own form. (He was placed inside Zeus' thigh in the G-certificate version. In the X-rated, he was sewn up into a part of his father's anatomy that had the young god later in life called *Enorches*—literally "among the testicles," or, if you like, "with balls.") The infant god emerged when his gestation was ripe. Hence *Dionysus*, "twice born." With mortal mother and immortal sire he had, so to speak, a foot in each camp and so could bestow on humankind the nectar of the gods.

A strange birth, then, and an even stranger life for the god of plenty, abundance, ecstasy, and indulgence. He was perhaps the most human of all the gods. Worshipped in the intoxicated revelry of the Dionysian rites, later the Roman Bacchanalia, in *enthousiasmas*, "divine possession." This glorious abandon in bibacity ensured a devotion in his followers more intense and cult-like—in every sense of the word, ancient and modern—than that enjoyed by any other deity. And, equally, inspired fear in those who believed that such excesses would inevitably lead to a breakdown of sober social order. Dionysus had one such, his cousin Pentheus, torn to pieces by the women of his own family, displaying an intemperate temper that is the dark side of his boon to mankind. This episode provides the subject for Euripides' celebrated play, *The Bacchae*.

Dionysus was a paradoxical and problematic patron. Through his cultivation of the soil he was celebrated as the bestower of civilization. But we can only imagine that charge over nature, fertility, agriculture, wine-making, inebriation, orgiastic celebration, and law and civic order fit uncomfortably within a single divine portfolio. Dionysus was also patron of the theatre, and much of life's best theatre—comedy and tragedy, romance, satire, farce, and burlesque—is played out every day and night by ordinary folk, not actors, inspired by their imbibing of all manner of different wines.

Because of the worst of his press, the *Dionysian* nature subsequently became one side of a widely used philosophical dichotomy, in opposition to the *Apollonian*. Apollo was also a son of Zeus and god of the sun, of prophecy and poetry, of healing, and of purification. He represents light and reason, then, contending with our urges towards darkness, disorder, disarray, and dissolution. (Callasso again—"Dionysus is not a useful god who helps weave or knot things together, but a god who loosens and unties.") Logic versus passion, culture versus nature, restraint versus boundlessness—a classically Freudian opposition. This is the line taken by Norman O. Brown in his hugely influential *Life Against Death*, in the chapter, "Apollo and Dionysus." In Freudian terms Brown sees Apollo as the spirit of sublimation—by which our orgiastic urges are channeled into more acceptable expressions. "Sublimation inhibits pain by keeping experience at a distance and interposing a veil between consciousness and life," claims Brown, and later, "the Apollonian preserves, the Dionysian destroys, self-consciousness." This is a destruction Brown welcomes—on the side, as he is, of id, instinct and ecstasy unbridled by shame and restraint. In the perpetual tussle between Pleasure Principle and Reality Principle, Brown comes all out (as others have and will continue to do) for the pursuit of pleasure. This is a common misreading of Freud. He did not regret that the constraints of reality must compromise pleasure—his own life is illustrative of this, just as his own work was acknowledged by him to be a continual sublimation. As Philip Rieff points out in *Freud: The Mind of the Moralist*—"It is the 'education to reality' or what amounts to the same thing, the restriction of pleasure, that teaches freedom and at the same time sets the limits of freedom ... Far from advancing the ethical hedonism with which he is mistakenly charged, Freud in his psychology of pleasure indicates the futility of hedonism."

The conflict of Apollo and Dionysus is inevitable and inescapable—and the two gods within us must make the frequently fractured and uneasy peace that defines the human condition. So Nietzsche, in a rare display of even-handedness, saw the value of both lying in their balance. In their fusion, Dionysian madness and Apollonian reason, was the great tradition of dramatic tragedy forged. More recently Camille Paglia, in her weighty tome, *Sexual Personae*, hilariously celebrates the Dionysian with references to the *hygra physis*, the chthonic, omophagy, and *sparagmos* (in order—"liquid nature," the seething pull of the underworld, the eating of raw flesh, and the ritual tearing to pieces of a victim—yeah, we had to look them up too). Her bottom line—the god of wine was a transvestite.

It is true that Dionysus has frequently been depicted as girlish in appearance. Caravaggio's famous work shows a figure that looks like nothing so much as a somewhat-more-than-tipsy painted male prostitute. In his film *Caravaggio*, writer/director Derek Jarman has a young, debauched and debauching Caravaggio express to what extent he has embraced the god's life's theme as his own—"I built my world as divine mystery ... Found the god in the wine and took into my heart. I painted myself as Bacchus and took on his fate—a wild, orgiastic dismemberment. I raise this fragile glass and drink to you, my audience. *Man's character is his fate*." (This film was marked by the very first appearance of the translucent Tilda Swinton, who subsequently graduated from indie film muse to *Narnia* White Witch and Oscar winner.) This ambiguity of appearance was what, so Ovid tells us, had the young god abducted by pirates—their intention to use him as, then sell him as, a catamite. In this instance Dionysus decided to display the trappings of divinity, holding the boat fast with vines that encircled the oars and masts, and driving the seamen mad so that they leapt overboard, only to be turned into dolphins. Ah, that temper again—though when you're a god, clearly you can do what you like to anyone harboring unsavory intentions towards you.

Caravaggio also created this painting's debilitated twin, *The Sick Bacchus*, during, or so it's said, his convalescence from an illness exacerbated in no small part by a lifestyle of indulgent excess. Now the god's apparent youthfulness reinforces the painting's seedy rankness, complexion stained by an unseemly green taint. Art critic Simon Schama captures the work's lurid and stomach-twisting confrontation of its viewer—"It's a picture not of immortality but of its opposite: decay. With filth-rimmed nails he offers us a bunch of grapes, the bloom rendered so perfectly that we can see how far gone to rot they are. And the rot is not especially noble." Do the moods of the god of wine infect his painter, or has the painter himself usurped the god, his influences and their consequences?

A differently androgynous, though no more sober, depiction of Bacchus is by Michelangelo. It's an early sculpture, and by all accounts not a favorite among art lovers. The likes of Vasari, Ruskin, Stendhal, and Shelley have all objected to the figure's expression, variously categorizing it as "the face of vice," "lewd," "coarse and without charm," and "drunken, brutal" with an "expression of dissoluteness." Hardly the "divine possession" sought by his followers, much less the transcending sense imagined much later by Emerson—"I intoxicated / And by the draught assimilated, / May float at pleasure through all natures." (Though we just can't quite picture Ralph Waldo Emerson on a screaming bender.) In actual fact, Michelangelo has it to a tee—even down to capturing the most lifelike suggestion of the simultaneously high-stepping and leaden-footed stagger of the committed dipsomaniac. A gait equally well caught by Disney in *Fantasia*, in the Pastoral scene—personally, our first encounter with an image of Bacchus—showing a less-than-svelte, red-nosed jolly old fellow stumbling about the wine-making efforts of his attendant centaurs, sylphs, and fauns.

A god of different faces, then. Different attitudes, and different moods. So wine makes us, as it made the gods. And not just in the classical pantheon.

Way before Rome, way before the Golden Age of Pericles' Athens, it was Noah who had claims to being the world's first vigneron—according, at least, to Genesis. The first to savor wine's transporting effects, and the first to suffer its consequences—making somewhat of a spectacle of himself being "uncovered within his tent" for all to witness his naked shame (not a pretty sight when you consider that, by the Bible's own arithmetic, Noah was pushing 600 years old at that point).

Then during the ascendancy of Rome under the Caesars, and long after that when the Empire had become Christian—wine, and no other beverage, persisted as the liquid of miracles and of the sacraments.

Three

The Happiest of Happy Accidents

"No thing more excellent nor more valuable than wine," said Plato, "was ever granted mankind by God." Victor Hugo however, with the benefit of hindsight and an Enlightenment mindset, begged to differ—"God made only water, but man made wine."

A gift of providence, then, coming from above? Those who agree with Plato won't be dissuaded by us. Or was it rather an ingenious invention of man? But this would imply a creative process that almost certainly didn't occur. No, as is so often the case the truth lies somewhere in between. Wine was neither gift nor invention. It came to us by accident. Happy accident, it's true. The happiest of happy accidents.

Imagine for a moment our far distant forebears. Consider Ugg the young cave-guy—a strapping lad and, though in his teens, a mature provider for his family clan. While a dab hand at harvesting a mastodon carcass and keeping cave bears at bay, Ugg's a bit of an unreconstructed chauvinist, preferring to stick to the "hunter" side of hunter-gatherer, leaving the more back-breaking gathering work (albeit with a lower mortality rate) to the females of the clan. And that's why—on the basis of absolutely no evidence whatsoever—we believe that the first winemaker, the accidental winemaker who nevertheless brought this great boon into the world, was a woman. Let's call her Daisy. She's carried for days, maybe weeks, a badly cured animal skin bag half-filled with fruit—we'll say, for argument's sake, they're grapes. With all the banging about against Daisy's back, being dropped when the clan stops then picked roughly up again, the fruit in the bag is now a little the worse for wear. It has been squashed, crushed, pulped, and, with no shortage of wild yeasts around, wonder of wonders, fermentation has set in. One evening around the fire, Ugg notices Daisy taking a quizzical sniff at the bag. He figures, with characteristic cave-guy sensitivity, that whatever she's got, he wants. We can only imagine that Daisy would have had too fastidious a taste to actually sample the stuff herself— it can't have been the sweetest smelling nectar. But Ugg has no such olfactory and gustatory scruples. Watch him take a belt from the skin bag . . . the intent squint of connoisseur concentration crosses his ugly mug for a moment . . . another belt, and he follows that with a few descriptive grunts alerting his companions to the beverage's "pleasantly diverting feral character." The others all want to try it, but Ugg's not having any of that. He downs the lot, and sometime later his slightly unbalanced capers provide enormous entertainment to the rest of the clan. Though Ugg wakes next morning feeling poisoned, that in no way diminishes his ever-after passionately pursued attempts to replicate his state of the previous evening.

So Daisy, here's cheers. *Salute! Santé! Skaal!* And our apologies for not knowing the Neanderthal for "raise a glass."

That's all it would have taken. Then human ingenuity stepped in. It's characteristic of who we are that discovery should lead immediately to refinement of method. The inquiring and questing nature of human psychology sees invention inspire experimentation towards improvement—all the while aspiring to perfection. How, then, to make this precious new liquid all it might be?

There are anthropological theories that link "the importance of alcohol in a ritual feast" to the invention of agriculture and cultivation of crops. And agriculture resulted in arguably the most profound reshaping of how humans live. It provided the impetus for abandoning nomadic ways to embark on the next stage of our development— settlement, society and social organization, even civilization itself.

How is it that clearing and ploughing and sowing and reaping can claim to be the very basis of all advancement that followed? Because staking a land claim, and cultivating that land, forced humans to confront each other and, in doing so, confront ourselves. For the first time a society of strangers became both inevitable and necessary. According to Plato's *The Republic*, "Society originates . . . because the individual is not self-sufficient, but has many needs which he can't supply himself." Community could no longer be based solely on the deep-rooted obligations of blood. The moral philosopher Jean-Jacques Rousseau called the family unit "the most ancient of all societies, and the only one that is natural." The Romantic Rousseau saw civil society as problematic, famously stating, "Man is born free, and everywhere he is in chains," those chains forged by the demands of civilization. In contrast, the pragmatic Thomas Hobbes, of *Leviathan* fame, had preferred to focus on civilization's liberating aspects. He saw the natural state—before inclusion in the group altered personal imperatives forever—as *bellum omnium contra omnes*, the "war of all against all." "In such condition there is no place for industry, because the fruit thereof is uncertain: and consequently no culture of the earth." The peace that replaces this incessant struggle (an uneasy peace at times, it's true) must come at some cost—an unavoidable sacrifice mankind had to make was "this Right, of doing anything he liketh." The concept of competition is not entirely neutered—that would *not* accord with our natures—but is given the perspective of cooperative benefits. And so the so-called "social contract" came into being—the grafting together of rights and responsibilities for the greater good of all. It didn't happen by design, it happened without meaning to happen—an implicit agreement finding its way over time, two steps forward and one back, advancing sometimes by tradition and sometimes by necessary adaptation. While the likes of Hobbes and Rousseau could not be reconciled as to the merits of socialization, neither disputed that the social contract lies fundamentally at the heart of community, culture, and custom; of division of labor and ensuing trade; of manners, social mores and moral standards; and, in the end, of all . . . of our very governance and law.

So cultivation of the vine had as its direct and inevitable end the cultivation of ethics and our moral sense—indeed civilization itself. All this, born of the whim to give up the wanderer's life, settle down and sink some roots, then plant and tend and harvest. No wonder our old forebears felt the need for a drink.

What is *civilization*? In his mind-bogglingly comprehensive, *Ideas: A History from Fire to Freud*, Peter Watson observes, "In the classical definition, civilization consists of three or more of the following: cities, writing, the specialization of occupations, monumental architecture, the formation of capital." Let's take our pick of three, then. "Cities" arise from agriculture-based settlement. "Specialization of occupations" was expanded by the far greater abundance of vocations subsequently available, not just in tilling and tending the fields but all the affiliated occupations that grew up in support of agricultural practice and the infrastructure required for the growth of villages into towns into cities and even city-states—all towards "the formation of capital," and the increasing of the common wealth. The political and social philosopher Thomas Malthus was a controversial fellow in his day and since, though his thoughts on what constitutes civilization seem eminently sensible. A society can be considered "civilized" with the attainment of four things—responsible government, rule of law, property rights, and universal education. Still, after all that we're not sure we don't prefer the more idiosyncratic model of civilization given by the award-winning Canadian novelist Robertson Davies, from his book *The Rebel Angels* (the following words put into the mouth of a Professor of

Physiology), "Civilization rests on two things . . . the discovery that fermentation produces alcohol, and voluntary ability to inhibit defecation." Thereby aligning drunkenness with cleanliness and so, we suppose, with godliness. Dionysus himself would surely approve.

Let's head back in time one more time. Not so far back as before—in fact, many generations on. The Roman Empire of Pliny the Elder was unquestionably "civilized" by all the above-mentioned standards. Daisy's fruitful discovery has come a long way. Different grape varieties have been identified and distinguished by the type of wine they produce. Regional affinities of varieties—for specific climes and conditions—have been recognized. Pliny points out in his *Natural History* that Cato the Elder, who held through his political career the lofty offices of Tribune, Consul, and Censor of the Roman republic, wrote treatises on his beloved subject of agriculture, especially viticulture—which pastime was "an occupation of the highest merit." Cato recommends which varieties to cultivate based on soil conditions and exposure to sun or fog. Pruning and other techniques have been employed to improve yield and quality of crop. And there have been improvements, too, in wine preservation and storage—including its keeping in oak barrels and so, by yet another happy accident, the felicitous love affair of wine and oak was noticed.

And there's one other development—one that will carry no surprises for the modern wine drinker. Wine by this time was inseparable from the *quality judgments* made of it. "The wines of Aminaea are in the top category because of their body and their character, which clearly improves with age." That "wines from Pompeii are at their best within ten years and gain nothing from greater maturity" suggests not only a sophisticated evaluation of the qualities that come with maturing wine, but an expectation of even more impressive venerability in wines from other regions. Pliny even cites the wines of his own culture's earliest era, listing the most highly regarded wines of the Homeric age. We earlier observed one essential aspect of human nature—that invention will be followed by further invention to refine the original discovery, improve upon that, and produce the best possible product. But there's another inescapable fact of who we are—once discovery is made, others will make judgments as to quality. And they will then make further judgments, judgments as to the standards by which all future judgments are to be made.

It's said that the oldest profession is . . . well, since most of you know we'll spare the delicate sensibilities of those who don't (and the blushes of that first courtesan of pre-history). An equally common cliché acknowledges espionage as the second oldest profession. Though human intrigue and duplicity no doubt go back to the very beginning of things . . . still, we can't agree. The desire, the need, the inescapable urge to pass judgment on what someone else has just done—*that's* the second oldest profession.

And so the wine critic was born.

Four

What's in a Number...?

This wine's been scored at 95 points from 100. That wine at 92. Which do you choose—and is it as simple as it seems? Think about that while we talk about this ...

It's a staggering thing to contemplate—that the most powerful and influential critic in any field at any time in history is a wine critic. We're talking about more than the power to make or break, though that's no inconsiderable thing in itself. No, here is the authority and influence to recast the worldwide winescape. And no one else, in any discipline or era, has done as much to shape and reshape tastes, decry and divert traditions, as much to establish and diminish reputations, as has Robert Parker in the wine world. Through the last century, prominent critics were, if not precisely household names, then at least moderately well-known, respected, and influential outside of their specific area of expertise—Bernard Berenson, Clement Greenberg, and perhaps Robert Hughes in the visual arts; in literature the American New Critics, the British F. R. Leavis and Frank Kermode, the Atlantic-hopping T. S. Eliot, and more recently a smattering of French postmodernists. These days, however, critics are seldom recognized beyond the cognoscenti of their particular field. For better or worse, then—and which might depend on whether you prefer heft or elegance in your wines— Parker is the colossus of critics.

There's a tendency today to want to quantify everything. That's what critics do—because it's what we demand of them. If they didn't exist ... well then, we'd have to invent them. We have a fascination—bordering on obsession—with lists, desert-island-selections, ratings and rankings. A recent *Time* magazine column provided a simultaneously humorous and insightful list of "10 reasons we make/read lists." The two most apt—or at least the two that most took our fancy—were "because the other guy is a moron" and "because we crave justice." Taken together, these two have the appeal of appearing on the one hand entirely irreconcilable and on the other perfectly complementary. Browsing at random through recent editions of some of the world's most prestigious wine publications, we see "Napa's 50 Best Cabernets—and 20 Rising Stars," "250 Top Value Picks," "Australia's Best Wines—More Than 200 at 90+," "Best Restaurant Wine Lists," "Cabernet Sauvignon Master Class—Greatest From Bordeaux, Napa, Chile, Washington, Italy," "Best of New Zealand's Exciting Pinot Noirs" (or should that be pinots noir?). You get the picture.

And we can't seem to get enough of this. We're drawn to see, in the light of the judgment of others—and expert others at that—which wines we recognize and which we don't, those we've had and enjoyed and those we've had and didn't, those we haven't/wouldn't/couldn't/won't, those we can afford (contented sigh), and those we clearly can't (sigh of an altogether different kind).

The compiler of a list—or the awarder of a score—is asserting their authority in this particular sphere of knowledge or experience. The reader of said list or rating acknowledges that authority and, furthermore, is hoping that some small part of the accompanying expertise will rub off on them. Ratings and rankings, then, are all about authority—who has it, how much they have, and how the rest of us can begin to share in the fruits.

One of the most significant influences of wine commentators is in defining and expanding *the language of wine* (about which, much more later). In *The Meaning of "Meaning,"* Hilary Putnam, philosopher of science, mind and language, speculates on a linguistic division of labor analogous to Adam Smith's economic division of labor—"to make a smaller quantity of labor produce a greater quantity of work," hence *specialization*, the cornerstone of every critic's efforts. The meanings of words in a specific field are determined and arbitrated by the experts of that field. In what area could this be more the case than in the wine world—where not just technical terminology but the senses of similes and metaphors are, to a large extent, standardized. The experts make the language that makes sense of wine; we make use of that language to make our preferences understood; and everyone drinks what makes them all happy.

There are, it's true, different channels of wine authority—winemaker, wine writer, sommelier, fine wine merchant—each of these relaying the language of wine, and the meaning of that language, to the broader wine drinking public. Their emphases might be different, according to context. They might articulate themselves differently in different situations, according to how they perceive the needs of their customer/listener/reader. But what emerges is a prescribed lexicon that can be at its best descriptively illuminating and at its worst a marginalizing jargon. It's in their charge, then—all those with perceived wine expertise—the language of wine, and whether and how well the rest of us speak and understand it. Whether we're all speaking the same language, so to speak. "'Not speaking the same language' is a virtual synonym for incommensurability," says cognitive psychologist Steven Pinker in his classic, *The Language Instinct*. He goes on to close the book with the following observation, "Knowing about the ubiquity of complex language across individuals and cultures and the single mental design underlying them all, no speech seems foreign to me, even when I cannot understand a word." Fair claim to make for such an expert in the field. As to the rest of us, when wine language is at its worst, its most extreme, its most dismayingly abstruse and bamboozling, then even when it's spoken in English to the English speaker, *Deutsch* to the German, *Français* to the French, and *Español* to the Spanish . . . it's still more likely to be all Greek to all.

We feel particularly inclined to seek out the recommendations of experts when our choice, and the statement we wish to make with it, is important to us. And furthermore, when acquiring that degree of extensive expertise ourselves would be excessively onerous or time-consuming. It's sobering to consider what's required in being able to claim legitimate expertise, let alone "mastery" in the area of wine (and before we go on, neither of your authors claims anything of the sort for ourselves—only a keen appreciation and a fascination in our relationship with wine):

- a grasp of the relevant history, going back to pre-classical times, followed by Europe's rise and then on to the emergence of the New World;
- geography, geology, climatology, and earth sciences;
- appreciation of the ineffable essence of *terroir*;
- not to ignore agriculture and viticulture;
- especially not overlooking a plethora of winemaking techniques and philosophies;
- not leaving out chemistry and bio-sciences;
- or forgetting laws, as they apply to the world's various appellation systems;
- then there's a keen aesthetic sense (something that some say can't be taught, or even learned, but is innate—or not);
- a finely honed taste;

- this last matched by a generous and genuine capacity to evaluate merits objectively, even when that style of wine is not that particular taster's personal cup of DRC;

- a voluminous memory for varieties, styles and vintages, even label-defining quirks, shortcomings or idiosyncrasies;

- and, finally, to ensure that your tasting will always be made in context, an alert and interpretive palate memory.

The ex-sommelier among us had this brought home to him in a way that was truly humbling . . .

After 5 or so years as a keen student of wine I was feeling pretty cocky in my knowledge:

- I felt I had Oz wines down to a tee, especially as I'd done my damnedest to get my head around the prevailing varieties and styles of remoter and less prominent regions;

- Bordeaux's a cinch; it's a grid, vintages along one axis, châteaux in descending order of 1855 classification along the other (okay, that won't fly with the Right Bank wines, but there's still an order and a method to their madness);

- Champagne's all about house styles and great years;

- what Aussie-shiraz-devotee wouldn't warm to the Rhône, especially as Australian shirazes are not all, as frequently believed, alcoholic monsters of mouth-blackening extraction—there's the verging-on-Burgundy style of the Hunter Valley and the pepper-and-spicy cool climate styles of Victoria;

- Burgundy's a mess—nobody really understands it, just uncover your style (for me that's Chablis for white and Chambolle-Musigny and Volnay for red) and then be prepared to spend a fortune in trial and error;

- Alsace is aromatics;

- ditto Germany, especially riesling—they even provide a hierarchical rating system for their wines of greatest distinction, *kabinett, spätlese, auslese, beerenauslese, eiswein, trockenbeerenauslese* (fair enough, it's not as easy as it looks . . . and, fair enough again, on second glance it doesn't even look easy);

- had some mnemonic I don't even remember now for remembering Italy's regions and varieties (Though, giving memory a bit of a squeeze, the final lines, or something like them, just popped back into consciousness—"for a slightly cheesy vino / try Sardegna's vermentino." That's "cheesy" as in hints of parmesan, not as in game show hosts. Now, don't let that put you off the whites of Sardinia. After all, it'd be a boring old world if all the Old World wines were cleaned up of their distinctive Old World quirks. Besides which, there's volumes to be said for a wine that takes you three glasses to decide whether you find it compelling or repellent.);

- South Africa is pinotage, that's all you need to know (clearly that's not so, and even less the case now as then—but novelty does have its undeniable draw); and, finally,

- moving on to get my head around the United States and I'm just about done ...

Well, you're never done, and that's no bad thing. Not even close to being done. I went one night to dinner with a colleague whose palate and knowledge I esteemed, and for good reason. He pulled out a Château Musar. In my ignorance I hadn't even heard of it, thought it was some obscure claret I'd never come across before. In my defense, the label design could be said to encourage that conclusion—and this was 20 years or so ago. Lebanon, of all places! Didn't even know they made wine there (only from biblical days, you donut). The wine was a revelation, in more ways than one. First of all, it was an exquisite drink—quite unlike anything I'd tasted. (Its creator, Serge Hochar, was Decanter Man of the Year in 1984, a year in which, through regional conflict, no vintage was able to be made.) There was, to be honest, just a touch of volatile acidity, though that has since become, to my palate at least, a defining and endearing attribute of the wine. "What's the blend?" I asked. As I received my answer, that was when it occurred to me—that to lay claim to a genuinely extensive knowledge, it's not enough to have tasted Musar, or any other wine for that matter. Even that tiny and remote corner of knowledge needs continually to be built on—topped up, as it were—down to each vintage's relative proportions of cinsault, cab sav and carignan, a little syrah some years. And more rarely still, but there all the same in some vintages, a hint of merlot, and perhaps some mourvèdre. The wine world is—in its every nook and cranny, in the sub-regions of sub-regions cultivating new taste experiences out of left field varieties—our wine world is so dynamic. So true mastery becomes a feat prodigious.

While impatience is excusable in youth, it's also enduring proof of that old chestnut that youth is wasted on the young. When you're starting out, it's mastery you're after—mastery, often for its own sake, as an accomplishment, wanted *now*. With greater age (or so we'd like to claim) comes greater patience (and creakier joints), and what matters more is the unfolding of genuine pleasure stretching out before you, never to end since new experience will never be exhausted. In those early days you can feel yourself in some respects *resenting* those varieties and styles that confound the neat compartments your tasting experience has been constructing. (As a student of art in schooldays, one of us went so far as to feel *betrayed* by Mondrian, on discovery that his earlier paintings—especially his romantically rendered foliage—did not fit squarely with the later iconic style of black lines and white and primary colored rectangles.) Later on, however, those are the wines that can carry the greatest appeal. Every atypical example, every wine that surprises, these release you from the need to feel you must know everything. They allow you to become instead a collector of experiences.

Tove Jannson is one of the greatest ever writers for children—in fact, at least one of us is convinced she's a more profound existentialist than Gide or Camus. In the first book of her famous Moomin series there is a character, the Hemulen, whose obsession is philately. He is encountered by Moomintroll one day in a state of melancholy. The unthinkable has happened, as he had so wanted, but now laments—"I have them all: every single one. My stamp collection is complete. There is nothing missing ... It's finished. There isn't a stamp or an error that I haven't collected. Not one. What shall I do now?" What indeed? As Moomintroll insightfully observes, "You aren't a collector any more, you're only an owner, and that isn't nearly so much fun." And so too for wine. Being the repository of *all* vinous knowledge might be impossible (though to speak to certain self-styled experts you'd never know it), but to many it would be eminently desirable. To us, however, the price you'd have to pay for that—the loss of whimsy, astonishment and occasional awe—would be vertiginously steep.

It has, for instance, been with high delight that we have encountered, over just the last year, no less than three styles and varieties previously entirely unknown to us. First of all, the proud tradition of quality sparkling wine produced in England. Who'da thunk it? Next, a floral, almost eye-wateringly perfumy New World example of the Italian variety fiano, famed in ancient Rome. And finally an exquisite sticky picolit, another grape celebrated in classical times but extremely rare today—given, apparently, to its genetic tendency to floral abortion, failure to fruit after flowering. May such surprises never cease.

Still, there must be experts, and they must be well informed. You can understand how Parker can feel the need to taste ten thousand wines a year—an ever-expanding range of new wines must be tasted, and many previous vintages of other wines assessed in their development. We'll write that as a number—10,000—just so those zeros can hit you with a sense of the scope of that kind of tasting. That's an average of 30 or so a day, day after day after day, rain, hail or shine, in sickness and in health. If that thought doesn't stagger you, try it for just two days in a row. Some days he'll taste as many as 100 wines. One hundred to be swirled, sipped and spat—twice. Plenty of other wine writers take on efforts similarly Herculean—or should that be Sisyphean? The necessary professional demands placed on the wine expert are not, for us, something to be envied. They must sacrifice a good deal of the simplicity of wine drinking pleasure—what the rest of us can savor with every sip we take, and should never take for granted. We amateur drinkers have the luxury of being wine sensualists in a way that wine professionals can no longer be. That is, it's true, their choice. But it is also, we can't help but feel, their loss. Or perhaps we'd do better to call it their sacrifice, made for the enjoyment of all the rest of us.

However much we rely on the judgment of wine critics, in spite of this (or perhaps because of it) many people feel less than fondly towards them. Is there another occupation (well, besides politician) towards which people take a greater delight in seeing supposed expertise skewered? A case in point is the worldwide response to an empirical paper of 2001 by Frédérick Brochet towards a doctorate in enology, with the unpresupposing title, "Chemical Object Representation in the Field of Consciousness."

In brief ... A white and a red wine were served up to be described by the participating subjects. Days later the same group was served the same white and another white wine colored red by the addition of a neutral, odorless food dye. At the second stage, the entire group described the characteristics of the red-colored white wine by typical red wine descriptive terms. In the experiment following, the same red Bordeaux was served to a group under two different labels—one far more prestigious than the other. Told that they would be sampling an ordinary table wine against a great wine, the group's responses reflected the differences they *thought* they ought to taste.

These results are hardly surprising, in the light of the psychological phenomenon of confirmation bias, by which we make interpretations on the basis of what confirms our preconceptions, and ignore those details that do not seem to fit. What was, however, surprising, is where this all went next, once word of these results got out. What followed was a technologically tooled-up kind of gossip. Spreading across the internet, the results were reported more and more breathlessly with greater embellishment and fabrication. Chief among those was that the experimental "subjects," never described by any other term by Brochet, overnight became "wine experts." This "fact" has since achieved a kind of urban myth emphaticness. What high delight! What *schadenfreude*! The emperor is buck motherless naked, with shame hanging out for all to see. Why is it that people so want to see wine critics humbled (or entirely discredited), that they will hyperbolize a perceptual experiment's findings? And why *wine* critics in particular? We couldn't conceive of a similar thing occurring in any other field. Is it because wine critics can make people feel insecure, even inferior, in a unique and specific way? What's more, in a way to which we are extremely sensitive, concerning as it does not just our taste (what flavors we respond to positively), but our taste with a capital 'T' (our discernment, style and so our sophistication).

And it's not just from their public that critics can cop a caning. Some of their own feel the need to flay their own calling. Not so long ago, no less a luminary than Jancis Robinson described wine critics as "parasitical" on the industry. She is, besides our own personal favorite to read, the editor of the *Oxford Companion to Wine*, and *Decanter's* Woman of the Year in 1999. (Given the unpleasant resonances of the word "parasite," many in that line will perhaps take scant comfort in the fact that a multitude of parasites work in symbiosis with their hosts, to mutual advantage. On the other hand, being described as parasites might seem a kind of faint praise in comparison with the Irish writer Brendan Behan's assessment—"Critics are like eunuchs in a harem; they know how it is done, they've seen it done every day, but they're unable to do it themselves.") We're convinced of the sincerity of those sentiments, coming from such an industry eminence, whom we don't for a moment imagine was exempting herself from her own criticism. Words of that nature are spoken to redress an imbalance—in power, in influence and in reach of voice. In fact, Robinson is in elevated company, there having been no shortage of high cultural commentators who have savaged the role of the critic—many if not most of whom had sidelines in criticism themselves. Coleridge, for instance—whose own magnum opus, *Biographia Literaria*, was a work of lit crit—held that those who had tried and failed in an endeavor, "therefore they turn critics." The German poet Rainer Maria Rilke also wrote a superior kind of criticism—of Rodin's sculptures in particular, having worked previously as his secretary. His most damning judgment, that little enlightenment is likely to be found in criticism—"Works of art are of an infinite solitariness, and nothing is less likely to bring us near to them than criticism."

While admirers of Rilke, we don't feel that the criticism situation is quite as bleak as all that. But reflection in this direction does beg the question—*What is criticism supposed to be*? Not a science, that's a certainty. Its results are not independently replicable. But then, it has never pretended to be anything of the sort, which is why those who dismiss wine judging on those grounds—failure in replication of results—are limbering up for the wrong fight. Marx thought criticism so fundamental a right, pursuit and pastime that he famously ranked it with satisfying the needs of our own sustenance—"to hunt in the morning, fish in the afternoon, rear cattle in the evening, criticize after dinner." Perhaps it was wine criticism he felt the urge to indulge in with his belly full. His parents owned vineyards in Germany's celebrated Ruwer Valley (and neighboring vineyards still produce a "Karl Marx Spätburgunder"—German pinot noir—with the bearded one himself gracing the label, raising a better-than-decent-sized glass for a sip). At university he joined a wine society, eventually becoming its president. And it's said that his initial interest in economics was piqued by the financial straits of the Mosel vintners, due to punitive duty regulations. At any rate, the status he accorded criticism is evidence of its importance as a form of self-expression. It is not an art—though at its very best it sits comfortably in such company.

Or might criticism be an art itself after all? In his essay "The Critic as Artist" Oscar Wilde uses a dialogue between two effete aesthetes to

work through his own personal views. The two voices give Wilde
license to express the internal inconsistencies of his own thoughts on
critics and criticism. The character of Ernest believes it self-evident that
"the creative faculty is higher than the critical." Gilbert parries with,
"no one who does not possess the critical faculty can create anything
at all." Ernest remains unconvinced of Gilbert's point, and the status of
critics—"But, surely, the higher you place the creative artist, the lower
must the critic rank." Gilbert, for his part, believes that the best criticism enthuses and reenergizes a discipline, for it is "the critical faculty
that invents fresh forms." (This, we think, has truth to it—the best criticism can kick-start new ways of seeing and doing.) The tendency of
creation, on the other hand, "is to repeat itself." Wilde goes on to use
the metaphor of wine to advocate for critics a light touch and a desirable degree of impetuousness—"to know the vintage and quality of a
wine one need not drink the whole cask." In fact, a good many books,
films, and works of art could be easily evaluated on the basis of a metaphorical sip (perhaps a methodology for the wine scribes to impart to
their fellow critics). Criticism, we go on to find, is by its mere existence
a statement of something's worth—anything that draws no reflective
commentary "should be left to the oblivion that it deserves."

Despite the fact that it's pure, unbridled Wilde, we're not convinced
by Gilbert's assertion that it's "more difficult to talk about a thing than
to do it," and doubt that too many winemakers would be sympathetic
to the notion. This dialectical exchange continues, sustained appropriately by a bottle of Chambertin, until it reaches Wilde's final evaluation
of the art of evaluation—"It is Criticism that, recognizing no position
as final, and refusing to bind itself by the shallow shibboleths of any
sect or school [*Whoa, there, Oscar*], creates the serene philosophic temper which loves truth for its own sake, and loves it not the less because
it knows it to be unattainable." This last point might give pause to critics inclined to award a perfect score in the face of a seemingly faultless
wine—but take heart, that Oscar himself describes the Chambertin as
"perfect."

Criticism is then, in the end of it all, itself. When pursued with dedication and application, and genuine consideration of the reader's
needs, it is a valuable contribution to a discipline's ongoing dialogue.
When not, well, just one more undeserving waste of space.

It's possible even to feel some sympathy towards wine critics, especially when you consider that they, by their own choice, burden themselves with an impediment that would be unheard of in any other
critical practice. They taste *blind*. That's not to describe their likely state
after tasting their way through a hundred wines (though we're no fans
of spitting ourselves). No, they deny themselves the knowledge of
what they're tasting as they're tasting it. Do they feel, like Oscar Wilde,
that "ignorance is like a delicate exotic fruit," and may therefore

complement the primary characteristics of the wine? Or are they forti-
fying their endeavors via the Orwellian maxim "Ignorance is
Strength"? Are they perhaps, with the Italian founding father of crimi-
nology, Cesare Lombroso, aspiring to enhance their enjoyment of the
wine under scrutiny, since "the ignorant man always loves what he
cannot understand"? What music critic would attend a concert to be
reviewed, in absolute ignorance of the program? What book reviewer
would have a colleague destroy the dust jacket, obliterate the frontis-
piece, title page, and any other distinguishing references so it might be
read and commentary written while oblivious to any authorial details?
Tasting integrity is the reason given by wine critics and reviewers.
And certainly the best of them take seriously the financial implications
of their assessment and the responsibility that brings (for an unknown
wine scored highly or, horror of horrors, a wine of first rank given a
third rate score). The notion is that they will be freed from the influence of their own preconceptions, and allot a score that is pure and
without prejudice. That might well be the case for those with the most
rarefied palates (and we'll ignore the question as to whether so rarefied
a frame of reference actually puts such judges out of the league of
instructing Joe Public on what tastes good). The more typically human
response, however, would be to scrutinize one's own base of knowledge as the wine being tasted is itself being scrutinized. Or to put it
another way, it would take a dedicated and single-minded taster to
ignore the insistent urgings of "What is it?" and attend only to the
question "What's it like?"

The connoisseur/critic/expert is an ever more ubiquitous phenomenon in our world today. There's one, and often many more than that,
for every season and reason. What we're all best off doing is making
use of the opinions of those wine writers whose palates seem most
complementary to our own. Use those opinions to broaden your own
exposure and experience, finding out—whether it's lauded or lam-
basted, fashionable or far from it—*what you most like to drink*. While we
find these further words of Rilke inspiring, "let your judgments have
their own quiet, undisturbed development," said development might
proceed in a more orderly fashion with the right advice from a sympathetic source. What's interesting is that it seems to be the most widely
recognized and renowned wine writers who are most inclined to
acknowledge the primacy of their audience's own tastes. Witness Robert Parker, "There can never be any substitute for your own palate"
and Hugh Johnson, "The best judge of the right styles of wine for your
palate is you" channeling the wisdom of the ancients as laid down by
Pliny the Elder: "The best kind of wine is that which is most pleasant
to him who drinks it." These kinds of critics have a confidence in their
own place in the scheme of things, and, therefore, feel no need to play
the partisan or proselytizer, at least as far as their readers are

concerned (some winemakers may well hum a different tune). Anyway, in our experience, you're more likely to find that it's the critics on the lower rungs of public notice who tend to put on the airs and graces of *ex cathedra* infallibility.

When relating a critic's judgment to consideration of your own taste, it's well to go beyond the numerical scores they give. Whether it's the overwhelmingly popular 100-point system (which is really a 50-point system, since just being able to be loosely described as wine secures a score of 50, and for all intents and purposes becomes a 20-point system, since anything scoring below 80 just isn't going to fly, at least by anyone who read *that* review), the "3 for color, 7 for nose, 10 for palate" system more frequently used in show judging, or the translation of a score out of 20 into a 5-star system (which, since half-points are frequently given, is more often than not a 10-point system) ... *no number can capture the nuance of a wine*. The experts know that, and for that reason they provide far more informative tasting notes—more's the pity that these are so often ignored for the quick-fix numerical snapshot. It's in these descriptions that you'll find the truer measure of a wine, and how it's likely to stack up as what you like, or not. It's a shame today that scores rule the way they do. Taking wine instruction "by the numbers," so to speak, is a dry and didactic kind of learning. There's little soul in it. Taking wine instruction rather from an expert's detailed tasting notes is akin to the method of the Socratic dialogues, the "maieutic" method of teaching, described by the philosopher Simon Blackburn as "the method of the midwife, merely assisting [them] to give birth to their own understanding." That is, we can't help thinking, a nice notion. Wine lovers pregnant with the sense of what they love, only requiring trained ministrations to bring forth their fullest imbibing pleasure. And midwifery, it seems, is an image that recommends itself to wine. Leon Kass, in *The Hungry Soul*, ponders how as "a psychic midwife, wine delivers us of hidden insights and affections." Since wine drinkers are all consenting adults with at least some of their own opinions and preferences, a form of wine instruction that plays to these, uses existing tastes as its basis, is not only likely to be more informative but, more importantly, more involving and more fun as well. Still, scores will endure because most people would riot if they were taken away. Well, perhaps not riot, but they would abandon in droves those publications that so dared, until a new breed of number-crunchers arose to fill the vacuum that nature abhors.

So there's still good reason for appreciating the efforts of wine experts, whatever their own motivations might happen to be. David Hume was, in his essay, "Of the Standard of Taste," inclined to think well, if a touch *too* benevolently, of the good taste and efforts of critics—"Strong sense, united to delicate sentiment, improved by practice, perfected by comparison, and cleared of all prejudice, can alone entitle critics to this valuable character; and the joint verdict of such, wherever they are to be found, is the true standard of taste and beauty." (In fact, Hume was such a skeptic of subjectivity that he took the "eye of the beholder" thing to its extreme, and opined that "to seek the real beauty ... is as fruitless an inquiry, as to pretend to ascertain the real sweet or bitter"—so it must be left to the expertise of critics to determine for us that desirable quality of sweetness in a Cinque Terre Sciacchetrà, or the slightly bitter-almond tang of a corvina-dominant Valpolicella.) But hold on a moment—we noticed that bit about "joint verdict" too. Joint verdicts aren't always forthcoming in the opinions of different wine critics concerning the same wines. (Admirers as both of us are of the great fantasy writer, Ursula Le Guin, we can't help but think of the solemn saying in her kingdom of Earthsea—"Infinite are the arguments of mages.") Still, that's hardly surprising in so subjective a sense as taste and, we suppose, the very reason Hume called for consensus as the true standard. And yet we still see plenty of examples of non-consensus, even when wines are judged in the ideal conditions of "a perfect serenity of mind, a recollection of thought, a due attention to the object." Even when all the critics are blessed with those characteristics of preferred discernment, "delicacy of imagination;" "delicacy of taste;" "quick and acute perception;" and, indeed, sport "organs" of taste "so fine as to allow nothing to escape them, and at the same time so exact as to perceive every ingredient in the composition." A tall order, you'd have to say. Moreover—and more's the better—it follows that if even the experts don't always agree then the pressure's off the rest of us. Infinite are the advantages of having experts.

With or without the assistance of experts, the rest of us are continually giving our own ratings of wine. Every time we purchase a single wine from among the array on display at a fine wine store, or make our choice of bottle from a restaurant's extensive list, or recommend a wine to a friend, we're applying our own rating. And if these tend to be qualitative and personal, a mixture of what we've heard or found from experience or read on a label, who's to say that's not as sound a basis as any for judgment? Such a rating in some ways carries more weight than any other, for we're saying *this* is what I choose to drink now, or what my friends should drink, over everything else that's available, or at least feasible. That's got to beat a gold medal hands down.

In choosing a wine, you're making a statement on that wine. And the wine is also making a statement on you. In *Distinctions: A Social Critique of the Judgment of Taste*, sociologist Pierre Bourdieu defines taste as "a practical mastery of distributions which makes it possible to sense or intuit what is likely (or unlikely) to befall ... an individual occupying a given position in social space." Taste then, and the statements made through its declaration, "functions as a sort of social orientation, a 'sense of one's place,' guiding the occupants of a given place in social space towards the social positions adjusted to their properties." Statements are made by alignment to one side or the other of a range of binary oppositions:

> between high (sublime, elevated, pure) and low (vulgar, low, modest), spiritual and material, fine (refined, elegant) and coarse (heavy, fat, crude, brutal), light (subtle, lively, sharp, adroit) and heavy (slow, thick, blunt, laborious, clumsy), free and forced, broad and narrow, or, in another dimension, between unique (rare, different, distinguished, exclusive, exceptional, singular, novel) and common (ordinary, banal, commonplace, trivial, routine).

While the making of statements with wine frequently possesses the impetus of elitism, that's a truly difficult thing to escape with any aesthetic judgments. Bourdieu's censure aside, people often intend the statement they're making with a particular choice of wine to reflect what they genuinely believe to be singular about their own taste. Choice becomes a kind of public self-expression. Okay, one benefit of ratings, and a psychologically appealing aspect, is that they allow us to bathe a little in the wine's own cachet:

- "Wine of the century, some experts say ... "handing the host a bottle of '61 Palmer (at least, we wish we had guests like that);
- "99 points/international trophy/5 stars ... "to your companions as you order a bottle from the restaurant's list; or
- "Prized for its rarity and cult status ... "when giving a (rather extravagant and intended-to-impress) gift.

There are, however, reasons for making a statement that go well beyond self-aggrandizement. The urge to ennoble an experience by sharing it is a legitimate and sincere statement made through a particular choice of wine. It casts distinction on the recipient of that generosity, and humility on its giver.

Wine is now an international multi-multi-billion dollar industry—not just in wine produced but in wine publications, auctions, courses, merchandising, and wine tourism. Scores and ratings play a major part in driving it, and that particular clock is never going to be turned back.

But imagine for a moment if it was ...

The late lamented Australian wine writer and iconoclast, Mark Shield, was no fan of numerical wine ratings. He suggested an alternative approach—a system of evaluating wine by comparison to music. The music that the wine most resembles, or the music it makes you wish you were listening to. Seriously ... or, at least, he wasn't being entirely tongue-in-cheek.

So, is that wine—whatever you're drinking, or thinking of drinking or remembering drinking—is that wine a symphony or suite, sonata or cantata, fantasia or fugue, blues, jazz, rock ballad, electronica, or even metal?

We once tasted in sequence one evening: a Michel Lafarge Volnay that was every bit the first movement of Beethoven's Sixth (peeping shyly at first from the glass, before tumbling out with all the freshness, vitality and joy of Spring); a Louis Jadot Gevrey-Chambertin Clos St. Jacques that was the last movement of his Ninth (very much an *Ode to Joy*, but Joy's deeper tones, approaching awe); a Beaux Frères from Oregon showing both the grandeur and bombast of Berlioz's *Requiem*; and a Felton Road pinot from Central Otago (New Zealand), that was pure Philip Glass (hypnotically insistent, or maybe insistently hypnotic).

A Joh. Jos. Prüm Eiswein brought to mind the Cocteau Twins' *Treasure*—all the delicacy and crystal fragility of Liz Fraser's voice, with deceptive depths and texture.

Gershwin's "Summertime" says open up a bottle of Beaujolais to ward off this heat. Not so cold that it'll dumb the wine down. Just the faintest skein of condensation on the bottle, sitting ready to be opened under the shade. No Nouveau, either, nothing so flippant or breezy. What's wanted is something more solid and circumspect—a Moulin-à-Vent or Morgon—more in sync with the song's languidness. On the other hand, the distinctly American *Rhapsody in Blue* wants a distinctly American vinous reference—a zinfandel, what else, (a full red, thanks, not that pink piss) with obvious berry fruit to pick up the more playful piano sequences and a long complexity beneath to mirror the blue notes.

Dylan's "A Hard Rain's a-Gonna Fall" is a rustic red with coarse notes that grows on you as you drink more and see how the whole hangs together—a Montepulciano d'Abbruzzo, perhaps. Bryan Ferry's cover, on the other hand—slicker, sexier, and certainly more melodious—is a decidedly modern wine, perhaps somewhat over-produced and losing some fundamental appeal in that.

Cabernet sauvignon is grape royalty. Nevertheless, there are continual attempts to erode its throne—from fashionable upstart varieties and blends and flash-in-the-pan faddish regions and styles. Still, cabernet persists, never failing to display its true class. Sinatra, then.

Such a rating system is, it's true, decidedly idiosyncratic. Don't look for it anytime soon in a wine journal near you. It is, however, a thoughtful and thought-provoking approach. Maybe much more so than appending a numerical score. More considered and personal and resonant also, and more likely to inspire the kind of debate and dialogue worthy of the wine being consumed.

Before we adjourn, let's return to our opening question. Which would you choose between the wine scored at 95 and one scored 92?

What if you were equally ignorant of each? What if you knew from experience that the 95 wasn't your style of wine? Then again, would it be harder or easier to choose if there were only a 1-point difference between them? What if that 1-point difference was between a score of 90 and one of 89? Surely that's a more emphatic difference than between 90 and 91, or 88 and 89? What about between a wine scored 87 out of 100 and one rated 17 out of 20? While the latter might seem at quick glance a higher score, it really converts to 85 out of 100. Though from there it becomes more, not less, confusing, since points out of 100 and 20 are not exactly comparable—that score of 17, while, in a relative sense, lower is actually higher and will nab a silver medal in show, while 85 is only good for a low bronze and 87 for a high bronze ... go figure.

So remember, whenever you find yourself relying on a score to advise your next wine purchase, the salient question to bear in mind isn't "What's in a number?" but rather "What's not ... ?"

Five

The Life of the Vine

> Of all the productions of the vegetable world, which the skill and ingenuity of man have rendered conducive to his comfort, and to the enlargement of the sphere of his enjoyments, and the increase of his pleasurable gratifications, the vine stands forward as the most preeminently conspicuous.

One hundred and fifty years ago a New World wine enthusiast spoke those words. He then echoed his own sentiment with the reflections of an Old World contemporary—"From the remotest records of antiquity, the vine has been celebrated in all ages as the type of plenty and the symbol of happiness."

Such celebrations in antiquity include the words of the Stoic Epictetus, who urged the impatient that they must wait for their fairest pleasures—"No great thing comes suddenly into being, anymore than a cluster of grapes ... let it flower first, then pour forth its fruit and then ripen."

And so we consider the life of the vine, before it attains its highest expression as wine.

The vines wake themselves from their winter dormancy. Now comes the budburst of spring. The sign of budburst's imminence is a kind of vinous stigmata, a bleeding of liquid from the cuts of the pruning shears. This is followed by the season's first hints of green in the vineyard, the emergence of shoots and leaves. What boons or busts is this vintage to bring—the most perfectly felicitous conditions, or drought, flood, frost or fire, hail or plague ... ? Spring frost is now the vine's greatest threat (and can, at its worst, destroy near-enough an entire crop). Spared this—by fortune and foresightful vineyard management—small clusters expose themselves to view. Barely formed and delicate, these are to grow into the grapes of this vintage. Some varieties burst eagerly out, while others display a greater natural reticence. What does early-budding chardonnay's impatience reveal about its wines, and what might this suggest about, say, the more cautious later-budding reds? (The seasons have always had a mystical draw for humankind. They mirror our days, each a season passing in miniature—dawn into noon into dusk into dark of night, a shadow of spring, summer, autumn, and winter. They reflect, too, the course of human life. The stories of the great heroes of old were regulated by the seasons—a season for each stage of the hero's life. Spring marks the birth of the hero—the phase "of revival and resurrection, of creation and ... of the defeat of the power of darkness, winter and death." Spring's story is comedy, and we can hear ourselves laugh as we emerge from the cold into the sun's slowly strengthening rays.)

With summer the buds bloom in flower. Pollination follows—flowers being, as they are, the sexual organs of plants. The winemakers of the ancients would offer sacrifice to the deities they feared or trusted most, to preserve the fragile flowering crop from shriveling frost and the violence of storms. (Modern vignerons, no doubt, have each their own protective practices and rituals.)

Fruit set marks the transformation of flower into berry. Only, however, the fortunate few—generally less than the flowers that fail. The unfortunates fall away, never to enjoy metamorphosis to grape and into wine. This failure in fruition is, aptly, known as "shatter." There's a sense of something broken, potential nipped in the bud so to speak, now never to bloom. Those flowers given to a bleaker and more introspective nature might ponder, with Samuel Beckett—"what is this shadow of the going in which we come, this shadow of the coming in which we go, this shadow of the coming and the going in which we wait, if not the shadow of purpose, of the purpose that budding withers, that withering buds, whose blooming is a budding withering?" (Summer is the season of high romance. Its motifs are quest, epiphany and overturning adversity. We follow the great deeds and triumphs of the hero, and the celebration of marriage and sacred transformation. "The romance is nearest of all literary forms to the wish-fulfillment dream"—that dream of perfect ripening in the mind's eye of the winemaker.)

Those flowers that enjoy the transmutation into fruit become the grapes whose ripening continues through autumn. Hard, green, and ungiving berries begin to soften at the stage of *veraison*. Grapes begin to offer up their perfume and flavor in the stage of *engustment*. The life-giving process of photosynthesis plumps the grapes fat with the sugars that will fuel their fermentation. Keats' "Season of mists and mellow fruitfulness" hardly captures the vineyard's poised sense of anticipation for the winemaker's call. Before this can be given, however, the winemaker must assess the grapes' composition—and in so doing compose in their own mind the final form of the wine they wish to shape. Finally comes the judgment—*"ripe"*—sweeping in the frenetic activity of harvest. (Autumn's form is tragedy and elegy. The hero, hanging midway between heaven and earth, is brought to their fall— the hero's death, so often made in sacrifice. So is each grape's picking a little death of sorts, but one that offers a greater redemption in the wine that will flow.)

Harvest done. The grapes—all of them, early ripening and late—are crushed now, their essence mingling with their fellows. All ready for the transformative magic of fermentation, that beautiful, natural alchemy. The crafting of fine wine will continue through the months of winter, season of dissolution. The vines, once more, resume their hibernation.

Through all of myth and history wine has been the heroic beverage. And it is the winemaker who is true hero of the story of each vintage.

With winter coming we must be patient. Take Epictetus at his word, we wine drinkers and the vines themselves. See ourselves through the months of cold—for how else can spring return again?

Six

In Vino in Memoriam

Bear with me a little. This is the voice you first heard, back on Santorini. Just looking to explore the memories that episode evokes.

Before that evening I'd never previously heard of those wines, assyrtiko and xinomavro. Perhaps their novelty was a part of what marked them for me. Have I drunk better wines? Undoubtedly. But I will still say that this persists as my most treasured wine drinking memory. Would tasting either wine again bring back that night with greater force and immediacy? I couldn't tell you. I've never tasted either again. Deliberately—or as deliberately as I can lay claim to, neither variety being likely to cross your path unless you seek it out in earnest. No, I couldn't tell you, because I wouldn't want to put at risk the perfection of the recollection as it stands.

Our memories are *ours*, truly and only our own at the deepest and most personal level. They are ourselves as we once were and ourselves in continuity and perpetuity. Recognition of this moved St. Augustine to proclaim, both in astonishment and in humility, "Great is the power of memory ... a deep and boundless manifoldness; and this thing is the mind, and this am I myself." No one else with whom I shared that evening possesses the memory as it resides in my own mind. Nor can I know what persists within their power to recollect. Was my waiter marked in the ways I was? It's doubtful. Likely he was preoccupied with the end of season and his imminent return to home and family. But he has his own past to nurture, as I have mine to burnish, hoard

and most of all protect. For what other possession could be more important and more intimate?

It's unsurprising that the scene from Santorini still seems so vivid—
it wasn't so very long ago that I was there and experienced that evening. But I can see, with the passing of time and as that time on the
island becomes more remote, I can see it becoming for me a seminal
memory. I can see, years on from now and even further on from then,
the scene arising to beckon me, making greater claims of influence and
emotion:

> There are in our existence spots of time,
> Which with distinct preeminence retain
> A renovating Virtue ...

These spots of time of Wordsworth are perhaps the most celebrated
notion across all his poetry. Each is a reviving in the poet's mind of
some past event or occurrence—one that might well seem trite or uninspiring to another, but for the one who lived the original experience
and re-experiences that again in memory ... for them these moments
past, these spots of time, have a deeply drawing resonance. Each
represents:

> A virtue, by which pleasure is enhanced,
> That penetrates, enables us to mount
> When high, more high, and lift us up when fallen ...
> Such moments, worthy of all gratitude,
> Are scattered everywhere ...

And it is, for me at least, the sense of gratitude that defined that
night and enshrined it above so many other memories. It is that gratitude which holds the greatest sway, as to how I will remember and
wish to remember that scene and its accompanying feelings.

We're not always, however, so in control of these things as we'd like
perhaps to think. Memory won't be protected. Instead it tends to rise
unbidden when it senses its own cue, whether we wish it to or not. I
was, some time after Santorini, startlingly taken back there, to that restaurant in that company and that mood. Something as slight as the taste
of an apricot brought the wine to mind, and with it a re-experiencing of
that evening's feelings. My own kind of Proustian revelation. But be that
as it may, I've continued to this day to avoid those varieties—dreading to
think of either of them tasting flat on my palate.

In *Remembrance of Things Past* ... (Neither of us has ever been quite
able to abandon this title, co-opted by Proust's translator Moncrieff
from Shakespeare's lovely Sonnet 30. We just can't get used to the
work's more recent, more accurate re-titling, *In Search of Lost Time*.) In

what Proust himself described as his "novels of the unconscious," the narrator Marcel has a similar experience of memory evoked by taste and smell, though one more delicately rendered. Visiting his mother, she serves him tea and little cakes called *madeleines*. The taste of the two together brings on an exquisite feeling of well-being. He tries to determine what in that taste had set off this state of mind. "And suddenly the memory revealed itself," a scene from childhood full of childish pleasure. He has been for a moment that child again, but he can't be only that. He is also the man who reflects on the past that he can only return to, and then only fleetingly, in memory—when it permits. (I'm moved, perhaps by the memory of my Greek waiter, to consider the Greek origins of the word "nostalgia." *Nosto*—"I return." *Alghó*—"I ache for.") "But when from a long-distant past nothing subsists, after the people are dead, after the things are broken and scattered, taste and smell alone, more fragile but more enduring, more unsubstantial, more persistent, more faithful, remain poised a long time, like souls, remembering, waiting, hoping, amid the ruins of all the rest: and bear unflinchingly, in the tiny and almost impalpable drop of their essence, the vast structure of recollection."

Proust's theme is memory (just as Evelyn Waugh says of himself—"My theme is memory, that winged host"—and is there, really, any other theme in literature?). So the artist Jean Cocteau was able to say of him that "the intonation of Proust's voice obeyed the laws of night and honey ... [and] conquered the hopeless sadness within him," and Walter Benjamin took up Cocteau's image to reflect that Proust "from the honeycombs of memory ... built a house for the swarm of his thoughts." These thoughts residing in memory, these moments of significance arising from out of the past, these scenes of personal epiphany, Proust calls *moments bienheureux*. It is through the lens of philosophy that we can see the true import of this term: "*Bienheureux* is an emphatic or superlative form of *heureux*, which is derived from *heure*, hour; the word literally means timely, and by extension favorable, lucky or fortunate, and finally, happy. *Bienheureux* thus means very happy, or blissful ... The *bienheureux*, in the plural, are the blessed, or the saved—those happy ones who have been lucky or fortunate enough to have received the grace of salvation."

My own recollection, if I'm honest, isn't pure. Even as I call it up I know it's been revised, distorted and elaborated. The scene shifts between two viewpoints, two modes of memory. For a moment I see things through my own eyes, and then I watch myself as merely one of three at the table and witness from outside myself my own engagement and reverie as I recall them. This vacillation is fascinating, something that draws you to toy with it (like switching perspective so in one moment a drawn cube seems to project towards you, and in the next to recede deeper into the page). *Field* memories and *observer* memories they've been dubbed, by Freud and subsequent theorists of mind—not, it's true, the most poetic terms. Observer memories are felt, for obvious reasons, to be more remote (an effective therapeutic technique in the treatment of trauma is to convert field to observer memories, flashbacks that can be viewed more dispassionately and with greater distance, to ameliorate the debilitating impact of the traumatic event and its recall). I can see why this should be so, but I'm not so sure. I don't feel any lesser attachment to the moment when it's viewed from a different vantage point. In fact, observer memories seem to instill an additional level of self-scrutiny—as you watch more closely how you were, or how you remember yourself to have been, or how you want to be remembered. Observer memories are proof positive that memory is a process of re-imagining and reconstructing. Memories are, according to Freud, "necessarily altered." So this mode of memory reveals the unavoidable corruption in remembrance. Yet even so, in a sense what happened is less important than how it's remembered. For the events of the past as they played out engaged who we were, while our current recollection comprises who we are now.

What wouldn't we give to experience again one perfect moment? To experience it *exactly* as before, innocent and unsullied by what's happened since. In *Brideshead Revisited*, Sebastian Flyte muses—in his youthful prime and primed by a bottle of Château Lafaurie-Peyraguey, "heaven with strawberries" as he says—"I should like to bury something precious in every place where I've ever been happy and then, when I was old and ugly and miserable, I could come back and dig it up and remember." Wish as we might, can we ever truly have that moment over again, even in memory?

Plato spoke of *reminiscence*. He rejected the notion that reminiscence is only a repository of past experience, preferring to see it as (consistent with his philosophy of Idealism) the soul's ability to comprehend the true Form of the world. His student Aristotle dismissed this, replacing Platonic Idealism with his own favoured Empiricism—a rejection of metaphysics, an insistence that knowledge can only be based in what we can observe. He made the distinction between *remembering* and *recollection*. The former is spontaneous and passive— memory comes upon us unbidden, evoked by some association. Recollection, on the other hand, is an active process—a deliberate attempt to recover the past.

This distinction was further refined by the German existentialist philosopher Soren Kierkegaard, in his 1843 essay *Repetition*. Kierkegaard distinguished between *recollection* and *repetition*. Recollection is a rolling back from where we are into the past. Repetition, however, would not have us retreat into the best of what's been, but rather attempt to draw that "best" forward into the present, and so reaffirm it for the future. "Just as they [the Greeks] taught us that all knowing is recollecting, modern philosophy will teach us that all life is a repetition." Kierke-gaard's alter ego in the essay, Constantin Constantius, begins his quest to recapture the past with a sense of (mildly qualified) optimism—"the present and the future contend with each other to find an eternal expression, and this recollecting is indeed eternity's flowing back into the present—that is, when this recollecting is sound." But isn't that *soundness*—and its perpetual unsureness—what is in question, eaten at by decision and indecision, certainty and uncertainty alike? Constantius attempts to prove to himself that a true re-enactment of the past is possible, by copying stage by stage and in every point of detail a previous trip to Berlin. He finds it will not, cannot happen.

This sentiment was later shared by William James, in many respects the father of modern Psychology. He addressed the notion of recapturing the past in his 1890 tome *Psychology*—in the chapter entitled "The Stream of Consciousness." (A note of clarification at this point. The term *stream of consciousness* was coined by James, but has come to be widely misapplied since. First of all it is mistakenly identified with the Freudian approach of *free association*, itself often wrongly equated with Jung's method of *word association*. Word association—a therapeutic cliché today that launches more jokes than cures—has the therapist speak a word and the patient respond, without consideration, with the first thing that comes into their mind—"mother ...," "courage," "madonna ...," "whore," "milk ...," "no thanks, a glass of wine." The second misreading of stream of consciousness is as a spontaneous, unpunctuated, ungrammatical and/or nonsensical outpouring of words. The classic example is in the writings of James Joyce—Molly Bloom's interior monologue which closes *Ulysses*, and the entirety of *Finnegan's Wake*, "What a mnice old mness it all mnakes!" Both of these misinterpretations read too much into James' intentions in coining the phrase. By *stream* of consciousness he was being more literal, if still metaphorical—consciousness flows like a natural watercourse. It flows at some times fast and others sluggishly, it gurgles and eddies and occasionally bursts its banks. It is everchanging but always clearly itself.) James laid out four "characters" of consciousness. The second of these is, "consciousness is in constant change." As to reliving the past, "no state once gone can recur and be identical with what it was before." Further to the point, "the same object cannot ... give us the same sensation over again." Every sensation and perception, every emotion experienced between then and now intervenes and taints the purity of the recollected state. Even the desire to re-experience in itself corrupts the memory of what occurred before, and what we would try to recapture once more.

More recently Harvard Professor of Psychology, Daniel Gilbert, has added a whimsical rhyme to the distinction implicit in memory's active and passive aspects. He distinguishes between *retrieving* and *reweaving* what we've previously experienced, and comes out plainly on the side of our memories being reweaved—"This fabrication happens so quickly and effortlessly that we have the illusion ... that the entire thing was in our heads the entire time" (reinforcing Aristotle's belief that memory belongs to "the same part [of the soul] as that to which imagination belongs"). We fill in our own gaps, without knowing what we're doing, in order to alter our own past and bring it closer to our own ideal.

So, that perfect night, that perfect meal, that perfect wine, that perfect company, that perfect mix—are they really irretrievable?

Smell and taste, of all our senses, are the most evocative of the past through memory. What the poets and philosophers knew intuitively, cognitive psychologists and neuroscientists have since proven experimentally. (Proust again, with an apposite insight—"The impression is for the writer what experimentation is for the scientist.") Recollections elicited by an odor or flavor carry far greater emotional weight than those triggered by a visual, auditory or tactile cue. In his book *Proust was a Neuroscientist*, Jonah Lehrer describes experiments demonstrating that "smell and taste are the only senses that connect directly to the hippocampus, the center of the brain's long-term memory. Their mark is indelible. All our other senses ... are first processed by the thalamus, the source of language and the front door to consciousness." When a smell or taste attaches to an experience in memory, it is unfiltered. That's not to say that memory doesn't frequently respond to some sight or sound or certain touch. Only that the memories drawn back by taste and smell are the more forceful and intense, and in essence the more moving. Little wonder then that wine, defined by our senses of smell and taste, can so powerfully urge forgotten episodes on us, or seem to provide a means to recapture what we once had and don't anymore. And in sharing wine, we can bring others with us into our own past, or accompany them into theirs.

I dined once with a friend who'd just returned from Europe. Her stay had been lengthy, and she'd got around. But from letters she'd sent I knew that she had loved her time in Tuscany most of all, staying for the most part in a villa near the medieval town of San Gimignano. I took her to an Italian restaurant with a good name and a broad if patchy wine list. Bought for her (by happy accident, as I hadn't recalled that she only drank white), bought for us a bottle of Vernaccia di San Gimignano, a white wine with reputation and pedigree from an overwhelmingly "red" region. She couldn't remember if she'd tasted *that* particular wine over there. It was, I couldn't really say more, a serviceable drink at best, refreshing but not lingering the way that better wines will. We talked as we drank, and when we'd knocked off one bottle she asked if I'd mind if we had another of those. She knew my horror of sticking to the same wine through an entire meal, but I was happy that she seemed to be enjoying it, and happy enough to bend my own rules for her. Into the second bottle she became more distracted and aloof in our conversation. As her reserve grew more pronounced I realized that whether or not she'd drunk this wine in Tuscany, she might as well have. She admitted later, much later, weeks or months, that the taste on her tongue had taken her back to what was clearly a dearly held period. I didn't push her further—some transient romance perhaps, or some less tangible feelings of purely personal significance, maybe the sense of reverence we experience (those of us from modern cities) when the past feels palpable all around us. Anyway, for her that wine had been transporting in every way it could be. That's not to say it wasn't without its pain—the regret of being there no longer and perhaps never again returning. But it was, she had no doubts, worth that sense of loss to recapture the once-having so intensely.

Gary Marcus is a Professor of Psychology with a novel way of looking at the human mind. Our minds are the way they are because evolution, rather than working towards some predestined pattern or grand design, has had to work with what it's got when it's got it. So our brains, and our associated higher functions, were built bit upon bit, advancing by incremental, haphazard and often temporary solutions, which were themselves then haphazardly adapted, and so too those adaptations, and so on, and so on ... In other words, our brains were not drawing-board designed for optimum function, but put together accidentally by evolutionary fluke. In explaining the tinkering ways of evolution, Marcus quotes François Jacob, awarded the 1965 Nobel Prize in Medicine—evolution "uses whatever he finds around him, old cardboards, pieces of strings, fragments of wood or metal, to make some kind of workable object ... [the result is] a patchwork of odd sets pieced together when and where the opportunity arose." Hence the title to Marcus' book, *Kluge: The Haphazard Construction of the Human Mind*. Kluge (rhymes with huge) is slang (as are so many expressive words), whose definition is given as "a clumsy or inelegant solution to a problem." "Clumsy," however, does great injustice to this kind of solution beloved of many engineers and experimental scientists and, apparently, Mother Nature herself—to save time, money and effort while still furnishing a contraption perfectly serviceable for the job at hand for as long as the job goes on (and what, you'd have to ask, would be the point of its lasting any longer?).

So have our brains developed—by stages, with necessity the shoehorn of invention, and all held together by the neurophysiological equivalent of chewing gum and bailing wire. Surprisingly, this isn't a model of the human psyche that offends in its inelegance, opportunism or occasional laziness. In fact, it's really rather endearing—with the additional virtue of explaining a helluva lot. Marcus goes on (to bring us back on point) to state, "Memory is, I believe, the mother of all kluges, the single factor most responsible for human cognitive idiosyncrasy." And within the mechanism of our memory, perhaps nothing is more idiosyncratic than how we jump from one idea/emotion/image/flashback/gut-feel/yearning to the next—by chain of association ("connecting trains of thought with chains of ought," to give Marcus a deserved final word).

Aristotle was the father of associationism—the theory (or mass of theories, or even *mess* of theories) seeking to explain how our minds make the connections they make. Or, more formally defined, the laws that determine "the mental connection between two ideas ... or memories, such that the presence of one tends to evoke the others." Aristotle originated the system whereby "three sorts of relationships serve as links in the chain of associations—similarity, contrast and contiguity." That is, when something is recalled other ideas and memories will follow because they are like to the initial memory, different in ways that are significantly contrary, or bound to the original by closeness (in time or space) at the time of its occurrence. David Hume, on Aristotle's model, saw an irrefutable parallel between memory and imagination, but saw these further as "the two different ways in which ideas work." He also posited three laws of association—resemblance (like Aristotle's "similarity"), contiguity (ditto to Aristotle's third law), causality (the antecedents and implications of the original event being remembered)—and seems, and a great shame too, to have done away entirely with association by contrast. These laws of Hume (similarity and contiguity becoming gradually more prominent in his thought, with causality relegated to a secondary condition of the other two) are regulated in our minds by our own patterns of *habit*—no flattering assessment to anyone who would like to feel the personal symbolism of their own associations to be endlessly complex.

Against my better judgment, such as it is, a chain of association of my own suggests itself. It begins with a wine, and goes full circle to end there.

Dinner in New York, with an old friend from Sydney I hadn't seen for years. Not really an old flame, since any combustion had been wholly one-sided. She'd moved there at the time I'd been carrying an entirely unrequited torch for her. A kiss hello at the bar, just the slightest brushing of lips, still enabling me to taste cherry with an intriguing bitter note. Put me in mind of a pinot. (She liked pinot. I knew that from our very first lunch, an excellent Mount Mary wine, which had echoed the shade but not the flavor of that day's lipstick.) I ordered a damned fine Rully (at a damned fine price).

Two days later, in the cab to J.F.K. Airport, her face in the dinner candlelight came to mind. A mind's-eye portrait. I didn't wonder what she was doing at that moment, since I believed I knew. She was at the

Museum of Modern Art (MOMA), at the Picasso portrait exhibition. I'd given her a spare ticket (they came as part of a deal I'd had with my hotel). Picasso painted the women he loved through his life—and clearly continued to paint them when love was well on the wane. You could chart the disintegration of yet another marriage by each wife's representation turning more sinister and insectile.

Those women, all barbs and stingers, brought to mind an even more disturbing piece, from MOMA's permanent collection. Alberto Giacometti specialized in bronzes of emaciated figures gathered together in public spaces but each clearly and irrevocably alienated from the others. It was *not* one of these pieces I was looking at. This—*Woman with Her Throat Cut*—was quite something else. A sprawling metal scorpion, simultaneously terrifying and violated, emasculating and pitiable. While meditating on the shock of that piece's confrontation . . .

Another image arose. "Gynecological instruments for operating on mutant females," from David Cronenberg's warped masterpiece *Dead Ringers*. Jeremy Irons well deserved the Oscar (clearly the film was just too much for the Academy, but they chose to reward him belatedly for his next film, *Reversal of Fortune*). He plays both Mantle brothers, twin gynecologists. Descending into a pit of despair and paranoia, the now-drug-addled brother Beverly has a metal-smith cast, from drawings of his own design, the most unsettling surgical instruments—"There's nothing wrong with the instrument. It's the body! The woman's body is all wrong . . . The patients are getting strange. They look alright on the outside, but their insides are . . . deformed. I had to deal with it somehow! Radical technology was required!"

This image is mercifully replaced by the vision of a much younger Irons, playing Charles Ryder in *Brideshead Revisited*. Visiting Brideshead, the estate of the Marchmain family, he is met at the station by Sebastian's sister, Lady Julia. It was his first meeting with the woman who would become his adulterous lover in another life many years on. While driving, she asks him to light a cigarette for her. "It was the first time in my life anyone had asked this of me, and as I took the cigarette from my lips and put it in hers, I caught a thin bat's squeak of sexuality, inaudible to all but me."

Performing the same act for my friend, after dinner, two nights earlier, I had experienced the same thing. And thought too that I wished I wasn't leaving in two days. A phrase from an early Ian McEwan short story voiced in my mind—"Overwhelmed with nostalgia for a country I had not yet left."

I don't know if my friend's expression, as we parted from each other, was knowing or teasing. I could still taste the wine on my tongue. So, I knew, could she. I stood there unable to move forward towards her. My hesitancy made this pause seem interminable, I couldn't collect my thoughts, further distracted by another phrase from another McEwan story—"in the pallor of her upturned throat he thought he saw from one bright morning in his childhood a field of dazzling white snow which he, a small boy of eight, had not dared scar with footprints."

I recalled that our very first lunch had ended very much the same way, with my timidity and vacillating intent. At least later that afternoon I'd had the company of an Irish barman I knew, who was always up for toasting the tribulations of others. "Don't worry about it, mate," he said, "it happens to the best of us. Nearly happened to me once ..."

Still life paintings of the 17th century were replete with images to evoke associations. A common feature of these paintings was *vanitas*—a reminder of the transience of life. Depicted objects symbolizing mortality include skulls, extinguished candles with their last disappearing wisp of smoke, hourglasses and other timepieces, and ... a wine glass. The amount of wine in the glass could suggest time's passing, or the imminence of death. Red wine could conjure up the notion of blood, by resemblance and religious significance. The ornateness of the glass, or a fracture or flaw in it, could warn of the inevitable fruits of debauchery (grapes were themselves a metaphor for both plenty and gluttony). And no explanation is required for the glass tipped on its side, with its abundance spilt out. Wine, then, as a simultaneous reminder of life and death.

There's a scene in the film *Sideways*, which elegantly captures this sense (and a scene we'll have cause to return to later). Maya, the film's sympathetic female lead, reflects that "a bottle of wine is actually *alive*, and it's constantly evolving and gaining complexity ... that is, until it peaks, and then begins its steady, inevitable decline." It's a lovely notion, wine as a living entity. And a poignant one, wine as a decaying entity, its decline from age, or poor handling, or our very act of enjoying it. As you drink it, it gifts you its last vestige of vitality. You get to, if you're fortunate and the timing is right and the circumstances felicitous, you get to experience that perfect point of evolution, the last gasp of beauty before it's gone and you'll never experience quite that again.

What other beverage do we talk of as if it's sentient? As if it *wants* to please, wants to be drunk at its best?

At the risk of seeming insensitively irreverent, we can't help also being reminded of something from Kurt Vonnegut's *Breakfast of Champions*. Vonnegut's alter ego, the science fiction writer Kilgore Trout, wrote a story "which was a dialogue between two pieces of yeast. They were discussing the possible purposes of life as they ate sugar and suffocated in their own excrement. Because of their limited intelligence, they never came close to guessing that they were making champagne."

Scopas of Thessaly once gave a banquet. Rich victuals were served, and the wine flowed. The poet Simonides recited a lyric in honor of his host, and included in it a celebration of Castor and Pollux, twin sons of Zeus and so demigods, brothers to Helen of Troy, heroes among the Argonauts on the quest for the Golden Fleece, living a punctuated immortality, one day upon the earth and the next below in Hades, and enshrined as Gemini in the heavens. Scopas, well in his cups at this point and resentful that the heroes had stolen some of his thunder, spitefully withheld half the agreed payment to Simonides, informing him that he could seek the balance from the twin deities. Some time later a message called Simonides from the banquet hall at the summons of two young men, of whom there was no sign when he went out to meet them. In his absence the roof of the hall came crashing down on the revelers, killing all where they sat. Simonides, remembering the order of guests around the table, was able to direct relatives to the remains of their loved ones (so they could perform the proper rites over the right bodies). Simonides is subsequently said to be the originator of the art of memory and "the method of loci"—"Noting that is was through his memory of the places at which the guests had been sitting that he had been able to identify the bodies, he realized that orderly arrangement is essential for good memory."

The method of loci is a mnemonic technique—a system for remembering with relative ease a great deal of information. It was popular in classical times for rhetoricians to commit to memory great swathes of speeches, and its popularity continued down through the Middle Ages and even on to today. The loci referred to, literally "places," were typically locations within a piece of architecture—for which reason the technique was also known as the "memory palace." First of all, a thorough acquaintance is made with the space to be used, down to each intricate detail of its decorations, distinctive features, nooks and crannies. Whatever one wishes to remember is then broken down into manageable pieces, each piece given a recognizable symbol. Each of these symbols subsequently has an association forged in the mind with a different feature of the memory palace. Recovering the memory then, in all its richness, proceeds as an imaginary tour through the memory palace.

The technique's a winner. Though ... let's try it as a *memory cellar*.

Think of a subterranean cellar. Lay out its floor plan in your mind. Descend into it, and construct the details of its catacombs just as you want. How you organize the bottles is up to you. You could go by region, or by variety. Still, that's been done to death with real cellars, and the memory cellar possesses all the possibilities of your imagination. I organize my wines by who I drank them with (and it never ceases to amaze and also flatter people when you remind them what was shared between you when you first met, first dined together as close friends, celebrated this or commiserated that ...).

The memory cellar is, I find, a mnemonic technique to sharpen palate memory. Palate memory is the capacity to *remember* a wine at a sensory level. To taste the ghost of the wine all over again. Or to project its presence once more onto your tongue. As you drink a wine, go down in your mind into your own memory cellar, place the wine where your own system says it fits ... and it can be brought out again and again to savor. It is a source of pleasure in its own right, being able to conjure from the past the best and most memorable wines you've enjoyed. And it gives context and perspective to wines you drink now and on into the future—whether they're alike to those other wines you've tried, or entirely different.

There is one respect in which wine can seem to work against memory, and we've all experienced it—with a little over-indulgence we can seem to lose the memory of some of the previous evening's events. Worry not. The psychological phenomenon of *state-dependent retrieval* ensures that we will likely recover those missing spots of time the next time we reach the same level of intoxication. That's certainly what the rats in the experiments have done—learning to run a maze drunk, unable to do so sober, then excelling once more with a few belts under the pelt. Shame for them, however—they were given their drink intravenously, and so denied the pleasure of its imbibing. Pity one of the lab technicians wasn't *au fait* with that Sardinian wine with a parmesan tang—the rats would have lapped it up. So, as you pass through the various stages of inebriation, search your mind for anything arresting from past wine drinking bouts that might crop up. Or you might prefer to take the sage advice of philosopher David Hume, and leave well enough alone with what's lost from memory by wine—"The follies of the last debauch should be buried in eternal oblivion, in order to give full scope to the follies of the next."

Mood-congruent retrieval acts similarly to state-dependent retrieval. In this case it's the emotional state that biases recall—a joyful mood facilitates joyful memories, and a dark mood calls forth memories of the same stain. My Santorini mood began this chapter. Fitting then that it close it too.

Keats' "Ode on Melancholy" brims with wine imagery. In the very first line the reader is enjoined "go not to Lethe." Dionysus was sometimes called the son of Lethe—forgetfulness or, more extremely, oblivion. The poet continues to urge against seeking oblivion—through "Wolf's bane ... for its poisonous wine," or "nightshade, ruby grape of Proserpine"—in order to escape the pain of melancholy and loss. And in a strange way that's what I've been doing with my Santorini wines—my avoidance driven by the fear of loss, not its reality. Perhaps I should instead track down those wines, embrace the inevitable and trust them to inspire and not to disappoint. Share the experience of these wines as they were shared with me. And in so doing, attach new memory to old association. As Keats completes his theme:

> Ay, in the very temple of Delight
> Veil'd Melancholy has her sovran shrine,
> Though seen of none save him whose strenuous tongue
> Can burst Joy's grape against his palate fine ...

The pain of never being able to attain what was had *just* as it was had is small price to pay for re-immersion in past pleasure. Drink all manner of varieties, then—assyrtiko, xinomavro, and every wine you've ever drunk with everyone you've ever loved—and forge new memories that honor, not spoil, the old.

(The author who was absent from Santorini still wishes he'd been there.)

Seven

The Nature of *Terroir*

The house of Psychology has no shortage of quarrels. But surely the most volatile issue—in its acrimony, vehemence, and breadth of relevance—has been the debate over "nature versus nurture."

The question of whether we are formed with our natures latent but inevitable, or entirely dependent on how we're reared and educated, straddles so much of what it means to be human. Have we free will, or are our actions all determined? What exactly are our thoughts, senses, feelings, beliefs ... and are they truly ours? Why do we act as we do, and how should we act as we should? What are we, and what should we be?

Wine has its own nature/nurture debate, and in the vinous sphere the arguments have been no less contentious. *Nature* is seen as what the earth puts in—*nurture* as what the winemaker draws out. Nature is what the grape is becoming—and nurture what the wine will finally be. Nature is the distinct sense of place. And nurture—the human hand meddling?

To ask of human nature, "well, isn't it a little of both?" is to ignore the fractiousness that the "nature" side of the debate creates. Steven Pinker, in *The Blank Slate: The Modern Denial of Human Nature*, expresses his intention "to explore why the extreme position (that culture is everything) is so often seen as moderate, and the moderate position is seen as extreme." He goes on to point out that "an honest discussion of human nature has never been more timely ... Throughout the 20th century, many intellectuals tried to rest principles of decency on fragile factual claims such as that human beings are biologically indistinguishable, harbor no ignoble motives, and are utterly free in their ability to make choices." Aristotle's *tabula rasa*—the "blank slate" upon which the influences of parents and educators will be written—was a metaphor that appealed to John Locke for the most virtuous reasons. To deny such a thing as human nature at that time permitted a liberation from the triple tyrannies of original sin, divine right of kings and human slavery. John Stuart Mill, inheritor of Locke's legacy, expanded its influence even further—into women's suffrage, education rights for minors, and improvements in the living conditions of the underclasses. The morality became a little twisted when the Behaviorist psychologists took it in a dehumanizing direction, giving us no more self-determination than maze-running rats (and transforming the Jesuits' maxim "give me the boy until seven, and I'll give you the man" into B. F. Skinner's "give me the specifications and I'll give you the man"—the latter which could well be maxim too to proponents of the "International style" of wine). Modern anthropology, under the influence of its disciplinary father Franz Boas, then sought to eliminate innate qualities entirely—a student of Boas declaring, "Heredity can't be allowed to have acted any part in history."

For things to be "a little of both" requires a defense of the integrity of both sides of the argument. And this is no less the case in the case of the grape. Here nature is summed up in a single word, and that word could only be French—*terroir*. Nurture is, on the other hand, the dimension of human intervention—educating the grape to be the kind of wine the winemaker wants. But even here the grape often has its own ideas. Just like us, the grape is no blank slate. Each variety has its own predisposition, which the winemaker can accommodate or contend with (you can't, after all, make a riesling from cabernet grapes ... at least not yet you can't and as for the future, well more on the genetic manipulation of the fruit of the vine in time).

Riesling is frequently seen as *terroir* incarnate—given its "ability to transmit the characteristics of a vineyard without losing [its] own inimitable style." It is distinguished in this from chardonnay, the variety upon which the mark of human interference sits like it sits on no other. So riesling is prized for its purity—and chardonnay for its complexity in breadth and depth, according to that winemaker's wiles (showing the steely restraint of Chablis, through the vacillating and varying degrees of Côte de Beune elegance and opulence and on to the biggest of those big-on-wood-and-malo New Worlders—and all the flavor shades that lie between).

Nature is what that keen Chianti-sipping native son of Tuscany, Galileo, was describing when he said, "Wine is a compound of light and humor." He couldn't miss the captured sunlight that resides in a glass of wine. By humor, though, he wasn't suggesting that every wine is a bottle of hilarity (much as it might seem so as the night goes on). By humor (Italian *umore*) he meant moisture—more precisely, the characteristic climate and geological conditions of that region. What Montpellier's *Institut Superier de la Vigne et du Vin* describes as "the interaction of climate, grape variety and the soil."

It can't be disputed, for all the consternation that the word can stir, that the concept of *terroir* has a distinguished heritage. Vitruvius, author of (among a great many other things) the most significant of all classical treatises on architecture, reflected on the influence of geological factors on the characteristic flavors of regional wines. He saw water as the earth's life force pulsing through the geological strata that are its veins. And Pliny the Elder, in his *Natural History*, reported the words of the physician Androcydes to Alexander the Great—"When you are about to drink wine ... remember that you are drinking the earth's blood." That's *terroir* right there—that quality of a wine that makes it seem the very blood of the rocks and soil and hills and mountain ranges, the earthy blood of all of that for the pleasure of our imbibing.

Still, without the gentle crafting of the winemaker's intent, *terroir* could whistle, and those grapes would be so much forage for the beasts.

Michel Chapoutier, whose "love for vines and wine and the awareness of the need to respect the earth and its *terroir*" is expressed in biodynamic commitment, whose family's roots have been sunk deep in the earth of Rhône for two centuries, who seeks also to release the charms of New World *terroir* ... this distinguished winemaker sees things thus—"*Terroir* is the combination of the soil, the climate which determines the quality of vintage, and the know-how that is rooted in long-standing tradition. Without winemakers, the notion of *terroir* is meaningless; without mankind, there can be no terroir." This symmetry of responsibility is, however, given a cautionary note—"but we also may be the cause of [*terroir's*] ruin." This interdependence is no gift, but a duty to preserve. Chapoutier's sentiments on the necessary symbiosis of *terroir* and human agency are echoed by high-profile New World winemaker Warren Winiarski—"I have given examples of what we do at Stag's Leap Wine Cellars to make the most of our *terroir*. The way the statement is made would suggest one could also make the least of *terroir*—or in other words, that one could make nothing of—or make it into nothing. Which shows that *terroir and man are inseparable*."

The sum and substance of *terroir* is captured by D. H. Lawrence in a poetic reflection on the poetry of origins—"Different places on the face of the earth have different vital effluence, different vibration, different chemical exhalation, different polarity with different stars: call it what you like. But the spirit of place is a great reality."

This spirit of place is a powerfully resonant message. It entrenches us firmly in the soil beneath our feet. For those winemakers whose families have worked that land for generations it's a kind of conduit through which flows philosophical nutrients from the very bones of those soil-tillers and vignerons of the past. And so it encompasses and revivifies age-old traditions, whose sense is indistinguishable from the earth's own essence.

Eight

What You Won't See on the Label

Let's peer into the secrets of the grape varieties, to get at the idiosyncrasies that lie beneath their skins ...

WHITES FIRST

Chardonnay: Some winemakers go at their chardonnay like cosmetic surgeons, nipping and tucking and firming and inflating well beyond what Nature's already given the grape. Such wines put us in mind of a wonderfully funny wine cartoon by the inimitable Ronald Searle—entitled "exceptionally full-bodied," an awe-inspiring and quite gravity-defying pair of breasts protrudes from a bottle, spilling abundantly over the label's best efforts to serve as impromptu brassiere. These kinds of wines were once, almost quaintly, described as "Dolly Parton wines." Perhaps it's time for the pop-cultural allusion to be updated, and what could serve better than "Pamela Anderson wines"—considering that chardonnay made in this style bears as much resemblance to the best offerings of Burgundy as Pammy does to a real woman.

Riesling: Frequently the ugly duckling. Difficult and recalcitrant in youth, by turns secretive and acerbic, like many an adolescent. But given time and careful keeping, can blossom breathtakingly.

Semillon: Ditto. Very much dissed as a dry table wine varietal, everywhere but Australia's Hunter Valley. Then its transformation can be as magical as riesling's. And, as with riesling, is a superior variety from which to make stickies (though sem-based stickies can, to our tastes at least, tend at times towards the cloying—think Shirley Temple at her most egregiously cutesy).

Sauvignon Blanc: Like a Tarantino film—difficult to take seriously, and too often a caricature of itself. *(This, it should be admitted, is the opinion of only one of the authors. The other is more than partial to the odd New World sav b, or a nice Sancerre.)*

Chenin Blanc: At its best, an excellent Vouvrey sec for instance, this grape is all crispness and zing—like taking a bite out of a barely ripe green apple then sucking on a river stone. At its less than best (and that's a wide and unstimulating palette, excuse the pun)—as tight-lipped, inscrutable and neutral as a Swiss banker.

The Rhône White trio—viognier, marsanne, roussanne: Diverting as solo acts, delightful singing together. At times, however, they want to hang out with red varieties too often, bunk in with the shiraz, grenache and mourvèdre (viognier is particularly guilty of this). Is this a delusion of grandeur, some kind of identity disorder, or is it just, as some insightful sommelier put to us one night—"every white wine really wants to be red!"

Pinot Gris/Grigio: The yin and yang variety. As Alsatian *gris* it offers rich creaminess and a gravitas befitting the gray tinge for which it's named, shot through with ashen yellow that calls to mind a dissolving bruise or a Turner sky. By contrast, Italian *grigio* is a light-tripping siren of a wine. In the New World, this character of multiple personalities turns somewhat pathological, as confusion over style makes for some schizophrenic wines.

Grüner Veltliner: The current cult fave of sommeliers everywhere. If a wine waiter offers you a blind sip of white, it's odds on you're being treated to Austria's soon-to-be-not-so-recherché variety.

Albariño: Wants to love you with seafood, in its Spanish manner.

Trebbiano: The good-time grape. Famously promiscuous, not to say ubiquitous. Turns up all over the place going by all manner of names. White hermitage, ugni blanc, castello, Saint Emilion, beau, thalia, russola, the list goes on and on … You mightn't know you've had it but rest assured you have.

THEN REDS

Pinot Noir: What's to be said about the winemakers' Holy Grail? It can be without peer, the most endlessly beguiling of wines. At the other end of the spectrum, beetroot juice adulterated with urine would be a preferable beverage. What other wine could be like sticking your face into a lavender bush, a jar of plum jam, a handful of fresh-picked mushrooms and a cowpat—or all of these together? At its best, overwhelming in its elegance.

At its all-too-frequently-and-greatly-disappointingly-less-than-best, well, to call it insipid would be an insult to the genuinely spineless.

Shiraz: It rules!

Cabernet Sauvignon: Smokers of the world take note—ordering the right cabernet might well be the only way left to enjoy the heady scent of tobacco in a restaurant.

Merlot: Pomerol aside, this classic variety (which blends so well with cabernet sauvignon and in so doing testifies elegantly to the Gestalt psychologist's cry "the whole is greater than the sum of its parts") is in danger of becoming (if it hasn't already) the alco-pop of the wine world. That's as much the fault of unadventurous middle-of-the-palate drinkers as it is of makers and marketers perpetuating the "inoffensive" style—demand, after all, has to cop some of the same stick as supply.

Cabernet Franc: When blended, this grape is a little like your kindergarten teacher (or perhaps like a dominatrix, if your kindergarten teacher was anything like Miss Anderson)—it imposes a taut restraint and discipline on the occasionally willful excesses of cab sav and merlot. This inclination to check unruliness and urge a little temperance perhaps comes from its parental status over its more famous cabernet progeny, sired on sauvignon blanc. When unblended—in the Loire and increasingly in parts of the New World—it's the epitome of structure and austerity. Still, in seeming ungiving it is not ungenerous—merely demanding that its imbiber tease out the pleasures on offer from less obvious hints than other varieties provide.

Malbec: When decked out in the sky blue and white of *Los Pumas*, can be an absolute belter—think of the Argentinean rugby pack scrummaging on your tongue. When from most other parts of the winegrowing world, more often than not a filler, a wallflower, not riveting on its own but there to make its company look more interesting.

Zinfandel: The red grape with Dissociative Identity Disorder. Spawned in Croatia, leaving its twin Primitivo in Puglia, Italy, it traveled to New England where it earned the named Black St. Peters, before becoming a modern staple of California. Zin's not entirely sure when it wants to ripen (tight green unready berries will share a bunch, literally hang cheek by jowl, with grapes that have reached plump purple perfection). Sometimes zin frocks up in party-girl pink (so-called "white zinfandel" must feel like the labor that Hercules always held was his hardest—cross-dressing and taking on women's chores for his sins). It can be frat-boy boisterous, as complex as a professor of Heideggerian ontology, or at its heaviest heavyweight can intimidate like a professional wrestler (whose signature move would surely be called "the ball-tearer").

Nebbiolo: The *nebbia*, a thick fog, rolls in over the hills of Piedmont when the grapes are finally ripening. Perhaps it hides the secrets of creating great nebbiolo from the rest of the world. On the old maps, fog-swathed stretches were marked "Here be monsters" ... and monsters well and truly are the great wines of Barolo and Barbaresco.

Sangiovese: A wine that grows wise as it ages, and may well end up entirely changing its nature. In youth it can dominate with the weight of a cabernet, even having the tendency to be a bit of a bully. With maturity, however, it has learned the subtle skills of seduction, and can entrance with the sublimity of older pinot.

Tempranillo: *Olé!!!*

Nine

A Flight of Wines

A flight of wines. As romantic as "a lamentation of swans," as uplifting as "an exaltation of larks." It should be wine's official collective noun. It's not, of course. But it still works a treat for what it is—a sommelier-selection of four, five, or maybe half a dozen tastes of wines that go well together or provide insightful contrast. It's an opportunity for wine drinkers to try something outside of their usual, without committing to a bottle. It's a chance to explore.

You can take a vertical flight—different vintages of the same wine. You can fly horizontally—same vintage, different examples of the same variety. Or you might find a flight that's more of a zigzag, just because that's the mood of the sommelier, who hopes it fits your own mood too.

It's such a pleasing word in the context. "Flight," you're afforded the opportunity to travel while never leaving your chair. And the notion of flights of fancy is appealing. It allows you to move beyond your more mundane fancies to be more fanciful, and try wines you mightn't otherwise try.

It's also a great way to discover the idiosyncrasies you find you like most in your wines. And idiosyncrasy here is too often underrated or overlooked. You'll know what we're driving at when you taste a wine that's so refined, so reluctant to court any disapproval from anyone, anywhere, that it's in danger of disappearing up its own punt (you know, that concavity in the bottom of the bottle).

What might we consider "perfection" in a wine? It's a term that's tossed around a bit—a wine might be deemed "a perfect example of the variety/vintage/*terroir*/style," or even more frequently "a perfect match with oysters/foie gras/caviar/bbq'd bangers." Champagne has a name as the wine for occasions because it's perfect for any occasion—in the words of Madame Lilly Bollinger, "I drink it when I'm happy and when I'm sad. Sometimes I drink it when I'm alone. When I have company I consider it obligatory. I trifle with it if I'm not hungry and drink it when I am. Otherwise I never touch it—unless I'm thirsty." Still, even if champagne is the perfect drop for any circumstance, what should we choose, hip-pocket permitting, as the perfect champagne? A friend once picked up, from a deceased estate auction, a case of '76 Salon—at an incredible bargain since no one else present seemed to realize what it was. The wine at this point was twelve or so years old. He cracked a bottle with one of us that night (and why not, with another eleven left?). As we sipped its exquisiteness, he explained that the wine had been scored at 20 out of 20 by the best wine magazines. Was the wine truly perfect, then? Well, we're not prepared to stake too much on the perspicacity of our palate back then. And perhaps, with no finer champagne to provide a frame of reference (if indeed one exists) ... if the Salon wasn't quite perfection *it might as well have been.*

The Oxford English Dictionary gives as one definition of perfect "free from any flaw or defect." But is faultlessness in a wine sufficient reason to acknowledge its perfection? A wine possessing no technical faults won't necessarily drink exceptionally, or even memorably. In fact, the absence of any discernible flaw might be, surprising as it sounds, a flaw in itself. The wines that truly engage are those with a true character of their own. Some individuality or uniqueness of statement, even if that be a little off-kilter. "I rather like bad wine," wrote Benjamin Disraeli, "one gets so bored with good wine."

This notion, the potential flaw in flawlessness, might be seen as a vinous particular of the Renaissance scholar Lucilio Vanini's paradox of perfection—that true perfection resides in imperfection. It was Vanini's contention that a state of perfection, aspiring to no further progress or improvement, was in fact a stagnancy. Imperfection, on the other hand, possesses the vibrant potential to improve so that all its attributes might come to complement each other more completely, hence ... (well, it wouldn't be a paradox if it was a simple thing to wrap your skull around). Perhaps Vanini's paradox of perfection explains a wine phenomenon that's frequently baffled us. That is, when a perfect score is given to wines that will undoubtedly improve, perhaps greatly, with greater age. Otherwise what's left for a wine scored 100 in its infancy, as were an unprecedented number of the '05 Bordeaux vintage, when it's opened at 10, 15, 20 years (whichever represents its optimum drinking age) and is then an entirely different wine, an entirely different sensory experience? Would that wine then be more perfect than perfect?

In his *Metaphysics* Aristotle outlines three different meanings of perfection. The first two aspects are related—that which is perfect must be complete (lacking no requisite element), and it must also be of such a standard that no other of its kind can be regarded as better. This is the meaning of "perfect" elaborated by Thomas Aquinas as a thing being perfect "in itself." Aristotle and Aquinas both distinguished this from a thing being perfect *for its purpose*.

As far as it goes for wine, the judgment of the first kind, of perfection in itself, is the kind of judgment made by wine critics. There is the aspiration to objectivity, an assessment in absolute terms, beyond context. For a perfect score to be awarded, the wine in a sense taunts the critic (albeit in the most engaging way) to find some, any grounds on which to deduct even a single point from its score. For most every other wine imbiber it's the other sense of perfection that matters—the wine's perfection for its purpose. This is a proudly subjective judgment, and the pronouncement of perfection requires only that, for this moment and mood and in this company, there isn't any other wine you would prefer to be drinking.

This highlights the special pleasure of the non-professional wine taster—we can revel in what appeals most to our own taste. Subjectivity is its own badge of honor, and there's no need to apologize for guilty indulgences. As observed by Immanuel Kant, the defining mind of modern philosophy (and very partial to a sip or several), "the judgment of taste is entirely independent of the concept of perfection." We may like what we like without justifying the "why." T. S. Eliot had the same idea in mind when he wrote "genuine taste is always imperfect taste"—idiosyncrasy of inclination is more interesting than a slavish adherence to the "taste" laid down by experts or etiquette, fad or fashion.

Whether or not you buy the notion that imperfection is perfection and vice versa, the small imperfections that make a wine its distinctive self are frequently more interesting than a wine that has no such quirks. These imperfections, additionally, give the wine drinker something genuine to hang your interest on—though we're not, of course, suggesting that a poorly made wine is ever likely to gain ascendancy over a wine meticulously made from quality grapes in an excellent vintage. For our part we'll take, almost always anyway, the appeal that comes from nonconformity. No suggestion that conformity is an evil in itself in wine. It's necessary, after all, in evaluating a wine, judging it in terms of its variety, region and vintage. We don't want our pinot to taste nothing at all like pinot is understood to taste. On the other hand, slavish and predictable typicality satisfies expectations without ever exceeding them, let alone twisting those expectations in new and diverting directions.

True beauty, in wine as in most everything, is *sui generis*. Peculiarity rules. After all, who of us doesn't wish to be loved as much for our imperfections as for our finer features?

Ten

An Unexamined Life, an Undrunk Wine

Found guilty and facing sentence for sins against the state, the philosopher Socrates chose to defend his life with passionate argument—"An unexamined life is not worth living." This observation secured his death and went on to echo down the ages. Who knows whether that provocative call inspired the winemakers of the time, fated as they were to lose one of their best customers, but it does suggest questions with respect to the pervasive influence of wine.

What has caused humankind to single out this beverage for all of the attention that we have? Is it because our impression of wine is one of the most subtle and curiously multilayered of experiences? Is it that wine actively engages all of our senses (and for any who ask, *what appeal to my sense of hearing*, we can only express our regret that they are tone deaf to the music of a wine well poured, and the clean crystal ring of glassware delicately touched in a toast)? Or is it more that wine is one of those experiences that urge reflection on us? To taste a wine without contemplating its characteristics and idiosyncrasies is to lose the opportunity to "know" it for ourselves. "Contemplation," contemplated the great Spanish thinker José Ortega y Gasset, means "to seek in a thing what it has of the absolute." And wine has much, if we're of a mind to find it.

It's a common thing, this tendency to limit our understanding of experiences. We continually cut short life's possibilities, heedlessly or with a restless urgency to move our attention around, as if fulfillment was measured by the number of experiences we encounter rather than their depth. The creator of *Alice in Wonderland* knew this well. In his final book, *Sylvie and Bruno*, Lewis Carroll has a character observe, "we lose half the pleasure we might have in Life by not really attending." So it is with wine.

Much of the lost pleasure referred to resides in the lost opportunity to relive experiences later in memory. Of course attention alone can't ensure a memory that will resist forgetfulness. Memorable experiences require framing, and the context has its part to play in recollection. A Mediterranean setting is one sure way to add a touch of *je ne sais quoi* to most experiences, and the Santorini incident is a case in point. But plenty of wines of the finest quality have been consumed in equally memorable settings, only to fade in time from the drinker's recollection, along with their significance. What saved the wines of the Santorini dinner from the same fate was their etching into memory by words. For all their synaesthetic harmony, only the words kept the physical and abstract elements of that evening and its wines meaningful and accessible.

There are many aspects of life where description serves to complete an experience; where not to capture an event in words is to risk it losing import—at every stage, from perception to meaning, understanding, and on to recollection. This applies no less to pleasurable events, and even more to those with claims to the aesthetic. When not captured in words—when, as the psychoanalyst Donnel Stern puts it, experiences are "unformulated"—they resist the call to recall and relive them. This is only logical. Words are how we engage with the events of our life. An event—a chance meeting, a meal shared, wines drunk, company enjoyed—any event that remains unformulated has been given no order, no context, no perspective, and so no frame of reference within our wider lives.

Describing an event, on the other hand, has the instant effect of enhancing the experience. The words themselves generate further layers of enjoyment, as our expression teases out other depths of meaning. "We can reflect on experience only when it exists in verbal form," says Stern, and later adds, "We know about ourselves to the extent that we can spell out in words what we are like, what our experience is like."

In the case of wine, by uncovering its covert qualities words enliven what we're drinking, positioning it within the context of other meaningful events in our life. So in reflecting on a wine, we intrude on our own reverie to give the fullest sense of what we've just tasted. And of course, hearing others describe the same wine in other ways adds further appeal to the wine and camaraderie to the occasion.

Firstly, then, we must give our attention—thereby expanding the parameters of the experience. In the case of wine, this is exploring its physical dimensions. Then comes reflection, which calls up our ideas. And finally, we assemble the words to describe those ideas. Take away attention, and the ideas are stillborn. Without reflection, ideas will be superficial. Deny the expression, and the most perceptive insights will fade like vapor trails before our eyes. Words are "pegs to hang ideas on," as the ever practical Henry Ward Beecher observed.

But what if we choose the "wrong" ideas and words—a possibility, even a likelihood when the novice sets out to describe a wine? It really doesn't matter. A wine expert and accomplished wordsmith may perhaps create a more elegant description and a truer one for them—but not necessarily more legitimate. The right words for each of us are those that mirror our own feelings at the time, having reflected on the wine we're drinking. If at a later time we revisit that wine it will be as a different person, on a different occasion, in different company, with a more experienced palate. We're able to elaborate the earlier ideas, or form different ones with different words. And again the next time. And so on—the present always an amalgam of what we are now and were before. And we *will* wish to revisit life and wine's best moments—as Stern ponders rhetorically, "Are we ever satisfied with interpreting our experience once?"

So, reflecting on and expressing our feelings about an experience gives it a past, a present, and a future—a life beyond the instant. The words are how we keep track of things, so we don't lose the past and the possible enjoyment or insight from its recall. "Words form the thread on which we string our experiences," said Aldous Huxley. The words we use ourselves, and those we hear others use, give an order to our ideas, and a meaning and context and memory.

And it is because all this has happened to others before us, many others and long before, that wine is the substance it is.

In Paul Torday's strangely wine-celebrating novel, *The Irresistible Inheritance of Wilberforce*, the eponymous protagonist is marked by a passion for fine Bordeaux that makes most obsessions look positively half-hearted. Yet while drinking great wines—an '82 Pétrus during a solitary dinner, for instance—he finds his reverie distracted, wandering ... When he returns to the bottle he finds it near empty, and berates himself for all the pleasure he has lost by sipping obliviously, not attending to what he was tasting and what that might have inspired.

Where does all this leave the solitary wine indulger? How, in the absence of companions, can most be made from the wine sipped on one's own? One of us, a live-alone bachelor, drinks wine on his own more than most ...

When I crack a bottle behind closed doors and in the privacy of my own mind, I'm reminded of a passage from Russell Hoban's novel *The*

Medusa Frequency. Hoban, an ex-pat American who gives life to London in his books, is a writer of warmest humor and humanity, and a personal favorite of ours. The book's central character, Herman Orff, is himself a writer as well as being what his all-too-briefly lover describes as "drinkiverous." Visiting a doctor, who asks after his profession, Orff is informed that writers "drink alone too much. People drink faster when they drink alone. [*Not true, I tell you; that's a damned lie.*] You drink alone much?" To his everlasting credit, Orff responds, "Well, I can't be bothered to go looking for people any time I want a drink, can I?" Still, a sense of society can be created in other ways. In order to breathe the illusion of company into my solitary imbibing, I find myself describing the wine ... to myself perhaps (especially when I'm trying to nut out what I really think of it), but more often as I would like to share that wine's experience with someone else. Different people come to mind, according to mood, and spark different descriptive approaches. This is, I find, one way of instilling an atmosphere of companionship into the ceremony of wine enjoyed alone (along with treating yourself to the finest glassware you have to hand, and taking time to decant when it's warranted, not just with older reds but to open up a young red and, on occasion, a particularly restrained white with underlying suggestion of more voluptuous body). I don't describe the wine just once. I talk to myself about it over time, putting into words not merely the first static impression but how the wine unfolds, changing what it offers and promises, and how it reveals more of itself. Though perhaps I'm just trying to avoid the charge of Satyrus (one of a number so-named in the classical world, and I'm really not sure which one)—"It is characteristic of degenerates to take pleasure in wine rather than in their drinking partners."

Not everyone, however, shares our views on breathing more life into wine through words. Emile Peynaud, famed French enologist and palate extraordinaire, takes exception—"It is impossible to describe a wine without simplifying and distorting its image." So, too, philosopher of wine Kent Bach—"Indeed, it is doubtful that words ... can really do justice to really great wines. Words might be useful for pinning down particular aromatic and flavor elements, but they do not seem adequate to the task of capturing what is distinctive about a distinctive wine, much less what makes a great wine great. They are just not precise and specific enough, even in combination." Even one of literature's giants laments at the inefficacy of language—"Human language," says Flaubert in *Madame Bovary*, "is like a cracked kettle on which we strum out tunes to make a bear dance, when we would move the stars to pity." The suggestion of all three is that there is only value in describing the perfect wine perfectly. Yet people create a greater sense of value in their lives all the time, by expressing, or attempting to express, what an event has given them or made them feel. It is the process of *trying to capture* that describes, albeit imperfectly, not just the experience we're trying to encapsulate, but ourselves in light of that experience, what it means to us and how it may have changed us. And, to return a moment to Flaubert—his protestation is, such is his genius, really the greatest proof against itself. The ultimate perfectionist of language, his own words don't lumber ridiculously as his so-rich image would have it, but do indeed soar to the heights of revelation.

Over thousands of years wine has inspired, and been the subject of, much philosophical discussion. Consider the ancient Greeks, who took wine together in Symposium—literally "fellow drinker"—as they discussed the great questions of logic, ethics and aesthetics. It has touched the imaginations of countless notables through history, and been written on surely more than all the other beverages combined. We now have symposia on the philosophy of wine, where learned academics of an equally esoteric and bibulous bent can formally debate wine's capacity for hidden meaning, and its social and cultural significance.

In comparison with such distinguished and scholarly inquiries, the *psychology* of wine might be thought simple. It isn't, but it does hinge on a simple proposition: that the sensory, mental and emotional associations evoked by wine, rich in depth and subtlety themselves, need to be encouraged and explored, or lost—in meaning and in memory.

So we say—and will have cause to say again—*you haven't really tasted a wine until you've put it into words*. Without that, with no contemplation, no reflection, no attempt to turn it into the words it deserves . . . then even the most noble wine, taken sip by sip, hasn't really been drunk, or lived, at all.

PART II

The Language of Wine

Eleven

Turning Wine into Words

Before ever there were words there were impressions. These are conveyed by our senses, and can be dangerously informative.

Emile Peynaud sounds a warning. In "Tasting Is a Difficult Art," he draws attention to "the problem of freeing oneself from the influence of external factors and the various forms of suggestion which might alter one's perceptions." But let it be said, this is decidedly *not* a concern for the happy amateur, the non-professional taster—whether novice, connoisseur or somewhere in between. Consider what Peynaud would forsake—the associations of the wine to be enjoyed, our past experiences drinking it, the quality and synergy of the meal with which we enjoy it, the company of its drinking, the ambience of the setting, the likelihood of that wine becoming linked in memory to the occasion, the prospect of ongoing pleasure in returning to this moment in our mind's eye whenever that wine, or one like it, is consumed in the future ... Such metaphysical considerations must not be allowed to divert the professional taster. But would we wish ourselves deprived of these wine-and-mind-enriching elements? Your choice—between pure pleasure or unbiased objectivity.

Turning wine into words is a contentious thing. How expansive can we be—or not? Devotees of wine-speak clash with its cynics, each damning the other's stance (with the cynics, it must be said, having managed to place themselves on the side of the righteous). As so often happens, both sides produce more heat than light. (Such an encapsulating image. It's at the same time enclosing and incisive, bringing to mind notions of misunderstanding and misrepresentation, the very stuff of controversy, and sitting so appositely in counterpoint to the wind-baggery that characterizes this particular argument. Okay, maybe we did go on a bit—but this *is* a chapter on words.)

When we're first assessing a wine we tend to retreat a little into ourselves. Along with initial impressions, initial appreciation tends to be private and silent. Anticipation may well have been honed by the wine's appearance on pouring into the glass—the green-tinged clarity of a young riesling, the butter-yellow lusciousness of chardonnay or deep, dense glass-staining purple of a heavyweight red (though don't mind if your pinot appears dull and faded—that most intractable of varieties won't always bother to put on its best face, but a drab appearance gives no hint as to the delights it may still offer).

Swirl the wine around in the glass. This releases the wine's perfume more intensely, and even if it didn't it would still remain a deeply satisfying action. As we form an impression of the wine, appreciation takes on a more vocal urge—the desire to share opinions and compare them to the responses of others. This broadens the scope of enjoyment to embrace vicarious pleasures as well as our own. Now, how do we convey these judgments? What vocabulary do we use to describe to others what we feel we're tasting? Peynaud has remarked on the difficulties inherent in trying to describe sensations that are not easily put into words. But that's surely not going to dissuade us from trying? (Having acknowledged their existence, we'll now ignore the carping of cynics as not conducive to this discussion.)

Wine tasters, whatever their level of experience, tend to couch their wine descriptions in one, some, or all of five descriptive dimensions:

- description by flavor,
- description by metaphor,
- description by geometry,
- description by gender, and fifth and finally
- attribution of human characteristics to the wine—anthropomorphizing it, if you like.

The chapters that follow explore these five dimensions of wine description, along with their hows, whys, and wherefores.

Before we move on, however—think how differently you might want to describe a wine to someone about to taste that wine themselves, compared to someone who's never tasted it and isn't just about to. There's likely to be a different focus on what you want to say about the wine, and what they're expecting to hear. In the first instance you'll more probably err on the side of expansiveness, and spice up your description with a touch of the metaphorical or poetic. You are after all, tasting the same flavors. It's the *essence* of the wine that you want to share. In the second case the need of your listener is such that expression is more likely to be pragmatic and informative, frankly, not fancifully, descriptive. That's until such time as the two of you actually share that wine and then the metaphors can come out of the closet.

This is not to put provisos on expression. It's rather to say that, as with all communication, circumstances will influence the choice of language when we describe a wine. A lack of recognition or acknowledgment of this is at the heart of much of the heat referred to earlier.

The language of wine has a long tradition. It goes back almost certainly to the first cultivation of the grape. And it's an honorable tradition. In fact, remove poetry and religious expression from consideration (neither of which could make claim to being an essential part of everyday language) and wine-speak sits preeminently. It surpasses all other experience-specific vernaculars, including those directed to music or painting or the other arts ... and even (gulp) the so-called language of love. In fact the latter, when not drowned out by grunts and shrill cries, is an especially ordinary competitor. The language of love is too often too saccharine. It's too often self-serving (for most of us or for the most part). It is inherently functional in ways that may be gross (with an off-putting vocabulary and plumbing metaphors to match). Invariably corny on replay (and they say the self-indulgent excesses of wine snobs are ridiculous), it's also highly un-poetical (even anti-poetical—forget Donne and Marvell, few are so silver-tongued). It is (perhaps mercifully) incoherent for the most part. It can, it's true, be highly amusing to one's partner if they happen to hear correctly (unless of course *they're* grunting or shrill crying, in which case your sense of the ridiculous will be severely tested). Woefully monosyllabic for obvious reasons (to fit neatly between the heaves), it's also limited in richness and no less in complexity by the paucity and basic similarity of body parts (this is *the* game breaker for wine-speak—the play where it streaks ahead). Then there's that alarming tendency to tail off limply (when satisfied, or through boredom or embarrassment—the I-can't-believe-I-said-that syndrome—usually a welcome sign of the restoration of some critical mental faculties). It's uninformed by said critical mental faculties (ipso facto), and essentially undeveloped since good old Ugg first set the model (though currently trending down if anything under the influence of Hollywood). The language of love is inconsistent and illogical ("lingering aftertaste" in wine language has a meaning, and usually the same one), just plain *stoopid* at times (sorry, you really had to be Sinatra to get away with that), and even optional (a subtle criticism—see previous chapter). Finally, and definitively, the language of love is immensely prone to abrupt endings (insert own script—we've all been there.)

The language of wine, on the other hand, suffers none of these indignities. It is rich and redolent, complex, generous, thoughtful, playful, idiosyncratic and poetic. Small embarrassments can occur, it's true—but hell, they do in the best of traditions. And when that happens, it's quickly picked up (see reference to cynics).

Bear in mind then, as you ponder the descriptive dimensions of the language of wine, that it's just a forerunner—a foretaste, if you like—of the real wonder. How we describe wine is one thing. How wine describes us is a more remarkable other.

Twelve

Flavors Weird and Wonderful

The most obvious description of wine is in terms of the flavors we detect. This dimension of flavor includes both the wine's nose and taste since, according to *The Oxford Companion to the Mind*, "flavor is usually defined as the overall sensation of taste and smell." History's greatest gourmand, Jean-Anthelme Brillat-Savarin, makes the same observation with greater pith and poetry in his *The Physiology of Taste*—"smell and taste form a single sense."

The very first times we raise a glass of wine to our nose, or even the first few dozen times, it smells of nothing so much as ... wine. It might smell like interesting wine, or possibly off-putting, appealing or unappetizing, but at this point our sense of smell hasn't learned enough, or become sufficiently sensitized, to discern the nuances of flavor. So too with its taste. And hardly surprising—few things worth doing, or at least doing well, come to us without some practice.

While chewing over taste, a brief digression seems in order. Consider the pre-Socratic philosopher Democritus, who gave us the concept that all matter is composed of "indivisible units" (*atoma*), and hence our conception of the atom (and in respect of wine, according to Pliny, "claimed to know all the different kinds of vines in Greece"). Democritus was what philosophers of mind would describe as a materialist, that is he didn't distinguish between the processes of the body and those of the soul or spirit—or, in more modern parlance, he made no distinction between matter/brain/sensation and metaphysics/

mind/thought. All our knowledge comes through our apprehension of the actions of atoms, and he additionally believed our physical senses to be absolutely fallible—"by the senses we in truth know nothing sure." As a materialist, Democritus was spared the convolutions of later thinkers who believed, with René Descartes, that body and mind were distinct and separate entities—hence Cartesian Dualism. The problem for dualists is *how*, if body and mind are entirely different in essence, immaterial things (thoughts, feelings, anything mental) can physically act on the material world. Democritus had given no credence to our senses, but at least believed that our perceptions reflected an external reality. To Descartes, by contrast—"Odors, smells and tastes are mere sensations, existing only in thought ... Such sensations represent nothing outside of our minds." Spinoza attempted to reconcile the logical inconsistencies of Descartes' "interactionist" style of dualism by proposing mind and body as parallel in their processes but in no way causal to each other. In the delightfully apposite words of one of our first year Psych textbooks—"Body and mind correlate, but they do not cause one another any more than the convex side of a glass causes the concave." And we will, we believe, leave it there. As to the question, *"How do you and I know that we taste the same thing when we're tasting the same thing*? Well, we won't be lured into that particular epistemological bog. Let's just say that if you can detect a delightful raspberry aroma in this cabernet and so can we, we're not going to wonder about whether our subjective experiences of "raspberry" are the same. That way madness lies.

When sipping your wine in the presence of connoisseurs or self-styled cognoscenti, you might be frequently distracted by a primal-sounding bubbling coming from between their pursed lips. This noise can be distinctly disgusting to normal people, but it's an immensely gratifying sensation in the mouth of the bubbler. The aim is to further aerate the wine in the mouth, thereby releasing more flavor. Not just for noticing by the tongue, but to stimulate the retronasal passage in back of your throat. This sends the olfactory bulb into paroxysms of pleasure—and you really are smelling inside your mouth.

What we are tasting and smelling are most often, unremarkably, fruit flavors, which require little explanation. Other less-than-usual flavors discerned in wines, however, veer from the neutrally unappealing to downright stomach-turning. Pencil shavings, forest floor (plenty of that in good Burgundy), barnyard, feral, civet, even skunk, and, as a 1973 Santenay Gravieres was once described, "of scatological aroma which then vanishes to be replaced by licorice" (are you licking your lips?). A singular flavor term is *garrigue*, which has no equal in the New World. It evokes the arid landscape of Southern France—Provence, Languedoc, and Southern Rhône—the dry scrub and tough wild herbs, rosemary and thyme, lavender and laurel. It is in a sense the essence of *terroir*, as if the landscape itself has made its way into the bottle.

Back to the cynics of wine language. Many object strenuously to the identification of flavors, fair or foul, in their wine. Roald Dahl, while giving us fanciful books like *Charley and the Chocolate Factory*, couldn't abide fanciful wine description, as an ongoing correspondence with *Decanter* magazine revealed. He particularly abhorred the likening of a wine's smell or taste to other fruits, flowers, nuts—anything that wasn't *grape*. In point of fact, wines do smell and taste like banana, apricot, quince, honey, pine, violet ... because of chemistry. Chemical compounds called esters give fruits their distinctive flavors. Esters are formed by the reaction of acids and alcohols. Acids and alcohol react during the fermentation of a wine, as well as afterwards during its ageing.

As you scent a wine's perfume and roll it over your tongue, get in the habit of looking beyond the obvious. Seek out nuance and subtleties. They're not, by their nature, showy. But they make up much of a wine's intrinsic character. A Puligny-Montrachet, for instance, might seem for all the world like face-slamming a bowl of peaches and cream—so delicious in itself that what else matters? Yet, isn't it the barely perceptible note of cinnamon, the tinge of exoticism, that's the making of that wine?

It also seems that discussion of flavor can include its absence. In his "Blind (Drunk) Wine Tasting," P. J. O'Rourke describes a certain wine, which shall remain nameless for charity's sake, as follows—"No flavor at all and yet it still tastes bad." And while not technically a dimension of flavor *per se*, observations of a wine's texture and mouthfeel often come up in this context. It's hardly a stretch to see why we would describe wine in tactile terms. After all, you can't very well drink a wine without touching it. Think of the sensations brought to mind in hearing a wine described as silky or steely, parching or prickly, grainy or grippy. As satirist Jonathan Swift once said of a delightfully chewy wine, "This wine should be eaten, it is too good to be drunk."

We are, as a race, a suggestible lot, and someone at a table identifying cloves in their wine (though hopefully not skunk) can set you to distinguishing just the slightest tang of clove yourself. If you think you detect it, then for all intents and purposes you do. No harm done and plenty of pleasure (provided, of course, you like cloves) with further pleasure still to come. Anyway, with practice comes greater accuracy—and drinking more good wine is the kind of practice nobody could object to. Experiments have suggested that it is not so much greater acuity of smell and taste that distinguishes experienced wine tasters from novices, but their greater range of experience and broader flavor vocabulary.

Never let anyone tell you a flavor you discern in a wine isn't there, as this salutary tale from Cervantes' *Don Quixote* attests. Two forbears of Sancho Panza's, who tells the story to underscore the lineage of his own perspicacious palate, were given a sample of wine to try from a barrel, and asked for their opinion. One tasted, the other simply brought it to his nose. The first described a flavor of iron, the second found a hint of Cordovan leather. The astounded winemaker felt obliged to defend the cleanliness of his barrel and the quality of his process, which certainly did not include the adding of those ingredients. Such flavors couldn't possibly be present in the wine. By and by, when all the wine was gone and the barrel cleaned out, a tiny key was found in it, hanging on a thong of (you guessed it) Cordovan leather.

The squire's story found favor with the philosopher David Hume in making his point that "a good palate is not tried by strong flavors; but by a mixture of small ingredients." And, in the case of wine, it's the subtlety of flavor within and the range of flavor between that gives it its depth of sensuous and aesthetic appeal.

"There are no more than five cardinal tastes," instructs Sun Tzu in the legendary, *The Art of War*, "sour, acrid, salt, sweet, bitter, yet combinations in them yield more flavors than can ever be tasted." You'll never exhaust the possibilities of flavor in wine, no matter how many wines you imbibe. That thought is a comfort, an inspiration, a challenge . . .

. . . Or, a terrifying threat. While working on your repertoire, sniffing and snorting your way from "aniseed" to "underbrush" spare a thought for the geuma-phobics of this world, those poor souls for whom the very act of taste itself—whether it's leather, iron, or raspberry sundae—is aversive and alarming. A surprisingly common affliction (according to those who earn a living from its treatment), the symptoms are said to be similar to a panic attack.

Is it possible that the taste gestapo of the wine world, those Dahl disciples, are really closet sufferers of this condition—smiling through their tears at our licorice and lychees and sandalwood fantasies? Never able to countenance the brambleberry or asparagus, the mulberry and cinnamon. Positively gagging at the thought of kerosene and mildew frolicking in their glass. And as for tree moss or pistachio hitting the old taste buds, instant upchuck (or "Technicolor yawn" for those esotericists more versed in vomitology). Bummer! Of course we've no hard evidence to support this hypothesis, but it has intrinsic appeal and if we scratched around we could probably make it work anecdotally.

From truffles and apricots to candle wax and cashew—if the flavors of wine seem weird and wonderful so much more are its other elements. The thoughts that wine will bring to mind are myriad and tough to ring around. We should wonder why that is.

Thirteen

"Bottled Poetry"

Can you hear, as the poet Baudelaire could, the wine's soul sing in the bottles? What promises it offers. It is "a song which is full of light and brotherhood." The wine is crying to be drunk, crying out to you to become drunk on its spirit. It wants to share itself, and have you pour it out in sharing with others. Wine is, in a way no other beverage can claim, a drink of fellowship. It inspires generosity, prompts and prods and even provokes it, and endows us with more when we are momentarily lacking. It is more than the simple sharing of an entity, goes way beyond the sharing of this quantity in the bottle before us. It is a mutual partaking in a unique experience.

"Wine is life," wrote Petronius, in a statement replete with meaning. Wine easily inspires such thoughts, and inspires us also to accept them for what they seem. It's a short step from this to see that to share wine is to share those things that are best in life. "Best," however, is a personal thing. Its consideration requires we take the bad with the good. For Petronius Arbiter—so called because of his time as the Emperor Nero's official "Arbiter of Taste"—it was a debauched indulgence leavened with cruelty. His place in history is down to his famed work, *Satyricon*, a loose parody of Homer's *Odyssey* that provides a licentious if witty depiction of the excesses of contemporary Roman society. Far from the poetic metaphor our minds want to project into his words, their true sense was crude and boorishly practical—the product of the buffoon-like character Trimalchio who built his repute as a bon vivant on crass depths of ignorance and vulgarity. Rich enough to indulge in the very best of wines, Petronius has his character serving the outstanding Falernian Opimian—claimed by Pliny to have a life of two hundred years—and reflecting in feigned wistfulness, "Wine has a longer life than us poor folks. So let's wet our whistles. Wine is life."

The love of wine has its contradictions. Wish as we might to idealize it, in others that is no necessary measure of worthiness. For every Louis Pasteur there's a Trimalchio. It's akin to admiring a work of literature then discovering the writer's feet of clay. And how often we're doomed to disappointment when we persist in probing into character. So many figures of genius lived their lives in dipsomania and debauchery. And all the while the wine flowed. Baudelaire is a case in point. He espoused the alleviative effect of wine, and wrote of it, of different wines and the characters who consume them to escape from life's condition. The Rag-and-Bone Men, murderers, lovers, and lonely men all had their particular wine. Still, while these orphans of society might seek in wine an easy oblivion, then "reel home scented with the reek of wine casks," they are neither so outcast nor so debased that wine cannot find some way to ennoble them: "Then through man's throat of high exploits it sings / And by its gifts reigns like authentic kings."

Baudelaire's contemporary Guy de Maupassant grants just such a rise on the wings of wine to the protagonist of his most popular novel, *Bel Ami*. A near-destitute ex-soldier, Duroy, is invited, by a chance meeting, to the house of an ex-comrade in arms who is now doing very well for himself. Out of sorts in the refined surroundings, it is the wine that finally allows him to add his piece to the table's conversation, to seek attention and finally to hold forth and earn the admiration of the party. He has chosen Burgundy over Bordeaux—the Grand Cru Corton from Côte de Beune over the distinguished Second Growth Gruaud-Larose from Saint-Julien—for his fancy has been particularly taken by this wine (and why not, indeed?). "He was beginning to experience a delicious sensation of physical comfort, a warmth that, starting from his stomach, rose to his head and spread through every limb until his whole body was glowing. He was seized by a feeling of complete well-being, a well-being of body and mind, life and thought." This episode marks the start of Duroy's rapid elevation in society, one that brings with it more of life's finer things, but the loss of some also. For his wine-inspired rise makes him, at different times, a dupe and fool, and a betrayer of trusts and love. His nickname, "Bel Ami"—good friend—is, by the book's end, the bitterest of ironies.

So, even while transporting, it may well chastise. Such is the resonance of wine and our reasons for drinking it. Horace, the greatest lyrical poet of his day, believed wine to be in itself a muse, and held that any poet worth the name must be a wine-imbiber—"No poems can please for long or live that are written by water drinkers."

Robert Louis Stevenson went even further. "Wine," he said, "is bottled poetry."

Perhaps it's this aspect that draws us to simile or fanciful metaphor, in an attempt to capture the essence of a wine. In Evelyn Waugh's *Brideshead Revisited*, Charles Ryder and Sebastian Flyte spend their summer holidays from Oxford educating themselves from the extensive cellars of the Marchmain family, encouraged by the faithful retainer, Wilcox. As their tasting progresses, their metaphors become more fabulous. One wine is shy like a gazelle, or perhaps a leprechaun, or like the strains of a flute's music by still water. Another is a wise old wine, a prophet in a cave. Yet another resembles a string of pearls on a pale female neck, like a swan, or then again like the last unicorn.

Think, then, when you drink a wine—what does it resemble? What does it make you think of? How does it make you feel, and what image best catches the essence of that?

Is this wine Raphael, Vermeer, Monet, or Hockney? (We put the question of artist-resemblance to a group of friends, while sharing a bottle of the Telmo Rodriguez Dehesa Gago 2005 Tempranillo, from Toro in Spain. While this wine divided the table, there was—to our surprise—near consensus on the artist it called to mind. Goya. Was it the wine's and artist's common homeland? Or perhaps the power of suggestion of a large letter "g" dominating the label. Was it instead the wine's disquieting effect—undoubtedly a wine of quality, but not an easy wine to warm to. It evoked the darker Goya, of the monstrous Saturn devouring his children, or the famous etching "The Sleep of Reason Produces Monsters." Or perhaps the slaughter-house, "Still Life With Sheep's Head"—the animal's carcass echoing the powerfully meaty flavor of the wine.)

Is this wine Hamlet (an indecisive pinot, constantly changing in the glass, vacillating between leading with its fruit or savory face)? Or is it King Lear (a venerable and distinguished *gran reserva* Rioja, of robust manner but drinking now just a little beyond its best)?

Is this wine a languorous swim in a blue ocean, a quest for some elusive truth, or an adrenalin-charged bottomless bungee-jump?

At face value such comparisons can invite laughter. But they are also an attempt to give meaning to an elusive experience by analogy— to pin down or perhaps expand those sensations, our own and those of whoever's with us, by likening them to something they're clearly unlike in order to get to a more poetic likeness. When industry veteran Matt Kramer says of an Échezeaux (a Grand Cru red Burgundy) that it "brims with the finesse and sinewy muscularity of a ballet dancer," we can picture the kind of muscularity he's suggesting, and certainly not that of a weightlifter (which might be invoked in relation to, say, Bordeaux, Barolo, or Ribera del Duero). We read the words, that descriptive phrase, and we think immediately of a strength possessing grace and seeming ease, without grunt or inelegant effort, no brawn or bulk but undeniable *presence*. Much has been said, or at least intimated, in a relatively few words—at least to others who share a similar frame of reference. As Steven Pinker observes in relation to metaphor, "We have to do two things with language. We've got to convey a message and we've got to negotiate what kind of social relationship we have with someone." Could you be convinced of some tempranillo's resemblance to ... an exiled king? If so, a temporary *folie a deux* is established, which may make little sense to anyone else, but could, one hopes, auger well for our more intimate complicity as the evening wears on.

Metaphors abound in the language of wine. And at that we shouldn't be surprised, given the claims made for the ubiquity of metaphor in everyday speech, from both sides of the theoretical debate. "It could be that 95 per cent of our speech is metaphorical, if you go back far enough in language," says Pinker. But there are metaphors and metaphors, and it must be said that some are cheaper than others. What communication message is conveyed when we read that a wine is "intellectual" or "sexually charged"? Or, from the metaphorical schema of construction (and even less constructive), when we are told that some wine is an "edifice"? Do such descriptors induce us to take the time to explore the image, or do we just dismiss them as sloppy or self-indulgent fillers? And on Pinker's other point, what social relationship is then created with the writer? We say "writer" because fifty cent metaphors are more easily tossed off in an article than delivered in a face to face way, with the consequent possibility of emerging with egg on our own if we can't carry it off.

Contrariwise, one of us actually wants to like the metaphor of "edifice" for a wine. On hearing it, a half a dozen different examples jumped to mind at once. It's hard to argue with the charge of deliberate obscurantism—but possible, when the metaphor works, at least to one's own mind. A favorite wine metaphor is from Jancis Robinson, of a wine we'll never get to taste, the '45 Pétrus—"Like velvet. But with a pattern on it." While velvet is more cliché than metaphor for merlot, it's what she adds that adds so much. You can on hearing that "pattern," even with nothing in your mouth, trace your tongue around the wine's textural crenulations. Words as proxy to give the average wine lover a taste for—but not of—an impossible-to-get-hold-of and impossibly expensive wine. Another wine writer, Bruce Palling, gives an ideal description of the red variety cabernet franc—"the equivalent of drinking a red Chablis"—then apologizes for its remoteness, "which isn't very helpful because it doesn't exist." Quite the opposite, the description captures the essence of franc's austerity, its leanness and reluctance to engage—particularly for those who love the white wines of Chablis as we do.

Familiar metaphors, those used in normal conversation, such as the oft-quoted example of argument as warfare "he attacked my position," are short hand communication devices recognized and accepted. There is neither the expectation nor requirement for careful reflection on the image being presented, because it is taken as understood—an intuition developed from experience. On the other hand, to refer to a wine as "passionately entwined" is to propose an image that pretends to familiarity and wants to trade on that, yet clearly hasn't earned the right. As a result it is more apt to confuse, annoy or intimidate than elucidate. None of this is to argue that metaphors have no place in wine language. Rather that they should have at least the objective of enriching understanding, and this is not easy to achieve in the medium of writing. Wine conversation, however, is a different matter. Here metaphor retains all of the potential richness of the figurative.

Anthropomorphic metaphor, such as our "exiled king," is a common and useful device for conveying impressions on wine. Appropriate too, given the many similarities between wines and us. "People cannot use a metaphor to reason with unless they have a deeper grasp of which aspects of the metaphor should be taken seriously, and which should be ignored," says Pinker. Here the underlying image warrants, indeed requires reflection, reflection that will be influenced by the context. The metaphor is an offer to lower one's guard and indulge in poetic conjecture, with a purpose. It's an intellectual exercise, as we circumscribe the image and decide on which aspects have relevance in the context. And it's an emotional exercise, for we must choose how much of ourselves we're willing to reveal. Entered into collaboratively, or even seductively, it will bring pleasure and greater insight—into the wine and your companion, and the possibilities in the relationship. Think how few other widely available experiences provide such opportunities for communication on so many levels. And this kind of whimsical approach to wine via metaphor can do wonders for your appreciation. Rest assured it's nothing at all like the tedious excesses of wine tragics, who tend to lack what's really needed here—the capacity to laugh at themselves, and a firm grip on reality.

"Personification ... is buried deep in winespeak," writes literary critic Ernesto Suarex-Toste, an observation that implies criticism. "Much of the farfetchedness of the genre lies precisely here." True enough. But however it might be ineptly misused, the poetic potential of wine is inherent—a part of its uniqueness as a substance and an experience. To ignore or deny this is to remove wine's most distinguishing feature. If the finest poetry provides an explosion of meaning, so too can the finest wine, as it engages all the senses and compels reflection, contemplation and the expression of our feelings. Poetry and wine are as collaborative as wine and memory—each feeding off the other's complexity to create something of worth that didn't exist before.

Fourteen

Why Wine Appreciation?

It's fitting that we speak of wine *appreciation*. But what does it mean?

Appreciation derives from the same Latin root as does *appraise*—and carries with it the sense of *setting a price on*, or if you prefer, assigning *value*.

Value can come in many ways, many of those unrelated to relative financial worth. The greater values are the personal and, dare we say, the moral values. And these apply to wine as much as to other aesthetic pleasures—wine shared with loved ones to honor an occasion, wine that recalls to mind a treasured memory, wine that exalts ourselves and our company, wine that causes us to probe deep inside our psyche. These are the wines that can expand our moral dimension (and, incidentally, make for the best drinking, whatever score they might attract in show judging). The value we place on them may be out of proportion to how they're seen by others, or even by ourselves in different circumstances. We regard them with appreciation, and remember them, not just for their material qualities, the characteristics that make them complex, but for how they touched us in immaterial ways, how they perhaps made of a mere gathering a metaphysical experience.

This is how we would wish to see appreciation. But some time in the late 18th century the water was muddied and *appreciation* took on the more prosaic and pragmatic sense of *rising in value*. Now if you've your own subterranean cellar, packed to the rafters with First Growth

Bordeaux and Grand Cru Burgundies and the finest German rieslings and the most sought-after Super Tuscans and cult Californian cabs and decades-worth of consecutive Grange vintages ... well, this is a meaning of *appreciation* that'll warm the cockles of your heart—and hell, the least you could do is have us round to crack a bottle or two. If, on the other hand, you're more like us, invading too early what you couldn't even really dignify as a *cellar* ... well, if you're like that, then this kind of appreciation is our mutual enemy, pushing prices up and up for the ongoing purchases of mature wines.

Such an understanding of the word serves to distort the meaning of value in wine, just as has occurred in the case of much art, prostituted perhaps beyond redemption. "Appreciation is a wonderful thing. It makes what is excellent in others belong to us as well"—an insightful observation widely attributed to Voltaire. But we would add a rider—not when the object of wonder must first be consumed to be appreciated. This is where wine parts company from other serious perceptual experiences—it makes voracious demands on the perceiver. The enjoyment of wine is a necessarily variegated thing. Lose the contribution of just one of the five senses, even the least of them, audition—the sound of a wine being generously poured, a bottle deftly uncorked, the "come-hither" sigh of champagne bead—and the whole is diminished disproportionately.

Yet the appreciation of wine in its noblest sense can also approach Chesterton's definition of gratitude, that it is "happiness doubled by wonder." Where, in keeping with the ambiguity of the experience, the response may be as light as a shrug of acknowledgement or something very near to reverence. "The aim of life is appreciation," Chesterton continues in his autobiography. Certainly the aim of wine is appreciation, and wine lovers can appreciate it on two levels. As *taste, judgment, and discernment*—of that wine's qualities (and quality). And as *gratitude*—to the wine's maker, the sommelier who recommends and serves it, and those companions who share and enjoy the bottle.

It's claimed by some (though rarely by artists themselves) that the appreciation of a piece of art (or music, or literature, or wine) mimics the psychological processes that led to its creation. Appreciation then takes on more than a sense of judgment or gratitude, and becomes a form of collaboration. Mark Steyn, aficionado of American musical theatre, relates the story of Cole Porter greeting the band leader Artie Shaw for the first time, with the words "Happy to meet my collaborator"—a reference to Shaw's iconic arrangement of Porter's slight-for-him number "Begin the Beguine" that henceforth defined the song musically. Could a wine drinker's appreciation of a wine have a similar defining effect? Unquestionably, we'd say—though clearly some more than others.

So where does this leave us in our appreciation of wine? Ralph Waldo Emerson claimed that nature and books belong to the eyes beholding them. "It depends on the mood of the man, whether he shall see the sunset or the fine poem. There are always sunsets, and there is always genius; but only a few hours so serene that we can relish nature or criticism." No blueprint can be laid down for appreciation. It depends so much on *our* mood. Sunsets and genius don't give up their riches casually. Nor does wine. But all repay the effort to appreciate them on their own terms.

Fifteen

The Other Side of Appreciation

Michel de Montaigne, that influential philosopher of Renaissance France, was well versed in the pleasures of the palate. "The art of dining well," he once reflected, "is no slight art." He also observed that "the most universal quality is diversity." And this is more and more the case on the wine lists of the world's restaurants.

Diversity's rise is evident in a far greater offering of foreign wines than at any time previous. The outlandish and the obscure were once the purview of only the most rarefied fine dining establishments. Now even neighborhood favorites have set their sights beyond their own borders, beyond even the perennials of Bordeaux, Burgundy and Rhône, Tuscany and Piedmont, Rioja and Ribera ... to Spanish albariño, Austrian grüner veltliner, Italian corvina, molinara, rondinella, lagrein, negroamaro and primitivo, the latter's North American twin zin, Greek agiorgitiko, South African pinotage, Chilean carmenère or even cinsault from Lebanon.

If you ask any sommelier what matters most in a wine, chances are they'll answer *balance*. Pose the same question about a wine list, and you'll more than likely get the same answer. Balance, at its best, comprises appropriate ranging across variety, region, appellation, country of origin, bottle age, price point, diner familiarity (or otherwise), and, logically enough, match to menu. An unbalanced list places limits on a diner's choices and thereby on their enjoyment. Still, essential as balance is, in the sommelier mind diversity's not far behind. Balance is *everything in its place*—to diversity's *a place for everything.*

That last parameter of balance—match to menu—is becoming somewhat more contentious lately. As wine's star rises on the culinary scene, there's occasionally conflict where there should be complementarity—sommeliers and chefs looking to outdo each other, and stamp their own fare as the true hero to the diner. Both should take a hint from wine itself. As balance matters greatly to both wine and wine list, it would seem that they have another equally desirable quality in common—*integration*. Integration at the dining table goes beyond a truce between plate and juice, to the ideal melding of flavors with every taste and swallow taken.

We were, one evening, weighing up the notion of wine list balance with a sommelier mate of ours with over three decades in the game. He wants, when he goes out to dine himself, he wants more than anything else to see a grape variety's full stylistic spectrum represented, and his examples befit a true pinotphile: "There should be sappy pinot, plum and cherry pinot, savory pinot and (personal favorite) *I can't believe it's a pinot* pinot"—that flattens the misconception of pinot as a vinous lightweight, and might appear on a list in the guise of a dense Central Otago, weighty Oregon, or some meaty Gevrey-Chambertin (diversity working hand in hand with balance).

Most diners will notice a lack of balance—a hole in the list, so to speak—because of the absence of a region/variety/style that they'd particularly wanted and had looked forward to ordering. We can only hope, in that situation, that the wine list in question has some compensating offerings. Then the sommelier can, as our friend has it, "steer the diner where they want to go, but in a way that might surprise them." So an unexpected variety, region, even country, can satisfy a diner's desired end—or to put it another way, what balance has overlooked, diversity might provide.

While balance and diversity can certainly be complementary, they can also grate against each other. A slavish adherence to some formulaic notion of balance can lead to a "paint-by-numbers" wine list devoid of surprises. Unbridled diversity on the other hand, unconstrained by any structure, can be simply, or not so simply, bewildering.

When it comes to a choice of wine, many diners don't embrace unfamiliarity for its own sake. For these the line between anticipation and intimidation is a fine one, and force of habit speaks loudly. William James likened habit to a mental rut—once habit is asserted "the alternatives will become harder to contemplate." That's because an inescapable aspect of habit is its seductive appeal to comfort and security, to the reassuring over the untried. Especially when faced with an extensive choice of equally mysterious wines. The diversity of a wine list comes with proportional responsibility—the less well known the range, the more adept the explanations required (and remember, it's the queer and quirky most likely to have customers asking *What the . . . ?*) It also comes with an unspoken promise to the diner—that any clarification is merely a question, or maybe just a sip, away.

Diners come to dine predisposed to be influenced by their floor staff. It's what we want. We're willing to place our dining pleasure in the hands of experts—but only insofar as we perceive our staff to *be* expert. And nothing says "professional" like expert knowledge and service of wine. Restaurant customers are disproportionately impressed by wine expertise—much more so than by the other skills and attributes that distinguish the best waiters. A *Cirque de Soleil* flamboyance in silver service, an elephant's memory for who ordered what and how they wanted it done, a winning charm and smile to match . . . all these, more's the shame, are expected, even taken for granted. Exceeding diner expectations, that calls for flair and flourish in the arcana of the wine list.

Those floor staff able to guide their diners down the paths less traveled won't wait for them to ask for directions. Very likely diners won't. Consider the likely mindset of someone contemplating the grape fiano, that venerable variety of Mount Vesuvius—*Does that rhyme with piano, or "Ti Amo" . . . what's it like, and will I like it . . . what the hell, there's a chardonnay I can't go wrong with.*

But an esoteric list, when presented enthusiastically and sensitively, its hidden gems made titillating not intimidating . . . that kind of list served that kind of way makes a diner's choice a kind of flirtation, or even—if you're a regular there—an ongoing courtship.

The wine list at Veritas in New York is certainly the most exhaustive (not to say exhausting) that we've encountered. Truth be told, it's 63 pages of un-put-downable, irresistible vino-porn for those so inclined. And the restaurant's 65 seats are on any given night serviced by four sommeliers—or as *Kitchen Confidential's* Anthony Bourdain blurted incredulously, "count them, *four*." While that abundance of wine expertise is admirable, it just isn't viable in most establishments. Still, diners should certainly not have to suffer the opposite extreme.

A brief time ago, one of us was phoned by a friend dining with her mother at a place that's been enjoying very sound reviews and will remain otherwise nameless, in the hope that this unedifying incident was an anomaly. This was an important dinner, and wanted wine to carry the occasion. The wine list was by all accounts extremely interesting, with a broad selection of locally grown Italian varieties, and an eclectic mix of wines from the old country—not just the usual suspects of Tuscany and Piedmont and the Tre Venezie, but Lombardy and Liguria, Apulia, Umbria, Marches, and (if memory serves) even Sicily (or was it Sardinia?). The waiter's response to a question was "I don't know anything about those wines"—neither apparently did anyone else there. Hence the phone call. Phone to ear, after reciting the entire list then giving an overview of dishes ordered, our friend had to relay to the waiter an explanation as to why the selected wine—a very nearly too-young Barberesco—should be decanted. Costing well over a century a bottle, the wine went on to be greatly enjoyed with the food. Still, one wonders, in the face of such unreassuring steerage through a well-compiled but frequently obscure list, how many other diners that night were prepared to chance their arm, and their hard-earned coin, on an unknown, unexplained wine. And what frustration (or worse) they likely felt with such abundant choice and unforthcoming assistance. (We can't help thinking of the sufferings of Tantalus in the lowest pits of Hades—banished there for the sin of taking the nectar of the gods from the god's own table, and sharing it with mere mortals:

> Now he hangs, perennially consumed by thirst and hunger, from the bough of a fruit-tree which leans over a marshy lake. Its waves lap against his waist, and sometimes reach his chin, yet whenever he bends down to drink, they slip away, and nothing remains but the black mud at his feet; or, if he ever succeeds in scooping up a handful of water, it slips through his fingers before he can do more than wet his cracked lips, leaving him thirstier than ever. The tree is laden with pears, shining apples, sweet figs, ripe olives and pomegranates, which dangle against his shoulders; but whenever he reaches for the luscious fruit, a gust of wind whirls them out of his reach.

And so he gives his name to that assailing state—*tantalized*—equal parts taunting seduction and perpetually torturous frustration.)

Diversity in a wine list offers so much opportunity, but unsupported by the floor so much is wasted. This is no criticism of sommeliers. Most do an excellent job, but can't be expected to be everywhere all the time. Just like their wine lists, they can also suffer their own share of being unsupported on the floor. There can just be so much about foreign wines that's so, well, *foreign* to many diners. Labels infrequently name varieties, the varieties themselves often offer few clues, and the various European appellation systems have their peculiarly idiosyncratic, if endearing, quirks. When these sorts of things are allowed to overwhelm the *frisson* of indulging in something new, the thrill of moving outside one's comfort zone, then diversity can wind up having the reverse of its intended effect—driving diners back to a narrow but consolingly safe repertoire.

In *The Origin of Species*, Charles Darwin speaks of "beautiful diversity," an essential characteristic to the survival of any species. In improving wine and its appreciation, perhaps there's an element here of vinous survival of the fittest. One thing's indisputable—diversity, all the weird and wonderful wines from all over the world, makes its unique contribution to the ongoing evolution of our wine lists, all our palates, and the evolution of the world wine industry overall. Dipping your toe in the great ocean of wine (and again, and then again) broadens appreciation of the wines from over the sea and those from closer to home.

Sixteen

For Better or for Worse

It's not by accident that we talk of the *marriage* of food and wine. And, as with all marriages, the outcome is often unpredictable. Awkward or transporting. Comfortable or volatile. Reassuring or disillusioning. Or it can be just plain inexplicable.

Next time you dine, serious food and likewise wine, consider what kind of marriage they make. A marriage of passion, say pinot and duck—or convenience, like your order of fish drunk with someone else's choice of cabernet? Easy harmony, ah fizz and oysters—or deep connection, osso bucco with a brooding Brunello di Montalcino? Opposites attracting or familiarity breeding whatever?

"Happiness in marriage"—in the marriage of food and wine, at least—need not be, as Jane Austen had it, "entirely a matter of chance." There are early warning signs, auspicious or otherwise, and to ignore these is to court deep disappointment. So Balzac—"The fate of a marriage depends on the first night." And that fateful match of wine with fish, flesh, or fowl will out in the first taste of the two together, and is ever after unlikely to improve. When the match is sublime, could it be better said than in Genesis, "and they shall be one flesh." (While in the mood for throwing about a few quotes on the union of two brought together as one, you'll excuse our refraining from any sappy, soppy "you complete me" bosh.) Samuel Taylor Coleridge had an intriguing notion of what might make for the happiest of marriages. And while it won't be well loved by all, we feel it offers some simpatico at least. "The most happy marriage I can picture or imagine to myself," reflected the old Romantic, "would be union of a deaf man to a blind woman." We take his point, at least at the dinner table. This would represent a pairing in which the wine's and the dish's quirks, excesses and idiosyncrasies—somewhat limiting on their own—are together elegantly complementary.

There are, it's true, food and wine matching rules. But these can be confusingly contradictory. Matching like with like, for instance, seems sound—light with light, rich with rich, delicate with same, robust dishes and a red with some grunt ... But you're exhorted also not to miss the opportunity for indulging in contrast—one of us wants a young, crisp riesling with pâté, to cut cleanly through the dish's richness, while the other prefers sauternes, to get a double hit of unctuousness. Consider, so they say, the sauce as much as the meat ... pair regional wine with their traditional cuisine ... try a touch of sweetness with salty dishes ... tannin cuts through fat. Chili and firm tannins are an abrasive, not to say a mutually abusive, match. The cohabitation of this couple is stridently discouraged. The oft-forgotten gewürztraminer is etymologically true to its German roots (*gewürz*—spice). It is a spicy little number itself, and matches perfectly—in that like with like way— to spicy Asian dishes from Chinese through Indian and down into Thai and its near neighbor islands. A meaty wine—shiraz, sangiovese, nebbiolo, tempranillo, mourvèdre/mataro/monastrell—wants a meaty dish. As for rosé, and there's no shame in having a glass of pink vino in hand—ladies, it's not a reinforcement of a fluffy stereotype, nor gents is it an admission of, shall we say, *confusion* in a big hairy lad. Rosé's really made its place—as a brilliant all-purpose picnic wine, a fit for everything from the smoked salmon through the pâté to the cold meats and on even to dessert, and as the perfect between-courses palate cleanser for more formal occasions, making far more sense—and giving far more fun—than the old-fashioned sorbet course. And sauvignon blanc, much maligned—by one of us, at any rate—is vinous savior to those ever contrary foods like goat's cheese, asparagus, artichokes, and well-dressed salads.

"The whole is greater than the sum of its parts." That's a popular truism to express the essence of Gestalt psychology. How true it can be with wine and food—when a wine and a dish equally exquisite come together to produce an effect that is truly sublime. Never to be forgotten—dinner at Tetsuya's, roast saddle of hare, Lindemans 1965 Bin 3100 Hunter River Burgundy, summit of food and wine pairing reached and if he die then, then he die a happy, spent, and sated man. On a more cautionary note, however, the whole may well turn out to be *less* than the sum of its parts. Try matching a chardonnay, however excellent, that's middle-weight or more with oak, with chili-laden Asian cuisine—the result is not propitious.

The marriage of wine and food has come even more to the fore with the ascendancy of the deg menu. *Degustation*—literally, the act of tasting. Consider the personal implications of degustation—that in pursuit of a wider and more exotic variety of tasting experiences, diners are willing to surrender that most personal of dining's offerings, individual choice. And chefs, for their part, can set about composing an entire six or eight or ten or twelve course culinary symphony.

The rise of degustation wine selections has raised the prominence and profile of the sommelier's role. Many diners will choose to follow the sommelier's expert recommendations—and so, relieved of all choice, can give over entirely to the indulgences of the evening. Others court the sommelier's approval of their own selection, and bask in acknowledgement of a well-made choice, feeling their own stocks rise in the eyes of their dining companions. A good sommelier always seems to know what's wanted. They're a quick study of the vagaries of human nature, and an insightful reader of a diner's needs. A good sommelier will guide their guests, or be guided by them, as best befits what they want this evening, novice or initiate, through the cryptic convolutions of Old World and New, region, appellation, maker, negociant, viticulture, viniculture, vintage, variety, blend, style, flavor, nuance. And they can always be counted on for their enthusiasm, astuteness ... and discretion.

A sommelier to one of us one evening:
"Is there anything you'd like to know about our wines?"
"Very likely," that one said—and then to the lass accompanying him, "What are you thinking of ordering?"
"I've never had Piggy on Pie before."
Thinks, *Neither have I, what the hell is it*? Looking for it on the menu, and imagining some sort of nouvelle re-interpretation of an English pork pie. Aha ...
"A pinot," suggested the sommelier, smiling only with her eyes, "would be just the thing for ... piggy on pie."
"Indeed," says our intrepid hero, who has decided on duck for himself, and orders a cracking Premier Cru Mercurey.
The lass, when mains were being consumed, declared the pinot and her, ah ... *pigeon* pie, to be wonderful together.
Memories of Charles Ryder in *Brideshead Revisited*, dining extravagantly in Paris—"It doesn't matter what people call you unless they call you pigeon pie and eat you up."

It's a noble lineage, that of sommelier. You can hark back to the 14th century and consider Sante Lancerio who held the post of *bottigliere* for Pope Paul III. Lancerio kept meticulous account of the best wines to grace the pontiff's table. And in doing so he initiated wine terminology—specific description of color, odor, and flavor and further still into the more broadly metaphorical characterization of wines, though not everyone will thank him for that. Nicholas Bidet, unfortunate name, was sommelier to Marie Antoinette and also found time to compose papers on the science of wine. He was a wine drinker first and Frenchman only after—"Champagne is my motherland"—in its way an admirable kind of nationalism.

Mention of Champagne, and other strands of our subject at hand, prompts a memory in one of us ... (And a warning from the other. This would be the perfect time to refresh your glass—open another bottle if it's needed—then put your feet up and get comfy. This could take a while.)

I've always loved that line of M. F. K. Fisher's, a wonderful writer and great celebrator of the culinary arts—"there is a communion of more than our bodies when bread is broken and wine drunk."

For me, some still life paintings really emphasize this sentiment. The freshly baked loaf torn open to show the impossible whiteness of its flesh, and beside it a glass brimming with gold or ruby. The absence of any human presence in these paintings seems to underscore the simple metaphysics of Fisher's view. The plain objects of nourishment have an essence that's their own, outside of any particular human taste or appetite.

Yet, for all that food and wine can come together in such felicitous circumstances, viewed individually they don't necessarily, to me at least, seem always like soulmates. I'm reminded for some reason of the flawless artistry of a Fred Astaire and Ginger Rogers dance, so smoothly flowing, so full of aloof passion and intelligence. But break that spell, and what you take away is the magic of one. Rogers provided the chiffon, the allure, the wholesome sex that completed Astaire's perfection. But the claim to perfection was his.

This disparity between food and wine, I had it brought home to me on a visit to Harrods some years ago. I was coming towards the end of a round-the-world trip that included South Africa, where I'd visited some of the great wineries of the Cape. In London, I got my business out of the way and, still flushed with the memories of the Cape wines I'd tasted—memorable chenins and cabernets, and my first fling with South Africa's singular pinotage—I decided to indulge myself in a morning at Harrods. Touring the store, admiring the rich remoteness of the merchandise, I splashed out on a tee shirt—an expensive item there, even on special. It was a Nicole Farhi brand, the clincher for me being that she was married to the playwright David Hare (we were at the time dabbling in some writing for the stage). Looking back it seems a somewhat desperate act for someone so determinedly non-superstitious, but it was an elegant piece and I wanted to make a purchase there.

A point of digression ... A couple of years later I was in Boston and rounded off some business with a visit to a notable restaurant, wearing my smart tee shirt under a jacket. I was refused entry by the Maitre d' on the grounds that the shirt had no collar. I looked around the dining room at other diners in their less than distinguished gear, albeit sporting collars, and began to marshal the arguments I felt sure would win my entry—"This is a Nicole Fahri," "Have you any idea what it cost me ... at *Harrods*?" "She's married to David Hare, the playwright ..." This tendency in us to be defensive, even protective of seemingly trite things that have a personal significance—when I see it in others I always find it a little touching. In myself I have to admit to finding it somewhat pathetic. Either way, to co-opt Nietzsche's words, it's "human, all too human." Anyway, as it turned out I put my reservation back an hour, went back to my hotel and changed. That's all I remember of that evening, and that restaurant.

Back to Harrods—I wandered around the store, ending up as I'd planned in the food hall and wine section. The sleekly expensive displays of food were impressive. They certainly inspired an appetite, but they didn't inspire me to abstract thoughts. The wines on the other hand, they had stories to tell, every one. Their different places of origin, different sizes and shapes of the bottles, the colorful patchwork of all their labels ... these gave the wines, paradoxically perhaps, an individuality compared to which the presentation of the foods seem artificial. Fred Astaire was a wine, I decided. Or all manner of fine wines. Ginger was the superbly lightly tripping accompaniment, the gorgeous dishes that paced and filled in the spaces of an evening. Together they were magical—but she needed him.

In Harrods it never occurred to me that the very next day I would test the truth of these musings on the relationship between wine and food. Before leaving on the trip I'd been offered an invitation to visit Moët & Chandon in Épernay. The offer came about from no merit of my own. An old family friend had a business that was a prodigious customer of their champagne. Ironically in fact, it had originally been offered to my son and co-author who was (to his enduring disappointment, thanks very much) unable at the time to take it up. Being able to go in his place generated a few pigs and strawberries barbs, to which I didn't argue, recognizing how slender my knowledge of wine was at the time—much the ugly sister compared to my *enthusiasm* for it. Had I not chosen to visit Harrods that morning in London, and not been caught up in philosophic reflections on wine, quite likely I would have canceled. I loath organized tours, though at least this one would have the merit of invisibility. I could disappear within an indulging crowd and indulge myself in unobtrusive learning as I pleased.

In any event, early the next morning I flew to Paris, checked into an expensive hotel (is there another kind in Paris?) and caught a train to my destination. The first sign that I'd underestimated what lay in store for me was the chauffeur-type waving a sign, "Dr. Mitchell." He took me to a Mercedes and we drove to the Hôtel Moët. The train had been a little late and clearly my arrival was awaited. I was escorted to a room where I met my host—charming man (French I think) with a title that gave an atypical cachet to P.R. Also present were three fellow guests. Two, it turned out, were prominent wine buyers—one of those, as it happened, the senior wine buyer from Harrods—and the third an ambassador from one of the Gulf States. My appearance was the signal to adjourn to an elegant sitting room, where the pre-lunch drinks were to be served.

With my invisibility gone, and any thoughts of inconspicuous education with it, my sole concern was to avoid the embarrassment of exposure as an imposter, and consignment to wherever the wine-ignorant are consigned in this area of France. In my defense, I'd like to believe I wanted to spare this embarrassment for my hosts as much as for myself—to seem unworthy of the degree of largesse we were clearly about to receive, that would be an unkind blow to the spirit of hospitality. Not for the first time, nor the last, I relied on the epithet "Dr." to muddy the waters. It can work a treat in such situations. You might be anyone, your expertise in any field. So I retired behind the persona, presenting a face of impassive companionability; and where I could, took on the added protective coloring of mimicking the actions of my fellows, so clearly at home in this private chamber of one of the world's great wine names. Thankfully the faking didn't have to extend to my enjoyment of the aperitif—an '85 Dom Pérignon. That year had started disastrously for the region, with extremes of winter cold and spring frosts, but ended in fine enough style to cap one of the great vintages of the 80s. My comments on the wine must have been more than a touch idiosyncratic. Perhaps they even raised a metaphorical eyebrow or two. Still, no one, not our host nor my fellow guests, was so ungracious as to appear bemused. I'd like to think they took my descriptive style as an endearing eccentricity. Pleasure aside, the episode was a window into how the other half lives, when it comes to fine wines. The intimate familiarity of the ambassador with the champagne of the moment, and a litany of preceding vintages, suggested that Dom Pérignon could easily have been the beverage of choice for breakfast in his set.

We were called to lunch to a lavish room decorated in green and found there another guest, Madame Simon, the predecessor of our host who had only recently retired after many years in the role. It soon became clear that this was to be an occasion of surprises. The venue, the very grand Salon Impérial, was not one typically used for occasions of such modesty. (There was talk that it was originally designed for a visit by the Emperor Napoleon in the early 1800s.) Then there was the pecking order of the day's repast. Astaire, it seemed, was to be the star; Ginger very much the accompaniment—still delectable, still superbly turned out, still delivering that pouting sex appeal, but seriously second. The wines were announced with much fanfare. Only then the foods that would accompany them, and the reasons behind each pairing. It was as though my idle musings in Harrods had been given both philosophical and practical legitimacy. Others had come to see what to me now was blindingly clear—that in the marriage of food and wine, the intellectual heft lay with the wine. Food, for all its sensual contribution to the partnership, was a cerebral lightweight. I toyed with other marriage analogies, Marilyn Monroe and Arthur Miller came to mind, but kept returning to Fred and Ginger, hugging myself for my prescience.

While we were in Champagne, and these wines were products of the château, they were not champagnes. They were still table wines—though as far as you could go from undistinguished *vin de table*. First a white, a 100% chardonnay Coteaux Champenois, a blend of various vintage years from the Saran vineyard. This wine was, quite simply, superb. Two days later I flew the Concorde from London to New York, in the course of which I consumed several glasses of an '87 Premier Cru Puligny-Montrachet that defied altitude's notorious flattening of the palate (the flight was far shorter than it ought reasonably to have been given the quality of the wine list). Different chardonnays, different circumstances, but demanding comparison. The Saran won hands down. The Épernay experience was like an emergence into Technicolor—Dorothy and Toto arriving in Oz, all eye-opening vibrancy. Or was that, perhaps, the effect of the starter? Or the magic of their match? It was a mushroom-based dish, simultaneously rustic and refined, and that's all I can recall. I do know that it was unbelievably good. I know also that it didn't believe it was there to play second fiddle to the wine. But this was lunchtime and I was already in two champagnes plus a top-up or two of the Saran, and it didn't feel right to question feelings I'd experienced with such certainty earlier.

Then came the main course—a rich beef dish perfectly done with accompanying vegetables that couldn't have been better paired. This was the support act to a red made from château-grown pinot noir, an '85 Bouzy Rouge, not sold but kept exclusively for oh-so-fortunate guests. Comparisons of whatever kind became superfluous. Now everything was perfection—the wine, the food, the conversation, the kind deference of the two hosts, even the encyclopedic knowledge of the ambassador on all things vinous—all seemed just right and proper and in perfect balance to the occasion. What had happened to Fred and Ginger? Why was the yin looking so yang? I began to think it possible that Marilyn had written *The Crucible*. Where was the clarity of earlier? Could philosophical insights be so ephemeral?

Dessert followed, served as a match to champagne. And how good was it? Superlatives fail. We left the ghost of Bonaparte and adjoined back to the sitting room for a truly unique post-prandial experience. And what an after dinner drink. A Marc de Champagne no longer produced, but made then by distilling the grape skins, seeds and stalks left from the pressing process in the first stages of champagne production. My companions were in raptures, breathing its fumes deeply, swirling and sipping and rolling it luxuriantly around their mouths. No keen spirit drinker, all I knew was that this wasn't for neophytes. This liquid could clear all the world's and history's sinuses. Smelling it, even as tentatively as I did, was like being caught between the immovable object and the irresistible force. But, funnily enough, the intensely spirit-y aroma (*aroma* ...? if a clout can be called a caress) was above all sobering. And that was useful. For it had been arranged that Madame was to take me on a personal tour of the cellars, 18 miles of wall-to-wall champagne classicism in the making. I learned at this point that the other three guests had stayed the night, and had their tour, *sans* Madame, the previous afternoon. Rather than envious, this made me feel relieved, less of a mountebank, and determined to make the most of what remained.

The cellars were dimly lit, seemingly endless arched corridors. I recall Madame saying that at a certain stage the wines were rotated each day for several weeks in the process of *remuage*—the gradual settling of the sediment that secondary fermentation produces, preparatory to its removal. They must have had an invisible army on hand, for we didn't encounter a soul. Occasionally muffled voices from what was presumably a guided tour were faintly discernable as we strolled the cellars, but my attention was entirely caught up in my companion. Our conversation was her life story, told in the context of the wines. Aside from her family, her life was the company, its wares and reputation, and all that it stood for. I asked what she would do now that she was retired. She was building a large house, a castle of sorts, in Brittany. There she would immerse herself in the classic history of her homeland. I remember my admiration for the depth of her love of France. No trace of hauteur, just extreme affection and pride, and a touching faith. I truly regretted her story coming to its end, drawn back again to our surroundings which had become part of the tale of the past few hours.

It was a surreal end to a strange day. We exchanged cards and I vaguely promised to call on another visit to France. I didn't of course. For the same reason perhaps that the Santorini wines were not initially sought out, the improbability of being able to recreate the mood of an experience, while knowing that anything less would be a disservice. "You cannot step twice into the same river." Heraclitus, and later William James, nailed it perfectly.

I made my goodbyes to my companions of lunch, now even more deeply immersed in their glasses. I didn't offer my card. Nor they. We knew our differences. I didn't envy them their lives, or their professional exposure to the finest wine. My time with Madame had given me what I thought was a uniquely different and personal perspective, a deep respect for something that could inspire such passion and imagination in a fellow being, and no less solid a basis for my Fred Astaire fantasies.

On the train back to Paris I feverishly wrote down in detail everything of that day. As to my insights on wine and food, I placed them aside to be reassessed, happy that I could somehow leave the test of that to dinner. I wandered the streets around my hotel for an hour looking at menus, before deciding in some surprise but also apparent determination that I would have a pizza. It was an indifferent meal, during which I consoled myself with the sanctimonious thought that any choice of French food after that lunch would have been a form of sacrilege. Who knows if that was my real reason, or whether in fact I had just become hungry and tired of the looking. By then all my naïve and arrogant convictions about the relative merits of food and wine had gone—fading as fast as they'd first appeared. I was sure of only one thing—that I *had* over the course of those Moët hours shared in the communion of which Fisher so famously wrote. And I knew as well that for such rare and cherished occasions, analysis of any kind, even retrospective, could only sully the experience and the memory.

The next morning, before leaving for home I went to the Louvre. I think I must have done that out of a tourist's sense of duty, since I recall little of the visit. My notes on the day at Épernay were subsequently lost . . .

The drinking of wine has always and ever been associated with dining. Whether boisterous occasion or intimate restaurant *tête à tête*, wine prepares us for what is to come. It is no more a mere accompaniment to food than a lover is a mere friend. Not all such relationships can play out to equal effect, and here the weight of mutual benefit falls more often to the food, while wine casts the spells that make or break the evening. It brings us into ourselves, and helps take us out as well. It shrinks the small world of the table as it opens wider possibilities— and all the while it blurs and accentuates that fine line distinguishing temptation and opportunity.

Seventeen

The Geometry of Wine

Flavor and metaphor don't exhaust the wine lexicon. We frequently find wine described in geometrical terms.

Balanced, symmetrical, round or flat, possessing angular tannins, we've even heard wines described as "lopsided." While having drunk more than a few lopsided wines ourselves, it's still more typically the drinker who winds up in that state.

Balance is a necessary virtue in a wine, and its lack a barely excusable vice. Recognizing, however, what's personally appealing as balance is a matter of personal taste. As Ann C. Noble (Professor Emerita, University of California, Davis) puts it—"The perception of balance is so individual. There can be an elephant on one side of the seesaw, and Tinker Bell on the other, and some people will perceive the wine as balanced because of the algebra of their brain." The modern debate over balance has come about largely due to the quest for increasing levels of ripeness in fruit, resulting in higher levels of alcohol. The New World is frequently singled out as guilty, as well as certain critics whose leaning is towards more powerful wines. Changes, though, in wine-making techniques and philosophies and fluctuations in the world palate have seen the Old World, especially with the so-called "International Style" wines, well and truly in this mix. Devotees of the ripe, high-alcohol style proclaim their preference for a "more is more" lushness. Detractors, of the "less is more" inclination, contend that the fine line separating ripe from overripe has been so far passed that it's in danger of disappearing way back where. They regret the loss of elegance, of nuance and subtlety, of wine's cleansing refreshment lost to the mouth-heat that high alcohol brings. Most of all they regret the loss of balance. This isn't to say that powerful wines can't display an admirable balance. It's by no means impossible, but it might be closer to that "camel through the eye of a needle" kind of thing.

The word itself, *balance*, can't help but bring to mind a set of scales (it might even incline you to hold your hands out, on either side and cupped, and then sway slightly from side to side ... but maybe that's just us). It's not, however, merely a weighing of one characteristic against one other. With wine the scales of your own taste are more like a spindle, with a multitude of extending arms, all in the most fragile equilibrium. A deviation in any one of those, and the whole may well come tumbling down—that is, the wine will be well out of whack, at least to your own personal preferences.

Balance in itself can't define the quality of the wine. All the various elements—fruit, sweetness, alcohol, acidity, tannin, and so on—need also to combine seamlessly with each other. That is, the wine should display *integration.* An interesting word. There's, at first, a mechanistic connotation—an image of cleanly meshing gears in a well-oiled machine. If that seems a little cold or soulless, there's another resonance—the wine as an organic whole. Something fitting and feeling *just so* in your mouth, something you can run your tongue around, feeling no intrusive peaks or troughs, only a biomorphic completeness. Through integration, balance becomes a *harmonious* whole.

Harmonious, now there's a lovely word. As lovely as the goddess from whom the name was taken. Harmonia was the daughter of beauty and war (though she seems to have taken more after mother Aphrodite, leaving sister Eris—Strife—to carry the inheritance of father Ares). And as wife of Cadmus and mother to Semele, she was grandmother to Dionysus, the god of wine—how apt. She was aligned in myth to the Muses, and there's a music to the word she leaves as her legacy.

That's not all that "harmony" means to us. Pythagoras, father of mathematics, saw musical harmony in mathematical terms. And so harmony in wine strikes us, too. A harmonious wine is in perfect proportion, all its elements in ideal ratio to each other.

The "golden ratio" or "golden mean"—represented by the Greek letter *phi*—expresses a mathematical relationship that has been embraced aesthetically through history, and "has been said to possess inherent aesthetic value because of an alleged correspondence with the laws of nature or the universe." The proportions of the Parthenon were governed by the golden mean, or as closely as imperfect human hands could approximate (*phi* being, like its mathematical sibling *pi*, intractably irrational). Leonardo da Vinci arranged the detail of his works based on his belief that certain bodily proportions within the human form were divine expression of the golden mean, and illustrations of his were included in the book *Divina Proportione* by his friend, the most famous mathematician of the day, Luca Pacioli. In this, as in so many things, he influenced many painters who came after, among them (though in entirely different ways) Dali and Mondrian. Even music—an art form of harmony in time, not space—had its adherents to composition by the golden mean. Musicologists have claimed this of Bach cantatas, Beethoven's Fifth, Mozart's sonatas, and select works of Schubert, Debussy, Satie, and Bartók. Does wine have its own golden mean, in balance and beauty? In liking a wine, even finding it beautiful, are we recognizing—if only unconsciously—the ideal proportion of all its aspects, with no spoiling overstatement or understatement. There is only consonance, no false notes. Such a wine is as compositionally pleasing as the *Suite No. 3 for Orchestra* or *The Last Supper*.

The golden mean was also a moral virtue in the philosophy of Aristotle—the desirable middle way between the extremes of excess and want. The essence of this is perfectly caught by the modern philosopher Julian Baggini—"Courage, for example, lies between the excess of rashness and the deficiency of cowardice. Generosity avoids the excess of profligacy and also the deficiency of meanness." It strikes us that the most engaging and fascinating of wines are those that flirt with extremes—opulence and austerity, for instance—but wend the ideal way between them, never falling into one side's excess or the other's unfulfillment.

Flat versus round is a common geometrical opposition used in description of wine. A wine will be deemed round, we've even heard such a wine described as *spherical*, when the mouthfeel is full and smooth all over. There are no sharp points that might require comparison to some less elegant 3-D polygon, no coarse or unintegrated tannins, no bitter pricking of other unkind phenolics.

Flat is a very telling wine word. It conjures up a sense of existential onomatopoeia. A flat wine tastes as we feel when we are not at our worst, but some way from our best—uninspired, uninspiring and unable or unwilling to express anything uplifting. When we feel flat, we're not the whole of ourselves. And a wine that's flat, while exhibiting no fault, gives us much less than it might.

There's a parallel here to a notion of the writer E. M. Forster in *Aspects of the Novel*. The most influential and enduring of these essays addresses characterization in fiction, and makes the literary distinction between "flat" and "round" characters. "Flat characters are sometimes called types and sometimes caricatures. In their purest form they are constructed around a single idea or quality ... The really flat characters can be expressed in one sentence." Flat, in Forster's meaning, is not necessarily pejorative. Context must be taken into consideration.

Because flat characters provide a valuable tool for filling out or moving forward the plot, they are frequently met in genre literature. And who of us doesn't like a good spy/crime/sci-fi/chick-lit bit of harmless self-indulgence now and then—just as we at times prefer pizza with a rough red over caviar and champagne.

Dickens is particularly cited as a master of flat characters (Forster even uses Mrs. Micawber in *David Copperfield* to define what it means for a character to be flat). His densely populated plots require many of them. Within the Dickens storyline they can engage, amuse, or appall. But take one such character in isolation from their surrounds and story, and you'd be left with someone singularly unexciting. So, too, with a bottle of wine not giving its best. Its mere presence as a mark of the evening's continuing conviviality may well be a reinvigorating and reassuring thing. But sitting back for a moment from the hubbub of the table's friendship and fellow feeling, to concentrate on this glass of wine you've just been poured … Well, without the accompanying company and confidences, it's a little disappointing. Not ruinously so, but the opportunity for enhancing the experience of all has fallen away with this particular bottle—to be resurrected, we hope, by the next.

We referred earlier to Russell Hoban's novel *The Medusa Frequency*. Hoban is a writer who delights in playing games with the round/flat character distinction, until it's turned entirely on its head. In this book the only round character is the protagonist, Herman Orff. So flat is every other character that Herman suspects they're interchangeable—a cast of a mere few doubling up in parts to play the multitude. "Economy" is how it's explained to him, by one of the interchangeables himself. "You have a chat with a stranger now and then, right? So do I, so does everyone. How many lines has the stranger got? Two or three maybe. There's really no need for a new actor each time, is there." Herman is further informed that, while a fully-fleshed and rounded-out character to himself, he is also, unknowingly, just an interchangeable bit-part to others—"Yesterday you were the conductor on the 11 bus and you also did quite a nice little tobacconist in the Charing Cross Road."

We mention this because it brings to mind too many wine lists we encounter. With all the wine available from all corners of the world, too often it seems that only a handful of brands get representation. There's no challenge to such lists, and worse than this, no sense of adventure. You could travel the world in the glass in your hand—but that opportunity's denied to you. The same names are plugged in to fill this and that slot. Lists we like to think of as *round*, on the other hand, possess the same virtue as round characters in literature—the capacity to surprise, over and over again.

Round characters and round wines, then, are endlessly surprising. That fact is surely the savior of even the most jaded palate. And the similarities don't end there. Consider what else Forster had in mind. Round characters possess a wide variety of qualities. Ditto the wines that most excite. The round character is complex. Ditto ditto. They bring us a distinctly different pleasure each time we meet with them, though our sense of familiarity loses nothing in that. The round character has, as Forster himself put it, *"the incalculability of life about it."* Could the pleasure we take in wine be any better expressed? Finally, and most definingly, the round character and the round wine are set apart by their capacity to *develop*, to change and so become with time something even more entrancing, and worth our deeper reflection.

We would always prefer our wines to seem round to us—and ourselves seem round characters to those we're drinking with.

Eighteen

Is It a Boy or a Girl?

Overheard one evening from an adjacent table, while not strictly minding our own business:

> He, "Would you call this wine masculine or feminine?"
> She, "I'm not sure what you mean."
> He, "How does it feel in your mouth? Work it around, use your tongue ...
> Majestic, would you say?"
> She, "I'd say pompous. So it must be masculine."
> *Touché.*

Wine is frequently—surprisingly frequently—rendered in terms of gender. Wines deemed to be assertive or even aggressive, weighty (sometimes ponderous), majestic, frank, candid, or forward tend to be described as masculine. Those wines viewed, on the other hand, as subtle and seductive, sensual and elegant, intriguing and elusive (not to say deceptive) tend to be described as feminine. Bordeaux, for instance, intense and brooding as they are, clearly fall into the masculine camp. Burgundies, endlessly beguiling, into the feminine. Even their respective bottle shapes reflect this association—the claret bottle's broad shoulders against the sinuous and swan-necked Burgundy bottle.

Bordeaux doesn't, however, have the masculine claim all its own way. The English literary critic and wine scribe, George Saintsbury, who gave his name to the famous Saintsbury Club, described the syrah of the Hermitage region as "the manliest wine" he had ever had. Though it's not entirely clear whether this was a pronouncement on the wine's own testosterone levels, or the feelings it brought forth in the drinker. Commenting on Saintsbury's observation in her voluminous *Wine Bible*, Karen MacNeil pushes the gender-identification further, detecting in Hermitage "that kind of salty, almost sweaty allure of a man's body."

Near neighbor of Hermitage in the Northern Rhône, Côte-Rôtie also produces powerful syrah-based wines. The most renowned grape growing areas, both steeply terraced hillsides, are the Côte Blonde—whose soil is, as the name suggests, of a lighter color—and Côte Brune, with darker soil. Local legend (too irresistible to doubt) has a nobleman of old bestowing one section on his blonde daughter, the other going to her sister of darker coloring—and over time the characteristics of these divided plots of land have come more and more to resemble their respective landladies.

E. Guigal, named for founder Etienne, is an iconic wine-producing family company based in Côte-Rôtie. Their most famous, famously rare and fabulously expensive wines are known colloquially as the La-Las—*La Mouline*, *La Turque*, and *La Landonne*. *La Mouline* hails from the Côte Blonde, and shows a feminine restraint, fragrance and finesse. The other two Las are Côte Brune—both deeper, darker, denser wines possessing astonishing length (*La Turque* perhaps a tad the lighter, for the inclusion of seven percent of the white grape viognier in its blend, while *La Landonne* is unashamedly pure unadulterated syrah). The sexual dynamics, however, become somewhat more ambiguous with Guigal's *Brune et Blonde*—a blend of both Côtes. So often opposites cancel each other out, but not here. Rather than appearing insipidly androgynous, this is simultaneously a face-buryingly voluptuous and proudly priapic hermaphrodite—and if that sounds wrong, then so many things ought to be.

In fact all across the wine world the gender distinction is not as clear as it might seem. Everything is relative. Within the feminine Burgundy, Chambolle-Musigny or Volnay will be regarded as über-feminine in comparison to the meatier wines of Nuits-Saint-Georges or Gevrey-Chambertin. And within Bordeaux, the cabernet-dominated wines of Pauillac on the Bordeaux Left Bank are seen as masculine to the iron-fist-in-a-velvet-palate merlot-dominated wines of Pomerol on the Right Bank. Moreover, within Pauillac itself, Château Latour is inescapably a masculine wine compared to the more elegant Lafite. And while not wishing to muddy the waters any more, there can, it seems, be masculine and feminine distinctions between the same wine across different vintages—how's that for having gender identity issues? Take Medoc wines in general, and compare the power and intensity of the '86 vintage to the supple finesse of '85.

Apparently there are not only degrees of masculinity and femininity, but different types as well. Legendary Italian winemaker, Angelo Gaja, patriarch of the Gaja wine family and *Decanter* magazine Man of the Year in 1998, speaks up for the masculine claims of the nebbiolo grape, responsible for the great Barolos and Barberescos of the Piedmont region. That arbiter of all things sexual, Freud himself, was inclined to "seek strength in a bottle of Barolo" when his spirits flagged (one can only wonder whether he turned to the supposedly masculine Barolos of the north or to the more feminine style of the south). Gaja has likened cabernet to John Wayne, and nebbiolo to Marcello Mastroianni. Let's ponder on what he could mean by this grape/actor comparison—and further on its legitimacy.

First of all, Gaja's not talking of the men themselves, but of their prevailing public images as established through their film roles. Now this isn't the time or place, nor have we the space, to examine Mastroianni's entire cinema career. So we've gone for his performance in Fellini's masterwork, *8 1/2*—a defining role, playing Fellini's alter-ego in this intensely autobiographical film. Interestingly enough, Mastroianni, subsequently dubbed the "Latin Lover" and renowned for his affairs with some of the world's most beautiful women, was originally cast by Fellini on account of his "terribly ordinary face."

Guido Anselmi—Mastroianni's character—is a director renowned for his "films of hopelessness." He is beset by nightmares and, even more disturbingly, by a creative block that he fears might be permanent, might in fact be the indictment of an entire career—"What if it's the end of a bluffer who ran out of talent?" Mastroianni has been sent by doctors to a health resort to "take the cure"—and from there he is attempting to bring to fruition his next project, currently a formless mess driven by intuition rather than ideas. "You wonder, what is the director really trying to do?" asks the odious Daumier, Mastroianni's collaborative writer (and surely not the first time those words have been uttered in relation to a Fellini film).

He seems to be searching for a female image that will solidify his own desires and give shape to what he wants his film to articulate. His dealings with different female characters betray the fact that he's really searching for a symbol more than a real woman. As a consequence, none satisfies his requirements and his needs—not Gloria, the overwrought philosophy student whose thesis deals with loneliness in the modern theater; not Carla, his vain and vacuous society mistress (whose face is insufficiently whore-like), for whom he feels an alternating attraction and repulsion; not the actresses he is casting for roles that don't necessarily exist; certainly not his wife Luisa (the delectable Anouk Aimée), at once muse and figure of enduring accusation; not her chiding best friend Rossella who talks to the spirits and claims to know Mastroianni's fate; and not a host of feminine presences from his past—including the repellent but perversely alluring rumba-dancing Saraghina—who bring into his waking dreams equal parts regret and self-recrimination.

These flashbacks, drawn from Fellini's own deeply felt past, are among the most affecting in the film. The happiest of these, in its simple innocence, speaks to our own present theme. The young Guido—the young Fellini—is lowered into a large wooden vat among a boisterous gang of other children, dancing and stamping in the macerating grapes and fermenting must. It's a kind of baptism of manliness—a bath in wine "will make you strong as a lion," a grandmotherly voice declares. Given Fellini's childhood, born and raised in the city of Rimini on the Adriatic Coast, in the region of Emilia-Romagna, best guess is that the vat contains the lambrusco grape, to be turned into rustic and pleasant peasant wine.

Back from his dreamscapes, Mastroianni seems to recognize himself that he is pursuing an archetype and not a flesh and blood female. He even glimpses a figment who embodies everything he wants, but cannot seem to will himself to act, "Let's admit you're pureness, spontaneity—What the hell does it mean, to be really honest." No longer trusting even his own instincts, he falls into bed in despair. And, as he sleeps, he is tended by his image of Innocence personified—"I've come to stay ..." she says, for us to hear and him to dream, "I want to set things in order."

A fateful confrontation with Rossella brings his creative crisis to a head.

> Rossella: "Why do you like stories where nothing happens?"
> Guido/Mastroianni/Fellini: "Everything happens in my film," and we can believe it, since we're at the impressively vast set of a spaceship, "I'm going to put everything in."

Then he turns on his own sentiment, and denounces his own aspirations: "I thought I had something to say. A film that could be useful to everyone ... that would help us bury all that's dead inside us. But I don't have the courage to bury anything." (What? His marriage, his affairs, a film drifting further and further from what he wants it to be? Or the increasingly intruding episodes from his past?)

"I have absolutely nothing to say! But I want to say it anyway."

Mastroianni's projection of indecision and of total emotional inertia does not, surprisingly enough, come across as impotence. There's a muscularity to his moral equivocation and vacillation. His flaws are pronounced, but pronouncedly masculine flaws. And this is at no stage more apparent than in the scene that follows a confrontation between wife and mistress, which turns surreally into a waltz. Mastroianni (ah, the prosaic predictability of male fantasy) imagines himself the Emir of his own harem, as the women from every stage of his life abase themselves in an attempt to satisfy their only wish—which is to satisfy his every wish.

This fantasy, however, soon evades his attempts to control it and compose it to his will. It mutates into a cacophony of bickering between the women for his attentions, before they turn on him. A whip-cracking Marcello is powerless to quell the revolt. Only a constant and indulgent wife stands by him. Or does she?

Then it is revealed—he *has* this much self-knowledge. He possesses this much insight into the desires that make him pitiful. This harem scene was to be the crowning scene of his own film. It was to be funny, then poignant, finally remorseful. He had always intended to display his self-blame by playing that blame (as he proceeds to do) through his wife's words—in his mind, and on the screen. When, on leaving him, she observes, "You needed an ending," so too did she. And achieving freedom from the bonds of marriage, which he both wants and doesn't want, doesn't ameliorate his punishment—to be confronted, in a single sitting, with all of the unkindnesses, abuses, and deceits of his life.

In the end, savaged by critics and companions alike—and unable to speak, explain or justify—he aborts his film project. While all the figures of his past—near and far—gather, symbolically white-garbed, he becomes his own soliloquizing leading man. The film finally morphs into a circus scene, this being, after all, from the film-maker who put his own name into the critical lexicon—*Felliniesque*.

To say that *True Grit* is a film of an altogether different type would be to stretch understatement well beyond its capacity to make sense. We have chosen this film as a representative role of the Duke's, since it was the genre of the Western that established his image, and additionally this was the part that earned Wayne his only Oscar—for all that he was by then, and says so himself in the film's final scene, "a fat old man." This is a distinctly linear film, with none of the convolutions of *8 1/2*. The morality is simple—so too the masculinity. Wayne's character, the eye-patch-wearing "Rooster" Cogburn, possesses his own flaws—brusque, unreliable, money-grubbing, and a booze-hound to boot. But the "true grit" of the film's title is his heroism, and a virtue that seemingly sweeps all else before it. (Wayne himself showed more than a little true grit, given that he'd not so long before had a lung removed.) It's through his grit that he can prevail over the bad guys, save the girl and save the day. And in being defined by his grit—by that alone and by no greater complexity or complication of character— he remains one of E. M. Forster's "flat" characters. There is no sense of personal re-assessment. No self-doubt or self-questioning. He experiences no redemption, or even a failed attempt at such, since no such attempt is apparently required. Self-examination ill befits the man of action. Soul-searching is, it seems, not what plays as manly in the Wild West.

The director Howard Hawks, who directed The Duke in *Rio Bravo* and *Hatari* among others, had this to say of his star—"John Wayne represents more force, more power than anyone else on the screen." If he's cabernet, then surely the Bordelais would agree with this sentiment—those on the Left Bank, at any rate. Columnist Charles Taylor, in an article "The 'Duke' and Democracy: On John Wayne" takes Hawks' thoughts further—"A performer who wields that kind of force, and has a physical presence to match, does not provide nuanced pleasure." For "performer" read "grape variety" and we have Gaja's point. Wayne's character comes across as emotionally hollow. How, then, does this stack up with the cabernet grape? It has to be said that some cabernet sauvignons display a similar hollowness, and have at times been unkindly dubbed "donut wines"—for the hole in their middle. It's one reason why the variety is so commonly blended with others that complement its characteristics and bring their own compensating attributes. This is something Angelo Gaja well knows—having introduced cabernet to his beloved Piedmont region, and even blending cabernet and nebbiolo together. (But what to make of the Mastroianni and Wayne love child?)

The Gaja *Sito Moresco* is a blend (near enough equal parts) of nebbiolo, cab sav, and merlot. With the distinguished and consistently high-pointed *Sperss* ("nostalgia"), previously a single vineyard Barolo, 100% nebbiolo, Gaja elected in the mid '90s to forego Barolo DOCG and adopt the humbler Langhe DOC appellation—in order to allow for the addition of cabernet. And Gaja's cabernet-dominated "Super Piedmont" is the *Darmagi*—literally "what a shame" in local dialect, its labeling expressive of Angelo's father's sentiments on surveying the hillside vineyard from which old nebbiolo vines were pulled so cabernet could be replanted.

Angelo's own commitment to cab sav, and his obvious sense of humor about it, suggest that his comments on the two varieties are intended to be more disarming than disparaging to cabernet sauvignon—though some streak of old Piedmontese parochialism might argue otherwise. Like *8 1/2*, nebbiolo is certainly enigmatic—at very least in the fact that its mysteries still elude the rest of the wine producing world. And while we've had our share of John Wayne cabernets, these by no means exhaust the range and variety of styles available. Angelo Gaja, by dropping a playful line hinting at deeper insights, was making a point while having a little fun. And it's a game we can all play, as we'll see in a later chapter.

So, where does all this leave the intrepid Lothario? Which wine to choose to advance seduction's suit? Opt, after all, for the authority of cabernet? Max Lake, medico, founder, and winemaker of the Hunter Valley's Lake's Folly, and author of the book *Scents and Sensuality*, has observed that after drinking cabernet sauvignon—but not other reds—the male body exudes a musky aroma, caused by the pheromone androste-none, which is irresistible to the fairer sex. Gentlemen, take note. That being said, as a prolific maker of cabernet we can't be entirely sure how firmly Max's tongue was planted in his cheek.

Should our would-be seducer, then, choose instead a languid pinot—perhaps hoping that the wine's own feminine wiles can out-flank those of his date, or maybe just surmising that she seems the kind of girl who might be inclined to jump the fence?

Whatever his choice (and whatever your own), with wine, as with so much else, persistence is a virtue. After all, who wants to seduce, or be seduced, too easily?

Nineteen

The Fifth Dimension

And so to the final, the fifth dimension of wine description—speaking of wine in human terms.

Galileo you'll recall, that native of Tuscany and dedicated drinker of the wines of Chianti, called wine "a compound of light and humor." "Humor" here (*umore*) is sometimes taken as a reference to the earth's moisture in that region, and related to *terroir*. Equally, it's as often taken to be a reference to the four humors once believed to define human character, identified by Hippocrates 400 years or so B.C. Refined by Galen some 600 years later into a theory of human temperament—"fusing the clinical and the theoretical"—it became part of a "Galenic canon" that lasted for more than a millennium. Still, sanguine, phlegmatic, choleric, melancholic … is this the wine being drunk, or what the drinking brings out?

Describing wine in terms of our own characteristics has proven a remarkably persistent inclination. This is despite the less than enthusiastic response from many in the academic world, a result of Maynard Amerine and Edward Roessler's influential book, *Wines—Their Sensory Evaluation*, which urged the replacement of such romanticism with a more scientifically descriptive approach. In fact, as *The Accidental Connoisseur*, Lawrence Osborne points out, to Professor Amerine (who had headed up the Department of Viticulture and Enology at the University of California, Davis) the only permissible wine description terminology should relate to its evident flavors. Eliminating the likes of "coarse" versus "elegant" as a descriptive opposition, or "rustic" versus "aristo-cratic," was intended to democratize wine. And that's a perfectly noble aspiration. We're all for the out-phasing of some of the wine world's more anachronistic and marginalizing practices. Still, we don't favor its achieve-ment by banning words and proscribing parameters of comparison.

And there are other vocal opponents of the personification of wine. This from Kingsley Amis in *Everyday Drinking*:

> When I find someone I respect writing about an edgy, nervous wine that dithered in the glass, I cringe. When I hear someone I don't respect talk-ing about an austere, unforgiving wine, I turn a bit austere and unforgiv-ing myself. When I come across stuff like that and remember about the figs and bananas, I want to snigger uneasily. You can call a wine red, and dry, and strong, and pleasant. After that, watch out.

(Perhaps less of a democratizing of wine than an anaesthetizing.)

An even greater cynic, our old friend Roald Dahl, known to be well partial to a fine Bordeaux, expressed his view of fanciful description deliciously in the short story "Taste." Here the villain of the story, a famed gourmet named Richard Pratt, was just such a culprit. The nub of the tale is a disgusting wager, between Pratt and his host (willing to bet his daughter's future happiness in order to "best his guest"), that the for-mer could not identify from taste alone a Bordeaux wine they were to enjoy with dinner. The gourmet proceeds to conduct a forensic-like analy-sis, interspersed with outlandish, and not always accurate, description:

> It is obviously a Medoc. There's no doubt about *that* ... Now—from which commune in Medoc does it come? That also, by elimination, should not be too difficult to decide. Margaux? No. It cannot be Mar-gaux. It has not the violent bouquet of a Margaux. Pauillac? It cannot be Pauillac, either. It is too tender, too gentle and wistful for Pauillac. The wine of Pauillac has a character that is almost imperious in its taste. And also, to me, a Pauillac contains just a little pith, a curious dusty, pithy fla-vor that the grape acquires from the sod of the district. No, no. This—this is a very gentle wine, demure and bashful in the first taste, emerging shyly but quite graciously in the second. A little arch, perhaps, in the sec-ond taste, and a little naughty also, teasing the tongue with a trace, just a trace of tannin. Then, in the after-taste, delightful—consoling and femi-nine, with a certain blithely generous character that one associates only with the wines of the commune of Saint Julien. Unmistakably this is a Saint Julien ...

This torture continues, until the denouement—

> Ah ... I have it! Yes, I think I have it! You know what this is? This is the little Château Branaire-Ducru.

This is something he'd known all along, having sneaked a look at the label earlier in his host's study, the best spot in the entire house to allow the wine to breathe, as he himself had recommended. Clearly he agreed with that wine industry truism—"a glance at the label is worth twenty-five years' tasting experience." The frequent sensual references—"obscene," "naughty," "teasing the tongue"—are no doubt designed by Dahl to doubly dishonor Pratt, and by inference the whole practice of fanciful wine description. And so was his comeuppance— orchestrated by a loyal family retainer wise to his deception.

It begins to be clear, and we've seen it before in the case of fruit flavors, that what offended Dahl was *any* form of wine description whatsoever—"Smell it! Inhale the bouquet! Taste it! Drink it! But never try to describe it!" More credible perhaps if the same character, from his notorious novel, *My Uncle Oswald*, hadn't then gone on to do just that—"like having an orgasm in the mouth and the nose at the same time." (Hey, forget how accurate it is—we're talking *principle* here.)

Few things are easier to parody than the perceived excesses of wine snobs—although using a wine collection as evidence of aesthetic taste, as the pathetic host does in Dahl's short story, comes close. However the opposition of Dahl and other cynics has not diminished the tendency to describe wine in terms of ourselves. There's more to this inclination than a belly laugh. We have a good deal in common with the grape. Wine's development over time mirrors the course of our own lives. In childhood, each a little troublesome, and more than a little indulged, every hint of promise viewed benevolently with pleasure and pride. In adolescence, well what can we say about this mercifully short span of turbulence and taciturnity? Then comes the payoff stage—the splendid emergence into maturity, truly the cream of existence for both. And finally, decline. Less than vigorous, wistful perhaps, but respectful and dignified.

In attributing character to wines, you might hear speak of a cheeky riesling, enigmatic semillon, overbearing chardonnay, demur pinot, grandiloquent syrah, profound cabernet, imposing tempranillo ... These aren't the whole of it, and they ignore nuance and the underlying traits that help make wines (and people) what (and who) they are. But they are valuable yardsticks, and reflect the same kind of character shorthand that we employ in categorizing and describing other people. Even a novice will not have to work too hard to understand such depictions in the context of the wines they describe. They become then a legitimate form of communication, whether written or spoken. And in projecting character traits onto the wine, they add an element of expectation and anticipation. Much as a thumbnail sketch of an individual may pique our interest in meeting them.

It's fitting that we tend to talk of the "character" of wine, rather than personality. A more than purely semantic point, made eloquently clear by the British philosopher Peter Goldie in his book *On Personal-ity*—"Character traits are importantly different from other aspects of personality ... The etymology of personality suggests veneer, appear-ance ... a mask of the kind that used to be worn by actors; character emerges when the mask is removed." We like to think of wine as pos-sessing character—defined by its various characteristics or character traits. Goldie again "A character trait is deeper ... and the judgment goes deeper too ... It reveals something ... that we are rightly inclined to say is concerned with their moral worth as a person."

There's a moral dimension to making wine. And also to consuming it. And the circumstances in which it is consumed. This is an essential aspect of what industry commentator Matt Kramer has described as a *wine culture*. Such a culture "is not an inevitable outgrowth of any other kind of culture, no matter how refined or evolved." Its legitimacy and sustainability comes from seeing fine wine as nothing less than "an expression of civilization." This is what makes the moral dimen-sion of wine an ennobling thing.

Not to say that our judgments, and the descriptions we use to give them voice, aren't problematic. Emile Peynaud describes wine tasting as "based on personal impressions where the key factor is the taster's own personality." So any attempt to describe a wine in human terms immediately begs the question—are we really describing the wine, or does the wine force us instead to describe ourselves? Sure, it's more than a little of both, but still it's a question worth the asking. Every-thing to do with descriptions of wine smacks of ambiguity, and this becomes even more of an issue when we engage in personification. So let's dig deeper. Are the characteristics we settle on an attempt to describe our own perceptions of wine? Are they more projections of ourselves? Do they reflect a synergy, some *gestalt* that occurs only through our own connection with the wine? Or do these characteristics, in some strange way, belong equally and independently to the wine, as much as to us?

We considered earlier the central scene from the film *Sideways*. After a dinner at which much wine has been consumed, and in one of those moments of intimacy you'd like every dinner to lead to, Miles (played by Paul Giamatti, who seems to specialize in misfits and urban antiher-oes) and Maya (the utterly comely Virginia Madsen) reveal how they see themselves, and perhaps the other, in the characteristics they distin-guish in wine.

"Why are you so into pinot?" she asks. "It's like a thing with you." Having prefaced that with, "Can I ask you a personal question?"—which it is. As pinotphiles ourselves, Burgundy, or the best of the New World: Sonoma, Oregon, Central Otago or Martinborough, Mornington Peninsula or the Yarra Valley—we love its changeable nature, and no wine changes more in the glass before your very nose. Savory and fruit flavors at first withdrawn then opening to lightly flirtatious, inexorably more sexy until it's outright wanton, seething between these states and showing now more of itself and now less, as if the most alluring thing was the object of your desire cloaking itself in more and more impenetrable layers. But enough of personal fetishes.

Miles gives some thought (or stalls while imaging what might be best to say, or how to say it), then responds in a monologue:

> I don't know. It's a hard grape to grow … thin-skinned, temperamental, ripens early. It's not a survivor like cabernet, which can just grow anywhere and thrive even when it's neglected. No, pinot needs constant care and attention, and in fact can only grow in these really specific little tucked-away corners of the world.

Winetalk becomes Miles' means of presenting the image of himself he wants Maya to see. His most obvious faults are acknowledged up front, as a platform for reinterpreting them. This is who I am. This is why it's not so bad—in fact in a funny way, it's to be admired. The pinot is Miles' psychological alter ego, fighting his battles, enabling him to rationalize and romanticize the fact that he will never be a cabernet, never have that commanding masculine presence.

"And only the most patient and nurturing growers can do it really, can tap into pinot's most fragile, delicate qualities." A subtle challenge here, of do you have what it might take? Are you up to nurturing me?

> Only when someone has taken the time to truly understand its potential can pinot be coaxed into its fullest expression. And when that happens, its flavors are the most haunting and brilliant and subtle and thrilling and ancient on the planet. I mean, cabernets can be powerful and exalting, but they seem prosaic to me for some reason. By comparison …

This is why it's worth it—why *I'm* worth it. Miles has been making a *terroir*-based argument for his own appeal and desirability. The wine he's consumed has worked as a kind of truth serum for Miles (*in vino veritas* indeed). And though his approach may be tactically sound in advancing seduction, we respond to the genuineness. This plea to be understood through the wine, as a person and a potential lover, is anthropomorphism in reverse—dramatically upending and extending the more routine convention of anthropomorphic metaphor. Rather than being simply an object of projection, wine becomes the standard against which human character can be assessed.

Maya's response is equally personal, but pragmatic. It's the pragmatism of her gender when it comes to relationships—about men or wine—and her attitude serves to further emphasize Miles' obsession.

"I have a really sharp palate ... and the more I drank, the more I liked what it made me think about."

Here there is no personification of wine, no subservience, not even a feigned equality. The focus is on Maya. The grape is to be appreciated, for what it is and for what it makes her think about and feel, but she won't idealize it. No reverse anthropomorphism here. Maya doesn't measure herself in terms of wine. She sees wine solely in terms of what she brings to their association, the qualities of a superior imagination and palate.

"I like to think about what was going on the year the grapes were growing, how the sun was shining that summer or if it rained ... what the weather was like. I think of all those people who tended and picked the grapes."

For Maya the grape is a plant, a living organism true, but neither a product of the gods nor some psychological offshoot of humanity. It doesn't exist to define us, it's dependent on us, on the people who plant it and tend it, all the way up to its metamorphosis into liquid—a glorious pleasure-giving liquid, but still liquid, confined in a bottle.

Even her reflections on the life of the wine—"constantly evolving and gaining complexity ... until it peaks, and begins its steady, inevitable decline"—for all their rhythmic momentum are dispassionate. So we're not surprised when she delivers her punchline—"and it tastes so fucking good." Or if we were, we aren't in retrospect.

Miles and Maya have gone further with wine than merely to describe their preferences. They have each in the same way used wine to examine their own lives (even to expose those lives), to articulate what they value out of life and to express, in a sense, their personal value systems. In their discussion of grapes and wine, Miles and Maya have spoken, really, of nothing but themselves. And how different are their notions of human character. Miles lives his life in a metaphorical twilight zone, his own fifth dimension. He is in thrall to the grape. It *does* define his character, as he would see it (with a capacity for capriciousness that a real life Maya would do well to think twice about). Wine (though for *@#%'s sake not merlot), gives meaning to his life. More than he's gleaned from his failed marriage or an unsuccessful writing career, both of which he'd rather deny. Wine provides another dimension into which he can escape—one that is not merely comforting but to his mind has the additional appeal of being logical. And who is to say that he's wrong?

Identifying himself with the wine, offbeat as it might seem when set against Maya's down to earth realism, works on our sympathy—and for good reason. The notion of a fifth dimension is one that a multitude of people readily accept. However rational or irrational may be the conceptualization, the idea itself carries with it the aura of mystery. Something beyond our normal ken, and strangely enticing, just because it is beyond the humdrum and always incomplete normal. Who wouldn't like to believe that the cosmos comprises more than just our visible three dimensions, plus Newton's time? Whatever the other might happen to be, is less important than the thought that it could exist. A singularity beyond our understanding but potentially within our reach, that could add who knows what to our lives? Such a hope manifests itself in all sorts of ways, some with the bonus of intellectual and social acceptability. We are few of us immune.

Perhaps our tendency to see seductive and complex phenomena in human terms reflects the same kind of restless urge. It's a way of giving our existence more depth, more aspects of interest to explore and more promise in the offing. In which case, wine is a special case of this. Certainly we've reacted to the blessings of wine in an all-embracing way—compared to other phenomena—to the extent of constructing a language (with all its faults) and a hierarchy of scholarship and expertise. We've forged a relationship with wine that straddles the commercial and the aesthetic, while affording special status to a special partner. And for its part wine sits comfortably on the pedestal we've given it. The grape carries the goodwill of having being seen to exist alongside of us throughout history, benefiting from but also aloof from our intrusion. (What does *terroir* confer if not a sense of self-righteous impregnability?) Unlike other aesthetic pleasures—literature, painting, sculpture, music—which can't escape their dependence on human creativity and ingenuity, wine trades on the ambiguity of its origins. And this is reflected in its influence.

How far can this hold on our imagination go? Can our connection with wine, beyond the sensory and intellectual excitement, help us to better understand our own psychological makeup? What can wine tell us about ourselves ... that is more than wishful thinking?

PART III

How Wine Describes Us

Twenty

Games People Play

"Now I've Got You, You Son Of A Bitch!"

Only kidding. Or, more to the point, it's only a game.

Back in the 1960s the psychiatrist Eric Berne wrote an extremely influential book, *Games People Play*, which took a novel angle on the psychology of human relationships. Based on a psychotherapy model called Transactional Analysis, its vision of social interaction involved three ego-states: the Child, the Parent, and the Adult. The book's immense popularity was largely due to its insightful (not to say inciteful) and frequently humorous examples of the games people do play with one another in everyday life—their rules, plays and counter-plays, and how the players all keep score.

Defined in colloquial terms by Berne as "a series of moves with a snare," a game can be classified across a range of variables: the number of players, the flexibility needed, the level of intensity, the tenacity with which players will persist. Underscoring the appeal of such divertingly dysfunctional activities—including particular favorites such as "Kick Me," "See What You Made Me Do," "Frigid Woman," and that most frustrating of all, "It's Your Decision"—is the level of gamesmanship involved. Players mask their real intentions, and not always unconsciously. Destructive? When carried out habitually and persistently, no doubt. But consider how boring life would be without it. A game-free relationship, even if one were possible, would be decidedly lacking in *frisson*. And sometimes it's just more fun not to have to play at being grown-up.

Wine conversation doesn't have to revolve around a game. But games can lead to deeper and more enlightening insights—into the wines themselves, and the people drinking them. As Berne's book shows, our minds are wired to embrace these kinds of rituals.

So why not play . . .

JUDGING A BOOK BY ITS COVER

In what ways does the label reflect, or not, the wine inside? Think style and design; content, color, and calligraphy; detail versus minimalism; humor at odds with gravitas . . . and never forget that elusive and intuitive aspect of the label's "feel."

Take Château Mouton-Rothschild (and we don't mind if we do). Each year since 1945 a world-renowned artist has been invited to decorate that vintage's label—the artist receiving a case of the wine for their efforts. What relation might these artworks have to the wine in their bottle?

How, for instance, do their respective labels portray the vintages of '85 and '86 (renowned respectively as feminine and masculine in style, as you'll recall)? The '85 works its feminine wiles delightfully—the Belgian artist Paul Delvaux, a surrealist by nature if not by name, renders one beautiful woman in blue reverently presenting a bunch of grapes to another beauty cloaked in reverie and red. Does the '86 carry off masculinity with the same brio? Well, no . . . though that's no artistic failure. Bernard Séjourné's work seems also to convey a sense of the feminine, but a distinctly disquieting one (at odds with the movement he founded, "The School of Beauty"). Where the Delvaux harks back to a Post-Impressionist influence, this painting proclaims its late-20th-century status, both stylistically and thematically. To the left are two overlapping faces, undeniably female but with a strong cast to their features, no doubt drawn from the women of the artist's native Haiti. A high moon illuminates the scene eerily. Compositionally balancing the faces, and revealing them for what they are, is a mask turned away from the viewer. It's the stark emptiness of its back concavity that's so disturbing. By themselves the faces on the left possess a calming Madonna-like closed-lidded knowingness. Alongside the contrasting back hollow, however, their long swan necks appear severed, and their inscrutable visages are undeniably sinister . . . if sinisterly beautiful. Both are works of art to ponder. For us the Delvaux inspires an expansive mood (and impression of the wine), an emergence into sunlight. The Séjourné, on the other hand, elicits a deeper, darker and more brooding kind of contemplation.

We can't easily ignore labels. The reflective insistence of wine will eventually draw us to a consideration of even the most unobtrusive. And our impressions of this will then intrude on our impressions of the wine. The objective of all labeling is to evoke a response. Why should it be different or less subtle for this the most subtle of substances?

Particular favorite works adorning the Mouton labels are the Henry Moore '64 (best known as a sculptor on a grand scale, there's an intimate reverence to three pairs of elegant long-fingered hands cradling sacramental goblets), Cocteau's '47 (detailing both the sheep of *mouton* and the grapes of the estate), a characteristically ethereal Chagall for the great vintage of 1970, and more recently Italian sculptor Giuseppe Penone, whose 2005 label reveals the distinct imprint of the winemaker's hand on the vine.

The Leeuwin Estate Art Series, from Margaret River in Western Australia, boasts a chardonnay often described as the country's finest. Even greater claims than that have been made for it—this from world wine legend Hugh Johnson, "I don't know of any other New World Chardonnay that has such consistently balanced precision and potency." A newly commissioned work graces each vintage of the chardonnay, cabernet, shiraz, and sav blanc—each work designed to "capture something of the wine in each painting," says the estate's Marketing Director, Simone Horgan-Furlong. She elaborates, "Sauvignon Blancs ... tend to be playful works done in light pastel colors, while the Cabernets tend to bear darker, bolder works." As to the riesling, four different *Frog* paintings by artist John Olsen adorn every vintage, and each captures the lively refreshing zing of riesling. That wine's been going down a treat for years, and we have to confess ... one of us has to confess that, by association, he quite literally begins to salivate at mere sight of the label—who said Pavlovian conditioning was just for the dogs?

Another favorite riesling producer, on the other side of the world, is Alsace's Josmeyer. They too regularly commission new works to adorn their labels. What stays consistent, however, is the color scheme for each variety—expressive of that grape's character. So an austerity-defining blue is signature of the Josmeyer *Le Kottabe* Riesling (named for a game of skill and chance played with wine in classical times). The pinot blanc *Mise du Printemps* evokes the spring of its name, as do the blooming spring colors of green, yellow, and white. The more autumnal pinot gris, named *Le Fromenteau* for its medieval ancestor grape, is decked out in hues that evoke Keats' "season of mists and mellow fruitfulness" and the season's melancholy drift towards winter. Poetry also attaches to the last in the series, the gewürztraminer *Les Folastries* (placed so since it was what we last drank, 2003 vintage, table consensus loved the vanilla and honey notes on the nose, opening into a teasingly elusive rose petal, with a rich palate—bordering on unctuousness but saving itself by drying off to a long, clean finish with an understated tang of butterscotch). The dominance of red might well allude to the wine's varietal spiciness, but the wine's name suggests another association. France's greatest poet of the Renaissance was Pierre de Ronsard, "prince of poets" in his day. And among the poems of his book *Les Folastries* he penned the lines—"Pour those roses in this wine. In this good wine pour those roses, and drink one to each other, so that the sadness present in our hearts will find an end."

There's no need to restrict this game to artist penned and painted labels. Design can have commercial, more than aesthetic, aims.

Some Old World labels are very "Olde Worlde." They reflect a history, sometimes one of centuries, and heritage isn't such a bad old marketing tool. The appeal here is to an insistence on and persistence of tradition. And those New World labels that have remained unchanged for decades, even half a century and up, can come across as either classic or as "traditional" in its stodgiest sense. Old World labels that sport a very "modern" look are often making a statement about the style of winemaking that's gone into what's inside— technologically pristine, fault-free and clean, "International" rather than *terroir*-bound. We've found, for instance (only anecdotally, but consistently)—drinking Vernaccia di San Gimignano with Tuscan-loving friends and family—that the "older" style labels accompany an older, more traditional slightly oxidized style of wine, while wines adorned with more "modern" looking labels (more "Newe Worlde" you could say) present a crisper purity of fruit more typically associated with the New World.

You needn't restrict your reflections and suggestions to one bottle at a time. Try mixing and matching for comparison. How does a traditionally labeled Old World wine compare with an "Olde Worlde" labeled New World wine? (We've two lined up side by side for cracking—an Haut Médoc Cru Bourgeois Superieur, Château de Malleret, and a Margaret River Fraser Gallop Estate cabernet, both from the '05 vintage that excelled in each hemisphere. Their respective labels could be modeled on each other—down to the finely etched line drawing of the estate house holding pride of place. We're smacking our lips at the prospect of how these two wines will stack up against each other, and how our label-based expectations will play out.) Or perhaps contrast an Old and New World wine both bearing more modern bottle design, edgy or minimalist or funky or fun-punning. On the other hand, you might pitch for an ironic switch—modern styled design on an Old World wine, versus its vice versa from the New World ... or the flip side to that match, old Old against new New. The possibilities are ... well, not exactly endless, but abundant for the games to be had.

Ah, books and their covers. Go to town, then, and see how you go. Deconstruct the significance of your wine labels as you imbibe. You can see there whatever catches your eye or your fancy, then see it all the more clearly on your subsequent bottles.

Then there's ...

THIS WINE'S LIKE...

We mused earlier on how wine can be aligned to music, and the expressive and apposite comparisons that come to mind from this. So, what else might wine remind us of?

"A great wine is a film, not a snapshot."

Hubert de Boüard, proprietor of Château Angélus in Saint-Émilion, is alluding here to wine's development over time, the unfolding of its narrative if you like. Wine, like film, has its opening—no pun intended—its developing towards denouement, its peaks and troughs of pace and revelation. But let's take his notion, wine as film, and run with it. And why not, since the '82 Angélus was Daniel Craig's new blond Bond's wine of choice in *Casino Royale*.

What's the movie in your glass, then?

The Godfather sweeps all before it. Given its director's foray into wines in the area, we're bound to say it's a Californian cabernet. And the film's age warrants a reference closer to its time. The 1973 Stag's Leap Cabernet Sauvignon then, since the film came out only the year previous. That's the wine that won the so-called Judgment in Paris in 1976, over fierce French competition and to serious French consternation. The wine continues to distinguish itself, once more trouncing the beret-wearers in the competition's 30th anniversary taste-off. Both film and wine seem just to get better with age—do they even have a use-by date?

You don't have to be a wine buff to play. The game demands no pre-existing knowledge or acquaintance with the wine in question. Just go with what taste and imagination suggest ...

A fine German riesling might be the art-house classic *Last Year at Marienbad*—cold and austere, impeccably stylish but aloof, not necessarily easy at first to engage with or warm to, but then ...

No need to be a cinephile either. Less esoteric filmic references can be just as spot-on ...

Rocky is an uncomplicated feel-good wine. Most likely a big Californian chardonnay, heavyweight without being serious, perhaps even a little flabby (Sly wasn't really "buff" until the sequels). But for all that it still finds itself receiving accolades and awards over more accomplished competition—remembering, and still not quite believing, that *Rocky* won the 1976 Best Picture Oscar over *Network*, *All the President's Men*, and *Taxi Driver*.

Certain shiraz and blends, from the Old World and New, might cry out Jerry Bruckheimer—blockbusters, explosive and overblown, but strangely unsatisfying in their lack of restraint. In wine, and movies too, there's still a place for a little subtlety between the fireworks.

The Lord of the Rings almost demands a New Zealand comparison, but we just can't give it one. It's mammoth, massive, enough spectacle (read alcohol) for three features—and (for all that their cabernet's coming along nicely) they just don't make that style in the Land of the Long White Cloud. A zinfandel at the monstrous end of the zin spectrum, then. Bound to spawn its imitators, and to call it larger than life is an undoubted understatement—still, a question as to its ageing credentials remains (big special effects, however mind-blowing on release, can be cruelly dating).

As to pinot, is there a more definitive film comparison than the Coen brothers? Idiosyncratic masterpieces (*Miller's Crossing*, *Barton Fink*, *Fargo*, *No Country for Old Men*) interspersed with the idiosyncratically unwatchable/undrinkable (*The Hudsucker Proxy*, *The Big Lebowski*, *Intolerable Cruelty*).

Another pinot is *Chinatown*. It takes a while to figure out what's going on, like many a good Volnay or Chambolle-Musigny. Up front it's all long, cool Faye Dunaway cherry elegance, but as you look deeper into it a darker, seamier side is revealed.

The Third Man, that Orson Welles classic (as actor, not director), is an otherwise marvelous red wine with rather severe, unintegrated tannins—which set your teeth on edge, like the film's zither music soundtrack.

And we will, of course, do our damnedest to avoid the vinous equivalent of *Dude, Where's My Car?*

Music, film, books and writers, the visual arts and artists themselves ... fashions and fads, design styles and designers ... or on a different tack entirely, sports, sportsmen, cars if they're your kick ... even places you've been or long to visit. (Drunk back to back one night—the wines that is, not us—a '96 Pipers Brook Summit chardonnay boasting such a dizzying array of flavors that your head kept spinning well after swallowing, a real New York of a wine. Then a Bannockburn chardonnay of the same vintage—singularly, quintessentially the essence of peaches and cream, richly and deliciously contemplative in the way of the English Lakes district.)

So choose your category, and then see how you and your fellow drinkers see different wines in that light.

Moving to the more personally introspective, there's the pursuit of ...

ASSOCIATIONS

Marcel had his *madeleines*; Santorini its apricots, that brought back to mind a special wine and the occasion of its sharing. What personal experience does the wine you're drinking conjure up?

It might be some seminal event from your past. It might be something that's lain buried in memory for years. It might even be an experience that never was but might have been, if you'd had your way, or just a little luck.

"Crushed ants" is not an auspicious wine description. In fact, it's the kind of comparison that confirms the worst to most people about the excesses of wine language. We were skeptics too—until one of us chanced upon a wine, a Coonawarra cabernet in fact, whose overwhelming odor transported him in his mind's eye back to a long-forgotten camping trip, a nearly extremely painful encounter with a rampaging bull-ant and the nostril-pummeling pungency of formic acid after grinding the angry little bugger into the dust.

A pinot's perfume might call to mind an evocative scent. Or a cabernet's depths of color an unforgettable shade of lipstick. Champagne can bring up a host of past celebrations, but the strong yeasty aroma of autolysis has (for us) brought up the image of fresh-baked rolls bought from an early opening bakery on the morning of a never-ending evening. And we once observed of a pumped-up durif, a.k.a. petit syrah, that it quite counterintuitively evoked the association of European cult movies—that wine was the equivalent of the late-night, deep-throated voice-over (introducing, for instance, a film like Jesus Franco's classic of sapphic exsanguination, *Vampyros Lesbos*) ... "the following film contains *adult themes.*"

Our imaginations are rich in all kinds of possibilities. So if you play it, why not play it to the hilt. Be as romantic, poetic, insightful, illogical, zany as you like. Who's to gainsay? It's your memory. Feel like making a statement to the table, to a certain someone, about yourself? Recast your persona? Here's your chance. A free ride, and they'll hang on your every word. Reputations have been cemented on less.

Finally of course, for the brave, or the foolhardy, there's ...

CHINESE ROULETTE

Taken from a game played to plot-making-and-breaking ends in Fassbinder's 1976 film of the same name.

Turn your thoughts to yourself and your drinking companions. If this wine were a *person*, who would it be? And the reasons. Wines, and people, possess a multitude of attributes. Any adjective used to describe an individual could be used to describe a wine. So chance your arm, there are no wrong answers and difference of opinion is simply sauce to discussion.

The same wine might, for instance (a Cornas from the Northern Rhône, say, or a Piedmont Barolo), be fairly described as generous, opulent, effusive, untamed, hedonistic, overbearing, bombastic, or opinionated ...

Equally, a young Chablis might be viewed as recalcitrant, enigmatic, tight-lipped, diffident, terse, reticent, or promising ...

Numerous New World chardonnays are masters, or mistresses, of overstatement—in your face, demanding attention above all others but when they get it ... it turns out they've not got much to say.

Now, match the characteristics.

Of course comparisons will become more outlandish as the evening unfolds and more bottles are uncorked. No doubt more pointed, and even more to the point. Though couples may take the opposite tack, turn it to a seductive game of chess—think Steve McQueen and Faye Dunaway in *The Thomas Crown Affair*—where the prize is control and the loser the first to show intent.

But you say you're concerned about sharp tongues and fallout of feelings in all this? Then play safe, and pick on celebrities instead. They're fair game for all.

And celebs can even play themselves. Sam Neill's an actor of art-house-to-blockbuster-and-back-again fame. He's also a wine devotee more serious than most, with his own Central Otago vineyards producing the Two Paddocks pinots, which do both the region and the variety proud. Interviewed in *Selector* magazine, he described a game in which wines are matched to especially admired women. And those matches go well beyond what he'd serve to whom. Choices reflect the essence of the chosen belle. Naomi Watts is a "very cool and crisp and elegant" Chablis. Kathy Bates, a Châteauneuf-du-Pape "from the best part of the vineyard. Best part of the hill. Full and rich, every performance satisfying." Helen Mirren, "one of those very austere South Australian rieslings." (And who could argue with d'Yquem for the Queen?)

All very nicely said. But we don't always feel the need (and nor should you) to be so generous with our targets.

Who might this be (raising a glass of an undistinguished and obvious sauvignon blanc)? Self-promoting, endlessly attention-seeking, outrageously popular, entirely vapid, and eminently forgettable?

The latest posturing supermodel ...?

A reality TV host ...?

Yet another DUI crotch-flashing popstress ...?

An equivocating and ingratiating politician ...?

Enough! Over to you. Take your pick. We have a date with "truth." (By the way, don't drink that glass. Send it back.)

Twenty-One

"Truth That Peeps over the Glasses' Edge..."

The classical historian Tacitus had this to say of Rome's ancient adversaries from Germania—"They formed their counsels (to make a resolution of war) while they were drunk, so they would not be lacking in vigor, and reflected on them while sober, so they would not be without understanding." Interesting that the ancient Persians were of the same habit, but with the flexibility of doing it the other way around, according to Herodotus—"any decision they make when they are sober, is reconsidered when they are drunk."

Perhaps our modern leaders should down a little more wine in their geo-political decision-making. ("Who prates of war or want after taking wine?" asks Horace rhetorically, and Plutarch gives his view on the subject of treaty-making—"Agreements arrived at over a glass of wine are the most sacred and inviolable of all agreements.") For all of that, nothing to do with wine and truth is ever straightforward. As Oscar Wilde informs us, "The truth is rarely pure and never simple." Those Germans and Persians no doubt had advisers reading entrails while urging them to tie their fates to a game of spin the bottle—just as, for our sins, we have our game theory and mathematical models. But truth is tricky—look at the each way bets of the Delphic oracle—and wine can have its own agenda.

In searching for truth through wine, you'd do well to consider what truth you're after. Don't panic, we're not about to launch into a tedious epistemological exegesis. We merely want to consider the simple, or not so simple, possibility that truth comes in different packages when wine handles the delivery, and it may or may not be the same truth we think it is.

That classic link between truth and wine—*in vino veritas*—was, it's rumored, first uttered by Pliny the Elder. He's most renowned for his remarkable, and remarkably compendious, *Natural History*, which happens to include references to 91 varieties of grape. Pliny was suffocated by vapor (would that be *vaporized*?) when venturing too close to Vesuvius at a particularly inopportune moment. "In wine, truth," indeed. He would have done well to follow his own counsel—a few goblets of the tasty *numisiana* from the region might have opened his eyes to the tragic truth about volcanoes. (Aren't undignified demises a bitch, the way they tend to distract from one's achievements?) Moving on for inspiration to another classical maxim, one that has a truer, if more dispiriting, feel—*in vino disertus*. Loosely speaking, "wine loosens the tongue."

We are no fans of this one. Some forms of truth are dubious, the currency of spies and twilight figures, not to mention suspicious spouses. They truthfully reflect no credit on anyone—including the wine, which should learn to keep better company. Of all the versions we'll deal with this most gives the lie to the notion that "truth never hurts the teller." Not that it does much for the receiver either. So we've chosen, perhaps a little sniffily, to label this "ignoble" truth.

Admittedly the esteemed moral philosopher Immanuel Kant took a more benign view of vinous tongue-loosening. "It also opens the heart," he asserted, "and is an instrumental vehicle of a moral quality, namely frankness." But then he would, wouldn't he? Ignoring the interesting side issue of which could be less important, being Frank or being Earnest, and with due deference to the great one (after all we do rely on him heavily from time to time) we've given this version its own label. After a brief flirtation with "open-hearted" truth, we settled on the more feel-good "let's-piously-spill-our-guts" truth.

And, as the pitch goes, that's not all. "Holding back one's thoughts," the great man continues, "is an oppressive state for a sincere heart; and many drinkers do not readily tolerate a very temperate guest at their revel, because he represents an observer who looks out for the faults of others while he hides his own." Well, where to even start in assessing the duplicity implied here—how to find the words to describe the anally fixated craftiness of those teetotalers and their odious truth that won't speak its name. (Instead of bitching about the high spirits of others, they should take a leaf from *Brideshead Revisited*—"The wines were too various ... it was neither the quality nor the quantity that was at fault. It was the mixture. Grasp that and you have the root of the matter. To understand all is to forgive all.") "Constipated" truth proposed one of us. But the contrarian of the partnership, proudly anal himself, empathetically plumped for "what-am-I-doing-here-with-such-an-intolerant-bunch-of-losers" truth. And this it is.

Little wonder the symposium of the Greek philosophers was fuelled by plenty of wine—an abundance of frankness has heavy merit in philosophical debate. And none, it seems, could keep pace with Socrates. In Plato's *Symposium*, Alcibiades complains of Socrates' perpetual sobriety, not a result of abstemiousness but rather an enviable capacity— "He will drink any quantity that he is bid, and never be drunk all the same." Quite unlike the picture given in Monty Python's *Philosophers' Song*, "Socrates himself will not be missed / a clever little thinker but a bugger when he's pissed."

The theatre has long seen the plot enhancing value of the vine. In Shakespeare's *As You Like It*, Rosalind exhorts her suitor not to fall in love with her, "for I am falser than vows made in wine." Now, vows made in wine (and we've made our share) get pretty bad press. But the question remains whether they, and their intentions, were sincere at the time (likely story or not, that's it and we're sticking to it). Not easy to arrange an empirical test of this. Even if a sober control group proves purer than the driven snow and a drunken experimental bunch behave like absolute sods, as the man said, it boils down to intentions. (For situations of this kind we suggest you keep Immanuel Kant handy as a character witness—*he must have been telling the truth sir, after all he was drunk*. That should close it out.) "If-you-let-me, I-promise-I-won't ..." truth seems to best reflect the intrinsic ambivalence here. And a word of warning, people will believe what they want to believe.

We seem to be racking up a lot of negatives, and this for an attribute that came in with such a rock solid reputation. And we fear it will get worse for truth before it gets better, for it's a fact that wine all too frequently hangs out with sin. You might say, so what? What would life—especially the good life—be without a little sin? A place for every sin, and every sin in its place ... True, but there's such a thing as guilt by association, and to be separated from sin only by wine leaves truth, well, somewhat compromised.

So where to start? Lust we think has earned the pole position—this after all is its second appearance on the bill. As the Roman poet Terence put it, "without Bacchus, Venus is cold," and one can only figure that the bulk of "vows made in sin" are made to this end. Euripides is even blunter, "Where there is no wine, love perishes," and perish that thought. But, and a troubling "but" indeed, as Shakespeare's porter in *Macbeth* cautions us, drink in excess has contrary effects on libido— "Lechery, sir, it provokes and unprovokes: it provokes the desire, but it takes away the performance." Now this calamitous side effect, if it's true (and it could be just a line put out by the other side), would seem an aspect of the grape damned worth fixing (pull in the best medical minds—this has genuine Nobel potential). But for now, what should we call it? Nothing too poetic or romantic, and nothing that mocks the delicacy of the situation. "Unwelcome" truth is appropriately flaccid, but truth shouldn't have to be prosaic. What's needed is something that captures the poignancy—"bloody hell" truth perhaps, or "bugger me" truth. Ah, yes, feel the despair.

From Lust it's a short hop to Greed. True birds of a feather—neither knowing when to stop, not stopping when one knows, only stopping when one must. It's a well-known supposition that greedy people are light on with the truth. And wine? Well, greed and drunkenness is surely not a good look, and a surefire recipe for untruths. A guilty verdict for wine then, but truth gets off with a warning.

Vanity? We once witnessed a table of women, terribly glamorous and all frocked up, drinking Dom Pérignon ... *through straws*! So as not to smudge their lipstick on the rims of their flutes. This proved a "revealing" truth.

The Envy of course was our own. *We* would never desecrate a great wine in that way, so *we* were more deserving of it. That's the "honest" truth.

Wrath? Anger in one's cups is best not spoken about—"Wine kindles wrath," from Seneca, 'nuff said. Gluttony? Is it any less when the substance gorged on is liquid? Sloth? Just wait for tomorrow's hangover—and that's the "sordid" truth.

It's time we tried for some balance. Wine and truth can't be all negative. So esteemed a churchman as Cardinal Richelieu (*Eminence Rouge* and power behind Louis XIII's throne) was moved to declare, "If God forbad drinking why would he have made wine so good?" Ah, "hypocritical" truth, the last refuge of the scoundrel.

Having exhausted wine and truth in the light of the seven deadly sins, what you ask is their status among the opposing cardinal virtues? Alas, bad news for our duo if they were hoping to make some ground up here, for only one is worth considering—and that's temperance. Our old mate Democritus believed "Moderation increases enjoyment, and makes pleasure even greater" (you can make up your own mind on that). And Seneca was prepared to shrug off his stoicism long enough to get tipsy, but not obliterated—"Upon occasion we should go as far as intoxication ... not total immersion." Can truth then be "sanctimonious"? You betcha.

The twin faces of wine, the sinful and the virtuous, find reconciliation in the observations of English philosopher Roger Scruton. He makes the thoughtful point that no other mind-bending substance known to man can be enjoyed as much in its imbibing as in its effects. Think about it. With any other intoxicating fare, the aim is to get off one's face. (We note the protests of single malt whisky drinkers, but ... well, it is, isn't it?). Wine, therefore, can be fairly considered "the virtuous intoxicant."

And so, with the oxymoron of "philosophical" truth off our chests, we can turn to serious truth and Robert Browning.

> No more wine? then we'll push back our chairs and talk.
> A final glass for me, though ...

Thus begins "Bishop Blougram's Apology"—a one way conversation between the bishop and his dinner companion, the narrow, ambitious and doubting scribbler Gigadibs. In this dramatic monologue, wine and truth coalesce to peel away the public exterior of a worldly bishop to reveal the figure behind—authoritarian and materialistic certainly, but honest in his hypocrisy, a big-hearted, devious and matter-of-fact man.

> So you despise me, Mr. Gigadibs.
> No deprecation,—nay, I beg you sir!
> Beside 't is our engagement: don't you know,
> I promised, if you'd watch a dinner out,
> We'd see truth dawn together? truth that peeps
> Over the glasses' edge when dinner's done.

G. K. Chesterton, one of his great admirers, observed of this poem that Browning "dethrones a saint to humanize a scoundrel." And what a humanizing it is, a remorseless self-unmasking of the bishop by the bishop. Does wine loosen his tongue? Well, as Emerson well knew, "A man will be eloquent if you give him good wine," and for Blougram, "Oh, there was wine, and good." But the loquacity here comes not through banal ill discipline—the good bishop could hold his wine like Socrates—but through the eloquent expressiveness that wine will unleash when voiced intelligently.

Does it open his heart? It opens us to what he believes. Even granted that Blougram believed "say, half he spoke," he knows the truths he wishes to confide. He knows the truths that should stay hidden ("for say they made me Pope"). And he reads well the truths of his companion:

> I am much, you are nothing; you would be all.
> I would be merely much: you beat me there.

How often, when truth peeps over the glasses' edge, does thoughtlessness take over—with truths blurted out on a warm glow's whim? Wine and truth in reckless combination will produce nothing gainful. Truth, when the product of wine, should be decorously dispensed like wine—never just splashed about. There are so many truths in the world from which to choose. So in choosing, as we must, we can easily do so honestly. The ever-practical Blougram: "truth is truth, and justifies itself by undreamed ways ... What need of lying?" What need, indeed?

Under the spell that is part of wine, our perceptions of truth receive a boost, become insightfully broadened. With such an expanded selection we can utilize truth more wisely, and select our words more persuasively. Pragmatism is everything when wine and truth combine, and this is brought to perfection in the bishop's honest skewering of Gigadibs. With the delicious bonus of his knowing that what he revealed would never be aired, or if it were, never believed. Pragmatism in spades.

There's but one more truth of wine to confront, and we are done for a time. This one we know all too well. Well enough to regularly deny, or even repress. We're referring of course to the after-effects. Ah, the much maligned hangover. Those physiological, mental, and moral oppressors that come together to pursue us like the Furies. Such dark consequences can sit askance with romantic and poetic notions of wine—until the penny drops—that it's all, of course, for our own good. Funny though how, even when we keep reminding ourselves of this, the pain still comes across like pure and simple retribution. Nevertheless, and perversely perhaps, we couldn't quite conscience a hangover-less existence. A painless post-inebriation, with no consequences or dire effects, is a common feature in sci-fi, especially those books with a Utopian bent. There's the soma of Huxley's *Brave New World*. In Philip K. Dick's *Do Androids Dream of Electric Sheep*, the "mood organ" allows for any mind state of choice to be rung up, and to be changed for any other at the turn of a dial. And in the futuristic Universe-state of Iain M. Banks' "Culture" novels, the altered humanoids possess their own glands to produce endless cocktails of intoxication—from which state they can pull themselves out at any time, and with no ill effects. There seems to us a joylessness in this lack of anticipatory recklessness. So we'll keep our hangovers—as if we've any choice—and just wish they didn't sting *quite* so much.

Kingsley Amis on the subject of the hangover calls it "that vast, vague, awful, shimmering metaphysical superstructure." There speaks a man *loaded* with experience. And only one so dedicated to the cause could make the extremely insightful distinction between the physical and the metaphysical hangover. We especially like his nomination of Kafka's "The Metamorphosis" as the literary model for the condition. The image of some monstrous vermin, which the unfortunate hero of the story wakes to find he's become, strikes us as about right—in fact it rings a bell. "As Gregor Samsa awoke one morning from uneasy dreams he found himself transformed in his bed into a gigantic insect." What an opening line. So frank, so unornamented, and so aptly matter-of-fact. So perfectly expressive of some mornings-after, and you can only wish that the unbidden interstitial visions assailing you are not flashbacks but simply the "uneasy dreams" of which Kafka speaks—if only. It's the helpless upended-ness that hits you first— turned turtle and it seems that all the world's effort, let alone what you in your depleted state might muster, couldn't turn you to rights. Your skin feels like a carapace, and your skull (inside which that infernal and insistent pounding will not stop), your skull appears to have become a kind of exoskeleton, egg-shell thin, so if tapped with no more than ordinary force ... out would spill what used to be your brains, no longer gray but a sickly green insect ichor.

Physical and metaphysical pain cry for a palliative (or more than one) and Amis is happy to oblige with suggestions. The metaphysical remedies are all prefaced on the (vaguely Puritan) assumption that we must feel worse (emotionally, that is) before we can begin to feel better, and are no doubt tongue in cheek, though it's hard to tell with Amis, but hell they're worth at least a try. Immersing oneself in gloomy literature is a starter. *One Day in the Life of Ivan Denisovich* apparently works a treat, largely through the sensitivity of its therapeutic message ("there are plenty of people about who have a bloody sight more to put up with than you"). Even a good thriller can serve sometimes to lift us from the mire of self-absorption. Another useful tactic is hangover listening. Ballet music (though he cautions against Tchaikovsky) and light operatic overtures are highly recommended, as are certain slow jazz tracks. Any diversion in fact that will drown the gloom you feel in even more oppressive gloominess. (One of us admits to seeking the metaphysical cure in an unlikely combo of Peter Greenaway and Arnie Schwarzenegger films.)

The physical remedies are also logical—immediate and vigorous sex for one—but the ingredients are not always on hand. And the writer is, as these writers are, firmly against substitutes.

The truth one confronts in the cold light of day is sobering, in more ways than one. "Let us have wine and women, mirth and laughter," urged Lord Byron, "Sermons and soda-water the day after." The hangover provides a moral barometer, a salutary warning for the future on where the limits are set. Elimination of the after-effects, even if possible, might bring consequences for the experience. Any risk of compromising the physical, aesthetic and intellectual pleasures of wine, and the benefits of its moral imperatives, and we say *vive la hangover*. We'll risk what Pliny threatens—"the intoxicated never see the sunrise and so shorten their lives"—being bigger fans of sunsets in any case. So bring it on—just don't corrupt the essence of our substance.

Amis makes his physical/metaphysical distinction largely for laughs (and the kernel of truth that lives in humor). In reality the two are parts of an unsplittable whole. More than overlapping, they superimpose themselves on each other, so that attempts to determine the truth of which feels the worse (guilt or nausea) is likely to bring on further waves of the other (nausea or guilt).

That's wine in truth, and truth in wine. "To understand all is to forgive all." Or so we can only hope.

Twenty-Two

A Beautiful Wine

"That's a beautiful wine," you'll hear people say. They may even, moved to hyperbolic ecstasy by true greatness in their glass, use a word like "masterpiece." If, however, you challenged them on that—on their sense of beauty, their taste in beauty and what beauty means to them—it's more than likely, almost certain in fact, that they'd admit to using the word beautiful quite differently to when they say "that's a beautiful painting."

Why? And more to the point, what is beauty? Poet and aesthetician Frederick Turner, in his essay "On Beauty," has a similar head-scratch:

> What nontrivial description could hold true for a beautiful Inuit mask, a beautiful man or woman, the laws of thermodynamics, an arcadian landscape, a picture of an arcadian landscape, a Bach canon, the Mandelbrot set ... a flowering chestnut tree, the theory of evolution by natural selection, an African ritual dance, and Yeats' "Byzantium"?

And, dare we add, a venerable Bandol and a young and vivacious Ice Wine?

Turner's point is well taken. For purposes of manageability, however, (not to say the preservation of our own sanity) we'll restrict our reflections on the aesthetics of fine wine to comparisons with fine art (music, literature, drama and dance inclusive)—paralleling the beauty forged by the artist's hand with that beauty fermented by the winemaker's.

Wine has, there's no doubting it, an aesthetic dimension. Its very standing as an object of our value judgments is proof, if proof were needed, of that. But few regard it as art. Those who do are taken less than seriously. The incomparable Robert Mondavi—mourned by all including the other wine giants in both the Old and New Worlds—believed that "when you can ... bring out the best of a given crop, I call it art." Plenty, in both the worlds of wine and art, beg to differ. Opponents of the notion take the view, "Well, he would say that, wouldn't he?" (Such critics wish to assert winemaking as a craft. And it's true that the term "artisanal wines"—referring to usually small-batch, traditionally and lovingly handcrafted wines—does seem some kind of concession from the winemaking fraternity that craftsmanship, rather than artistry, better represents their skills and efforts. But then again, perhaps that's just a becoming lack of pretension.) Consider next Fannie Farmer of *The Boston Cooking-School Cookbook* fame, in print for over a hundred years. She was convinced that "Cooking [and, by extension we believe, winemaking] may be as much a means of self expression as any of the arts." Monroe C. Beardsley—author of *Aesthetics: Problems in the Philosophy of Criticism, The Aesthetic Point of View*, and the highly influential, not to say phrase-making, essay, "The Intentional Fallacy"—gave tart retort to Farmer's claim. "We are told ... that 'cooking may be as much a means of self-expression as any of the arts,' but that only goes to show that there is more to art than self-expression." So the so-called culinary arts—the preparation of great dishes and the making of their perfect matches in the finest wines—apparently do not quite cut the mustard as *art*.

Once again—why? Or, why not? After all, we live in times in which even pop stars are awarded the highest honors for their "services to the Arts." An Elton John concert ... sorry, a *Sir* Elton John concert, then, or a night in with a bottle of La Chapelle (we know what we'd be opting for)? Which experience is more likely to provide a glimpse of true beauty?

Perhaps the most delightfully succinct definition of beauty ever given is that of St. Thomas Aquinas—beauty is "that which being seen pleases." To broaden beauty beyond the single sense of sight, we might for "seen" insert instead "perceived," or even "apprehended." The latter is closer to the notion of beauty held by 20th century philosopher Jacques Maritain. Maritain's deeply personal aesthetic sense was based on Aquinas, but influenced also by his friendships with working artists of the highest rank, including Rouault, Chagall, and Cocteau—not an uninteresting bunch to hang around with. "The intelligence delights in the beautiful," wrote Maritain, "because in the beautiful it finds itself again and recognizes itself, and makes contact with its own light." There have been, however, equally legitimate and resonant but far more problematic meditations on beauty. "The eyes delight in beautiful shapes of different sorts and bright attractive colors," observes St. Augustine, acknowledging the pull of beauty. Rather than be diverted, however, he prefers to remain alert in resisting temptation—"I would not have these things take possession of my soul." Dostoyevsky has the eldest brother Karamazov warn the youngest, "Beauty is the battle-field where God and the devil war for the soul of man." And Goethe was convinced that in beauty lay ambiguity—"Beauty can never be clear about itself."

Wine is not without its ambiguities, and our appreciation of it has its paradoxes. So, too, the senses through which wine articulates its beauty—taste and smell. Still, there are apparently other necessary con-ditions beyond beauty in order for something (a category of objects, or an object in itself) to be accepted as art. What, then, are those qualities lacking in wine?

Consider first the co-called "institutional theory" of art—that "any-thing which is in an art museum … is a work of art, and anything that is a work of art is in an art museum" (the profundity of philosophers is at times a humbling thing). Art critic Boris Groys sees aesthetic liber-ation in the fact that "so-called primitive artworks, abstract forms, and simple objects from everyday life have all acquired the kind of recogni-tion that once used to be granted only to the historically privileged artistic masterpieces"—all by virtue (if you could call it that) of their hanging on some gallery wall. "The artwork," he continues, "is an exhibited object." Now wine does make its appearance in galleries, though in our experience it's typically pretty insipid wine being poured at the openings of less-than-inspiring art. (Then again, neither of us can claim to be A-listers when it comes to opening night invites. Those tend to go to such patrons of high culture as soap stars, reality TV alumni, and celebrity hair-dressers.) Though, in keeping with Groys' sentiment, perhaps the act of all those guests necking all those glasses of whatever plonk's on the pour that night could, in its own way, be seen as a kind of performance piece.

Of course we couldn't allow such a silly theory to be the last word on the subject. So let's instead consider art from the viewpoints of its creation, and its appreciation.

First things first—how art is made.

There are, broadly speaking, two kinds of artist—the creative and the interpretive. This distinction isn't intended to rank creativity over interpretation. A poorly executed painting might be execrable, a badly written poem diabolical, whereas a passionately performed song or dance might be a thing of purest eye-watering beauty. No, the distinc-tion is not as to relative status *per se*. The distinction is from where they start.

Creative artists make something from nothing—sculptors (excepting Marcel Duchamp's urinal and all its "readymade" imitators), painters (with the exception of Damian Hirst's entire *oeuvre*), writers, composers, choreographers, and a certain kind of cinema *auteur*. These all begin with a blank piece of paper.

Interpretive artists, on the other hand, start with the piece of paper they've been given—directors, conductors, musicians, singers, dancers, actors ... and winemakers (let's give them the benefit of the doubt for the time being).

We find ourselves reminded of the efforts of Pygmalion, sung of by Orpheus in Ovid's *Metamorphoses*. Repulsed by the Propoetides—first women of myth to prostitute themselves—and as a moral withdrawal from their cavortings, the sculptor carves an exquisite female figure from finest ivory. So beautiful is it that he, who had sworn himself off women altogether, falls in love with his lovely creation—"Pleas'd with his idol, he commends, admires,/Adores; and last, the thing ador'd, desires." Aphrodite answers his prayers, and the figure is animated into Galatea, "she who is milk white," to become Pygmalion's wife and the mother of his child. Now wait just a minute, that'd make for an interesting new criterion for art—that is, to regard as art *any medium in which the creator could conceivably fall in love with their created object.* Pygmalion has made fair claim for sculpture. Painting's a no-brainer. Literature certainly qualifies—one of us having, in poetry, fallen for every incarnation of the "Life in Death" woman of Keats, Poe and Baudelaire (though surely no more than they did themselves), and also fallen in love successively with each female character, virtually on first appearance, in Lawrence Durrell's *Alexandria Quartet*. You almost feel playwrights should be in love with their characters, at least a little, if they're to really embody human feelings, failings, and strivings on the stage. Ditto the composer, and even librettist, of opera. Choreographer ... we hold with Yeats' adoration of Isadora Duncan, "How can you know the dancer from the dance?" At that point, however, when you come to scrutinize the interpretive arts, the proposition begins to unravel. In the case of interpretive artists it seems just a little self-serving, a tad narcissistic perhaps, for them to fall for themselves in performance. The exception would seem to be a director—who may be a tower of ego but is excused somewhat for remaining in the wings or behind the camera. And what of winemakers in this regard? Could they be touched, even moved, by their own creation? What would it take for the vigneron to become enamored to distraction by the fruits of their own hand?

Let's consider the winemaker's starting point as interpretive artist. They begin, of course, with the grapes ... but there is so much more than that. Also on the piece of paper they've been given are the vagaries of that vintage, whatever fluke or misfortune may have played with those grapes, for better or for worse. Then there are the winemaker's own viticultural decisions through every stage of the vintage, decisions which will now inevitably shape the kind of wine that will be made or *can* be made. There's the nature of the vineyard itself, our old friend *terroir*, along with every person in the past who's had a significant hand in shaping it and tending to it. There's the heritage of the winery, its history, reputation, and the world's view of its signature style. No less important is the winemaker's own winemaking philosophy, especially any developments or departures in that philosophy over time—stemming from correspondence or visits with other winemakers anywhere in the world, reading widely, drinking (one hopes more widely still), the odd happy accident and even one or two of those *eureka* moments all of us, winemakers included, wish would come our way more frequently. ("Hence," says Maritain, "the tyrannical and absorbing power of Art, and also its astonishing power of soothing ... it establishes [the artist] in a world apart, closed, limited, absolute ... This is true of all art; the ennui of living and willing ceases at the door of every workshop." *Every* workshop? Surely not. Nor every winery. Though unquestionably some, unquestionably some.)

So *those* are what a winemaker begins with. And from those can come something beautiful, inexplicable, even something sublime.

The concept of sublime, or more precisely "the sublime," has a long history in aesthetics. For the classical rhetorician Longinus the sublime is what entrances us, "what transports us with wonder" rather than what merely "gratifies us." Edmund Burke was the first to distinguish between the beautiful and the sublime, though with an unfortunate tendency, in an otherwise admirable philosopher, to trivialize the former and aggrandize the latter in rather risible terms. Immanuel Kant, though implicitly critical of Burke's "merely empirical exposition of the sublime and the beautiful," saw sufficient value in the distinction to make it a cornerstone of his grand aesthetic theory. Kant begins his aesthetic hierarchy from the bottom, with "the agreeable"—defining this via a wine analogy. The agreeable is a private and highly subjective response—"Thus he does not take it amiss if, when he says that Canarywine is agreeable, another corrects him and reminds him that he ought to say: It is agreeable *to me*." (Canary wine hails from Spain's Canary Isles, and while its reputation flags today it was some centuries ago quite the rage, especially the traditional sweet wines made from the malvasia grape. Shakespeare alluded to it in not one but two plays—*The Merry Wives of Windsor* and more famously in *Twelfth Night*, in which the coarse but curiously insightful inebriate, Sir Toby Belch, calls for "a cup of canary.") The pleasure we gain from the agreeable is the pleasure of gratification. The higher aesthetic dimensions, however, are not justifiable by purely personal gratification, but must be vindicated universally. These finer feelings are "of two kinds: the feeling of the *sublime* and that of the *beautiful*. The stirring of each is pleasant [decided understatement there], but in different ways ... Night is

sublime, day is beautiful ... The sublime *moves*, the beautiful *charms* ...
The sublime must always be great; the beautiful can also be small. The
sublime must be simple; the beautiful can be adorned and ornamen-
tal." Whether you find yourself moved or merely charmed by the best
wines you've drunk, the most evocative wines or those shared in love
and friendship ... well, that's a matter for your own taste and, perhaps, your own conscience. And Kant himself was no stranger to aligning aesthetic and moral judgment—Kant scholar Paul Guyer asserts his
claim "that the beautiful is the morally good."

Schopenhauer followed Kant's lead in employing a wine analogy to
explain an aesthetic point. In contrasting the distinct natures of explicit
versus implicit knowledge and experience, he claims "that philosophy
is related to art as wine is to grapes: philosophy provides actual wisdom, art potential wisdom." Wine here, while admirably used to make
a difficult idea clear and unambiguous, seems at the same time to be
getting short shrift. Wine, Schopenhauer appears to be suggesting, is
on a lower plane to philosophy and art. It may be worthy as a metaphor, but not as true comparison. It may illustrate, but not partake. We
prefer the approach of Oscar Wilde who, when it comes to wine and
philosophy, gives the dominant role to good old vino. This is unsurprising, given Wilde's disinclination to take things too seriously—not
to mention his nature as an intuitive, rather than a theoretical, aesthete.
In *The Picture of Dorian Gray*, over a sumptuous luncheon, the character
Lord Henry Wotton is holding forth (Wilde's description of Lord
Henry's speaking style reflects, apparently, his own style as his con-
temporaries have described it). He takes as his topic "Philosophy,"
which he personifies as a woman who might pine for her youth—"and
Philosophy herself became young." Lord Henry is mirroring his own
words of moments earlier, spoken to an elderly dowager to her delight,
that "to get back to one's youth one has merely to repeat one's follies."
And Philosophy has now caught "the mad music of Pleasure, wearing,
one might fancy, her wine-stained robe and wreath of ivy, [and]
danced like a Bacchante over the hills of life."

Now, before we move on from wine's creation to its appreciation,
and whatever your current feelings or beliefs concerning wine and its
status (or not) as art, one point is inescapable and inarguable—that
there are a multitude of objects, artifacts, manuscripts, or whatever else
accepted as art that have taken, in their making, nothing like the time,
precious attention to detail, hands-on master-craftsmanship and expressive artistry invested in the making of the finest wines. A collective
"So there!" from winemakers everywhere seems in order.

So, we've had our first things first. Now second things second—
what we make of art.

One of the strongest arguments made against wine as art is its transience. Elisabeth Telfer, author of *Food for Thought: Philosophy and Food*,

says that, "there are two reasons why transience might make a work of art less important. One is that it limits the contemplation that is possible. ... The other reason is that transient works of art cannot acquire the stature that a long-lived work of art can." Further to the question of ephemerality, Tim Crane in his essay "Wine as an Aesthetic Object" observes that "the mark of a great work of art is that it repays frequent visits. There is a sense, however, in which a wine cannot be returned to time after time." Never a truer word spoken. Wine is so quickly gone, so blissfully (and yet regrettably) consumed—and then no more. We can, of course, reach for another if we're so fortunate as to have one more wine of such distinction to hand. But ... same problem, now that's gone too. And even a bottle of the same wine, the same in every way, same château, vintage, kept side by side in the same cellar, decanted for precisely the same period ... is not the same wine, hence the old industry adage *there are no great wines, only great bottles of wine.* The beauty is in the drinking, not in the object (the bottle) held in your hands. And its "art-worthiness" disappears in the very act of expressing itself. Still, is this sufficient reason to reject wine as art? (And if transience is in itself sufficient reason to deny some work art status ... whoops, there goes Christo, all the wrapped coastlines and homicidal umbrellas, struck forever from the record.) Surely ephemeral pleasures have their own claims, and their own validity.

One of us, in Paris, at the Louvre, sought out the painting that moved him above all others, Gericault's *Raft of the Medusa.* He picks up the thread of his story ...

I sat in front of the painting for around an hour, perhaps a little longer. Come to think of it, about the same amount of time I'd take to enjoy a good bottle of wine. Every now and then I'd tear my gaze away, shake my head, look up and down the halls. I wondered, when Gericault himself came here to the Louvre as a young art student, had he any premonition that his masterpiece would one day hang in this pride of place, one day so soon after his too-soon death from consumption? It's the painting's block composition that instantly takes you, before you even distinguish the crew members one by one—this crew who've endured abandonment, the fiercest for-survival violence, cannibalism ... and now catch the faintest smear of a sail, salvation on the horizon but so faint it may well be illusory (and it will drop from sight, to their despair, before returning again for their rescue). The pyramidal arrangement of bodies seems at first a nod to neoclassicism, though in every other respect this work heralds, in scale and subject and tragic grandeur, all the sweep of capital "R" Romanticism. The figures, corpses and desperate survivors both, are depicted in such detail of anatomical precision that it's both shocking and, in its context, moving. (Delacroix, an artist in his youth when he modeled for this very work, described Gericault's smaller scale studies of lopped limbs as "the best argument for Beauty as it might be understood"—horror and tragedy transcending themselves in their triumphant depiction.) You can imagine the painter, still young but wasting away, all sign of the dandy long gone, his head now shaved to reinforce his self-sequestration from society (and mark a kind of private monasticism?). You can imagine him in his small rooms, body parts strewn about in various stages of decomposition (brought home for closer study from the morgue of the nearby Hospital Beaujon), inspiration for the artist to capture their twisted supplication. The force of composition thrusts up from the drowned corpses through various higher levels of hell, damnation, and desperation to that apex figure waving his shirt as a flag to rescue and redemption. (How scandalous at the time, for a dark-skinned figure to hold the focal point—a damning of slavery and plea for emancipation.) It strikes me now how compositionally similar they are—a painting, a wine. Certain key elements carry all else—color, line, light, arrangement (or fruit, weight, tannin, acidity …). Within and around these there is cohesion, integration, balance, sinuousness or angularity, contrasts and complements of tone and texture, jarring accents that for a moment stand out as if they don't belong but, when reflected on at greater length, reveal just how much emptier the work, or wine, would be without them …

Say he never returns to see that painting again. (Say he never drinks a particular wine again.) Say that in order not to corrupt its memory he denies himself any exposure at all to images of *Medusa*. That doesn't mean the experience has been lost. It's held in memory—where it can be returned to and relived and given meaning and savored over again. Like the memory of a favored wine. Where's the difference?

The argument against wine's transience is a relatively recent one. Before sounds and images could be recorded and transmitted, people's experience of all art was transient. Even the aristocratic patrons of Mozart and Haydn couldn't hear whatever music they wanted whenever they wanted—as we can by simply pushing a button. And anyone wishing to experience a great work of painting or sculpture had to physically visit it (no search engines at fingertips)—and lose its likeness again until they returned. All this is to say that not so long ago people experienced *all* art similarly to the way they experienced wine, similarly to the way that we still experience wine.

Where, then, does the "artness" reside? In a painting or sculpture that's easy enough to answer—it lives in the work itself, and some ghost of its art no doubt sits in images of that work (as frustrating and unsatisfying as a tasting note compared to tasting for yourself the real thing). A piece of music's "art," however, lives beyond even all the manuscripts on which it's written. And as to the art of poetry in an oral-tradition culture … the art is all around, in the remembering and the retelling.

So what are we judging in judging art? Take a performance of Chekhov's *The Cherry Orchard*. As we watch from our seats in the darkened theater, is it the work itself we're judging? This specific translation and adaptation? The quality of actors' performances, the seamlessness of roles all folding together into a greater whole? The staging and set design, perhaps (a line remembered, but not from where—"The Valkyries were all wearing diving suits")? Or the revolutionary use of multimedia? To what extent is the work a distinct artistic entity to that particular performance?

So too with our aesthetic judgment of wine. Are we focused solely on our subjective response towards an objective assessment? How expressive it is of its variety and region and the combination of these? How it reflects the style and reputation of its estate and maker? Or are we inclined rather to scrutinize our overall impression of all these elements, complicated not a little by the context in which it's consumed— the wine's "performance" you might call it (lead player, or perhaps support to the dish you've just been served).

Does wine resemble any one art medium more than others? As with painting, our focus expands and contracts, taking in the whole before attending to this or that particularly striking feature. Weighing balance and composition according to those features we choose to concentrate on or that seek out our own taste. There's parallel there, but the static form doesn't reflect the ever-changing dynamism of wine. In a temporal sense, then, perhaps wine better resembles some narrative form— film, literature or drama—in its development towards denouement, mounting complexity towards closure.

Or perhaps wine most resembles music.

"All art," as Walter Pater famously wrote, "constantly aspires to the condition of music." He goes on to explain that in music there is no separation between a work's subject matter and its form. Too often a work's meaning, its expression, rebels against its artistic shape and articulation. (In respect of the subsequent tendency to evaluate art solely on the message over the medium, Richard Wollheim states, "perhaps most primitively, we think of a work of art as expressive in the sense in which a gesture or a cry would be expressive.") Wine's message—which might be its *terroir*, its call to indulgence and fellowship, its reflective urgings—is also inextricable from its substance. Add to that the observation of philosopher of taste Carolyn Korsmeyer—"a discriminating palate is perhaps as hard to come by as a musical ear"—and you have quite the compelling case.

Hegel's a hoot, when you don't have to read too much of him or take it too seriously. He was also a great wine imbiber. So much so that, the story goes, he once turned up in the university town of Tubingen so off his chops that he had to be hidden by friends from authorities. He was then, so it's said, warned—"Hegel, you'll drink away that little bit of sense you've got left." (Anyone who, for their sins, has waded through—or attempted to—*The Phenomenology of Spirit*, might consider those words prophetic.) In the realm of aesthetics he has some fascinating notions of music. "If music is to express the depths of romantic feeling, it must make use of harmonic dissonance and discords." This puts one of us in mind of a certain wine drunk just recently.

A 1997 Paul Jaboulet Hermitage Blanc it was, opened over dinner with an old schoolmate. We enjoyed it for an hour or so, and it never stopped surprising. I'll say up front it wasn't anything like I was expecting, nothing like I've ever previously found roussanne and marsanne to taste. I wouldn't, however, have wanted it tasting in any way differently to how it did. At first I thought it might be slightly oxidized, though the color was good, and paler than I'd expected with that age. The first scent was what my friend, a psychiatrist, described as "ether"—a little wistfully, thinking of his med student days. Slightly candied orange on the palate gave way to a vegetal note that twitched between cooking onions and onion jam (more appetizing than might sound). A slight Fino sherry nuttiness complemented a tang of barley sugar until, just when I thought it was on its last legs, an intense purity of poaching stone fruit emerged, merging then further into fruit toffee, all the while that slightly spirit-y edge waxing and waning and each sip given satisfaction by a persistent but delicate acidity. After dinner we retired back to my place (his wife being, as they say, in the family way) to listen to a little music over cognac and cigars. Our conversation over the music—John Adams's *Violin Concerto*, Respighi's *The Birds* and *Church Windows*, the wonderful Ravel *Piano Concerto in G* (Louis Lortie's magical hands), and, new to me, John Corigliano's *The Red Violin Suite*—our discussion of this selection was no more or less enthusiastic (and at times intense) than our discussion of that wine had been at dinner. Its dissonances, taking Hegel's point, were much of its making, much of its persisting interest, much of what kept us returning to it to swap impressions. Beardsley has asked why there are "no taste symphonies and smell sonatas." Well, that wine was one—appreciated in time and over time, changing melody with development, certain harmonies rising then falling and rising again, fugue-like, and certain at-first-disconcerting notes showing themselves an essential part of the greater whole.

One music critic believes that, "unlike a novel or a painting, a score gives up its full meaning only when it is performed in front of an audience; it is a child of loneliness that lives off crowds." Wine, on the other hand, can be savored both ways—in solitary contemplation and in the generous warmth of company and companionship.

Perhaps "wine" as an abstract concept, like "painting" when we refer to no specific work, "music" when we're talking about no particular piece, "architecture" with no set building in mind … perhaps "wine" as an essence can be accorded its honor as *art*, while withholding that status from all the physical bottles which will in time be drunk and so gone. Wine could be an art without artifacts—or an art with many artifacts in a shrinking population as bottles are enjoyed. As to those bottles that are kept till past their best, surely the question of art becomes a moot one. Unless … if great wine might be great art, might bad wine be bad art?

Let's reflect on wine's artistic bona fides one more time, in the light of a more modern aesthetic formulation. As Steven Pinker notes, "the philosopher Denis Dutton has identified seven universal signatures" of art, recognizable across all cultures:

- Expertise or virtuosity
- Non-utilitarian pleasure ("art for art's sake")
- Style (standards of form, as significant for their breaking as their making)
- Criticism (the tendency of others to see value in making value judgments)
- Imitation (art imitating life, what the thinkers of classical days called *mimesis*)
- Special focus (in that it is set apart from the humdrum of everyday existence, and can therefore transform or ennoble that existence)
- Imagination (in both its production by the artist and its apprehension by its audience)

When this list is criticized, it tends to be not so much in terms of its comprehensiveness, but rather for being *too* comprehensive, for including criteria that are not met by all things that all people would like to regard as art. Certainly the advent by Marcel Duchamp of the "readymade"—via his "Fountain"-entitled urinal—would seem to fall short of the second signature, non-utilitarianism. (Duchamp himself was dismissive of those who misunderstood his intentions and who attempted to justify the relocated *pissoir* on grounds of artistic beauty— "When I discovered readymades, I thought to discourage aesthetics. I threw … the urinal in their faces as a challenge, and now they admire them for their aesthetic beauty.") The work possesses an obvious function, given that one could conceivably take a piss in it—though a purer aesthetic judgment might be to take a piss on it.

Wine, too, violates the second signature—though in a manner far more honorable. "All art is quite useless," opined Oscar Wilde. That's not the slur it's frequently taken to be, but rather a true art-lover's exaltation of beauty over utility. And perhaps in this we've found a genuine reason to deny wine the status of art. For wine does not lack for purpose. Not the purpose of inebriation—that may at times be its end, but never its reason. Rather, the purpose of marking ceremony and occasion, of honoring guests and distinguishing them in their own eyes, of making great food exquisite and memorable company indelible.

"Art is what you can get away with," said Andy Warhol (making Boris Pasternak's "Art always serves beauty" seem old fashioned, indeed blissfully naïve in the extreme). This reminds us that, unlike the art world, no one has ever deliberately made a bad wine in order to make a statement. By mistake, inexperience, lack of talent perhaps. But no winemaker has ever felt the (highly overrated) need to shock with pure, unadulterated, unambiguous ugliness. "Anti-art" was deemed a revolutionary movement in the second half of the 20th century—but could you conceive of (and would you want to) "anti-wine." "Imagination without skill gives us contemporary art," was Tom Stoppard's wry way of hitting the nail on the head in *Artist Descending a Staircase* (invoking once more the ghost of old Marcel). We all know though, that *both* imagination and skill are required in the makers of any wine worth the drinking.

Maybe there's the answer there. Or a different question altogether.

In a period of art distinguished (if that's the word) by Warhol's opportunistic cynicism, marked by the banality and asininity of Italian artist Piero Manzoni selling his own excrement (don't laugh, the Tate paid £22,300 for a single tin of the stuff just a few years back—proving, we suppose, that at least some modern art is quite literally shit)—the question shouldn't be whether wine is art, but *why would it want to be*?

Twenty-Three

Wine and Mammon

There's another attribute that wine and art have in common. They are the most obvious ways for the über-wealthy to demonstrate their "taste." (Fashion should be another, but you need only witness the egregious dress *faux pas* of many pop stars and actors to know that, well, money, fame, class ... you clearly can't have it all.) This observation, from a prominent Napa winemaker—"Wine and wealth follow each other around in the most obnoxious way ... And the wealthy *like* being told what to like." (Shades of Trimalchio and his Falernian Opimian.) So who is following whom, and could the follower be the one being chased? Is wine the stalker or the stalked? While reflecting on this, you'll recognize that one answer is the more interesting.

The once humble vine has come a long way. And it's worth remembering just how far. Pliny the Elder, reflecting on a banquet thrown by Pomponius Secundus for Gaius Caesar, observed with some distaste, "so much money is tied up in our wine cellars." An artless observation from a natural historian 2,000 years ago, but it shows the depths of the roots of our relationship with wine. We can read in these simple words all of the pride, bravado, and frustrated passion that characterizes collectors of wine, seemingly from time immemorial.

Because it has the image, like art, of an image-maker, it makes sense that wine should be prone to inflationary trends. (These days still, as in Wilde's time, "people know the price of everything, and the value of nothing.") At its top end, whether the producers like it or not (or profess not to but secretly do), sit designer brands all but unapproach-able to any but the wealthiest or most well-connected. Some industry insiders have estimated that, at current rates of top-end wine price inflation, in 50 years time a case of a First Growth Bordeaux could cost in the region of £10 million (mm ... we'd have to say depending of course on the economic circumstances prevailing). This is the Pétrus/ Yquem phenomenon, with the wealthy pursuing, or having to be seen having, a relatively few well-known and stratospherically priced brands. Though we would never argue that the acquisition of great wealth denies refinement, in the case of wine and what is seen as ac-ceptable drinking, it does act as a deterrent—as this anecdote, reported to us by a sommelier in one of New Zealand's premier restaurants, attests. In for dinner one evening, an ageing Brit rock star and super-model wife (just another in a long line that must make his alimony payments look like the GDP of a small South American country). She asks for the restaurant's most expensive wine, dismissing the somme-lier's attempts to dissuade her ... "I don't care what it is, I want the *best*." That happened to be a '59 Château d'Yquem—not much change out of five grand. It was poured for her to taste, and she less than deli-cately, without bothering to nose it at all, slurped it down and promptly spluttered it back up again (clearly not to her exquisite taste). She drank Salon for the rest of the night (that was the most expensive fizz on the list). Still, hubby coughed up for it, and the staff enjoyed a unique palate-expanding experience.

Oddly, or not, a character portrayed as the epitome of connoisseur-ship falls similarly prey to the Pétrus/Yquem syndrome, if in a less gauche way. Hannibal Lecter, from Thomas Harris' thrillers and immortalized by Anthony Hopkins' performances, is purported to be a man for whom the phrase "impeccable taste" could have been invented. But the Doctor, for all his supposed discernment, reveals the same label-fellating obsession as the unseriously informed wealthy. Rather than showing true individuality of preference, he's portrayed drinking those very two labels (as well as a Bâtard-Montrachet of unknown provenance)—and, in *Hannibal*, FBI agent Clarice Starling uses the predictability of these tastes to track Lecter down.

In our examination of wine and art, we had cause to consider the seven universal signatures of Dennis Dutton. Steven Pinker takes this further—"One of the items on Dutton's list ... is impracticality. But useless things, paradoxically, can be highly useful for a certain pur-pose: appraising the assets of the bearer. Thorstein Veblen first made the point in his theory of social status. Since we cannot easily peer into the bank books or Palm Pilots of our neighbors, a good way to size up their means is to see whether they can afford to waste them on luxu-ries and leisure. Veblen wrote that the psychology of taste is driven by three 'pecuniary canons': conspicuous consumption, conspicuous leisure, and conspicuous waste." Pinker goes on to give, as an evolutionary metaphor for these three canons of conspicuousness, the delightfully apposite image of the peacock.

So, what constitutes value for money? And further to the point—is a $5,000 bottle of wine 100 times better than a bottle costing $50, and what about the wine that sits at $50,000? Obviously the answer is no ... and yes. It's a question of what's being paid for here—name, prestige and pedigree, the surety of quality, history, the certainty of being envied. The reason for rampant inflation at the high end of wine lies in two avenues of avarice—greed for money and greed for recognition. In the case of the former, consider the gall of the Bordelais in attempting to gouge even dearer prices for the inferior '04 vintage than for the excellent '03. Or the phenomenon that occurs in both Old and New Worlds, of declaring a *vintage of the century* every decade or so, with a consequent price flight into the stratosphere, and of course an inevitable flow-on to subsequent (less hyperbole-deserving) vintages. In some respects, a producer setting an outrageous price (on the basis of relative scarcity or plain old *chutzpah*) is taking an "offense is the best form of defense" tack against critical reviews—few are likely to even get to sample wines priced at that extreme, and those who do are unlikely to look that particular gift horse in the mouth. *Wine Spectator* veteran, James Laube, describes such wines as "untouchables"—insulated from critique "due largely to a price mechanism that sets them apart from the broader market." The ramifications of stratospheric wine prices reach beyond those rich enough to be gouged. It's not difficult to sympathize with the outrage such media stories provoke in ordinary folk, who view the prices paid for expensive wines (after all, just a bottle of plonk) as obscene. This is a kind of class resentment we're sure wouldn't occur if it was something more obviously functional like a Dino Ferrari or Masarati under discussion.

Mind you, it's tough finding someone to cast the first stone. Experiments at Cal Tech and Stanford revealed that when drinking the same wine, with different sample groups believing it was a $5 or a $90 bottle, subjects expressed far greater pleasure in drinking the "more expensive" one. And results were not solely based on subjects' own descriptions of their responses—brain scans revealed greater stimulation of pleasure centers in the brain during the consumption of the wine they believed to be more exclusive. (It's not necessary to go through the ritual of hypnosis to demonstrate the malleability of people.)

It seems it's the lot of all we poor mortals to be biased toward a wine we're informed is expensive over one we believe is cheap. Well not quite all. There's one group of exceptions—those who practice inverted snobbery in relation to wine. So in thrall to the pursuit of extreme bargains are these people, they convince themselves that their home-drinking staple cleanskin/supermarket wine/unknown-cheap-and-cheerful is "every bit as good" as a wine 5, 10, 20 times its price. And they won't be gainsaid, or private in their triumph. The world must listen, and furthermore agree, that their cleanskin/supermarket wine/unknown-cheap-and-cheerful offers every bit the drinking experience of that wine caressing your palate at the same time it's giving your credit card a migraine. (Add the whiff of piety and ... well, you get the picture.) But the fundamental fact is that, unless the dearer wine in question is corked, oxidized or suffering from some other extreme fault—likely an uncharacteristic fault, or said wine could never have sustained and built its reputation and price point—then *No, your cleanskin/supermarket wine/unknown-cheap-and-cheerful, however much you might enjoy it, is most assuredly* NOT *"every bit as good as ..."*

Wine plays to the best and worst of human morality, and can make you question faith in human judgment. And it can be damnably obscuring.

All this is grist to the mill of the wine forgers—and here delicious examples abound. See, already we're following fashion, teetering on the brink of idealizing the forger. Which is not our viewpoint. Let it be said that these people are robbers, irrespective of the wealth or moral standing or tastelessness of those they rob. Put aside your Robin Hood arguments on moral equivalence, we shut our ears. That said, we do make an exception, in fact confess to a sneaking affection for one villain, the arch art-forger Eric Hebborn. His brilliant deceptions were not made to feed a habit of casinos or fast women (that we know of), or even to purchase art (which would sort of defeat the purpose), but merely to keep him in sufficient quantities of Chianti—of which his body stank when he was found dead, proof of his dedication. To give Hebborn the due we refuse others, he felt his forgery to be quixotic, and also if not a victimless crime then a crime with no victim anyone cared for, since any victims (dealers and wealthy collectors) were, he felt, complicit in the rape of the art world. Fooling them, he felt, was its own vindication. (You must admit he has a point, with respect to art.) So having reached the end of the roundabout in our argument, we'll leave it. (Well, no one's perfect.)

What *is* conspicuously gross and offensive in the stories of wine forgery and misrepresentation, is the typically weasely behavior of the parties concerned. The forgers indulge in barefaced denials, the experts suddenly mislay their expertise, auction houses place their hands on their hearts and point piously to precedent, and the aggrieved buyers ... well with a few notable exceptions they just want the embarrassment to go away, at any cost. (It's all in Hebborn's book, *Confessions of a Master Forger*—nothing changes. And what has, you'll find in Benjamin Wallace's *The Billionaire's Vinegar*.)

Some forms of wine skullduggery have their comical aspects, but not so the increasing practice of wine heists. Money follows fashion, and thieves follow money, so thieves become interested in what's fashion in wine, and act on it—like the vertical of Pétrus, vintages from 1964 to 2003, stolen from a Canadian restaurant. The threat of possible hijack led the merchants of Bordeaux to take no chances with the famed 2005 vintage. Such was the level of risk that insurance was out of the question, so shipments, even some of fewer than a dozen cases, were accompanied by a phalanx of armed guards and surveillance vehicles. Another cost of wine inflation.

A bizarre postscript to the wine forgery sagas has emerged in Spain. Scientists are working on an electronic tongue—no prurient sniggers please, this could well be serious. "The e-tongue, as it is called, can already distinguish the differences between chardonnay, malvasia, macabeu and airen grape varieties from different vintages." The device, which apparently makes use of "tiny synthetic membranes," can pick up the five human tastes and is thought might be useful in detecting fraud. We bow to the technology but surely a preferable fraud detection approach, especially from the point of view of auction houses and collectors, is one that doesn't require the bottle to be cracked to tell you that you've been ripped off.

And so back to the starkest aspect of wine as a pleasurable experience—that it must be destroyed, to be physically enjoyed. (Reason enough for its following the evolutionary byways and finding for itself a metaphysical identity.) Such a tragic quality makes fine wine surely the most decadently self indulgent of all luxury items. Art and property and jewelry and cars and planes and boats, you name it, these have the merit of being tangible. They may deteriorate and depreciate (and appreciate), but it's not as if they have a use-by date beyond which we take an axe to them. And before you counter with the argument of wine as an investment item, think about the remorseless life cycle. Where lies the aesthetic satisfaction in owning a bottle of wine you know is terminally ill? It seems rather like a concert one of us attended, by Sinatra, when he was in his seventies. Not only was it not pleasurable, but excruciatingly painful, to listen to a once great talent struggle through the repertoire. And made even more pathetic by that famed sense of timing occasionally disguising the terrible onslaught of age upon "the Voice." Who but a sadist or masochist would want a recording of that evening? The most intense feelings of nostalgia couldn't justify its revisiting.

Yet for some, the contemplative quality of wine leads to opportunity in sadness. How better to reflect on the ephemerality of our own lives than to take out and lovingly observe a fine old wine we know is dying—its grace and beauty fading visibly—and allow it to expire in dignity?

One of us firmly believes that's how he would act in the circumstances. The other, I fear, is more likely to assuage his frustration with a hammer, cursing himself and the thoughtless bottle (dammit) in equal parts.

Therapeutic either way. And, relative to other expensive experiences, worth the money.

Twenty-Four

The Tyranny of *Terroir*

Modern debate over *terroir* turns on disputes that are couched in ideal-istic terms—differing Old and New World wine making philosophies, Old World tradition versus New World technology, or even Old World authenticity versus New World promiscuity. But they remain essen-tially commercial. In the midst, each side vigorously protests the sup-posed tyranny of the other.

Not surprisingly, *terroir* advocates bemoan the insidious influence of critic Robert Parker. But closer to home they have also decried the enologist Emile Peynaud's prescient efforts to modernize Bordeaux wine making practices, continued today all over the world by his country-hopping protégé Michel Rolland. This was a consistent theme asserted and developed through Jonathan Nossiter's 2004 film, *Mondovino*. The film is well worth a look, and not only for its treatment of *terroir* and Old versus New World tensions. (But be warned. Its bum-numbing length can leave you feeling, as you stand up at the closing credits, that you've just sat through an entire Ingmar Bergman retrospective.)

It's the remorseless erosion of tradition in the "Internationalizing" of wine styles that primarily draws ire. This has, the claim goes, led to a monolithic vinous monotony and (less acknowledged, but surely more threatening) a stylistic monopoly—in which weight and size (of flavor, scale, alcohol, and wood) steamroll regional diversity, subtlety, and any element of appealing quirkiness.

The argument has merit, no question. Still, tradition isn't everything. History isn't an excuse for stagnation. The Old World's objection to the so-called International style is that it will supplant heterogeneity with uniformity. But shrill insistence that only the Old World possesses *terroir*, and that the New World most decidedly does not, is an encouragement of the uniformity they claim to fear, and a nail in the coffin of the heterogeneity they wish to protect. The sentiment of Madame Denise Capbern Gasqueton, proprietress of St. Estèphe third growth Calon-Ségur, illuminates the closed-mindedness of the extreme *terroir* case, and its inherent circularity—"I drink (foreign) wines. Very good wines are produced in Chile, for example, but they lack *terroir*, and *terroir* is what makes everything. A wine that is well produced is a good wine, but lacks complexity and other elements to which we are used." How do you say "thanks for nothing" in Spanish?

If Old World norms are *all that wine may be judged by*—then where, may we ask, does the tyranny start? (Overheard more than once at a tasting:

> Of an Old World wine—"This is thin, insipid, and uninspiring."
> "Eh bien, vous ne comprenez pas *terroir*" [Loose translation—"Oh well, you clearly do not understand *terroir*."]
> Of a New World wine—"This is fat, blowsy, and overblown."
> "C'est merde!" [Loose translation—"Of course! It lacks the distinction bestowed by true *terroir*."])

Must every pinot taste like Burgundy (you will frequently see wine writers make comments on some New World pinot along the lines of "while a lovely drink, lacks true pinot varietal character")? Is cabernet that demonstrates greater opulence in its youth than most Bordeaux necessarily inferior? Is white Burgundy the only measure of chardonnay? And must all shiraz, and its adventures with grenache, be an imitation of Rhône reds?

The reputation of these regions and their wines is fully justified. But their prominence does tend to cast an unnecessary pall over other wine styles and varieties and regions and techniques. They have become not only the *standard* by which other wines are judged, but the only *context* in which those judgments are made. These regions, in becoming identified with their traditional varieties, have in a very real and unyielding sense become the yardstick by which all others *must* be appraised. In a word, they have become "canonical."

The so-called Western Canon, that collection of the highest of high culture in art and literature, is celebrated by many as a sacred repository of civilized attainment from ancient days to modern times. But equally it's rejected by others for its marginalizing of works which, for whatever reasons, don't quite "fit" the elitist ideals. (As Harold Bloom in *The Western Canon*, laments, "Shakespeare, whose aesthetic supremacy has been confirmed by the universal judgment of four centuries, is now 'historicized' into pragmatic diminishment.") The traditions and inherited wisdom of the Old World are the wine world's canon. Enduring European styles and standards have set the benchmarks of quality and acceptability, dictating the basis by which other styles and standards "fit" or not. Hardly surprising then, that this canon too finds itself under assault.

As the *terroir* argument rages, it's not just New World wine adherents who are challenging tradition. Wine makers in some of the oldest wine regions of Europe have also kicked against the constraints tradition and tradition-based appellation requirements impose on them. These regional regulations to which wines need to comply if they are to claim the highest positioning, while originally designed to protect the integrity and quality of the region's output, now frequently do very much the opposite. The Sassicaia story is a salutary one (you might recall from *Sideways*, that an '88 Sassicaia was the wine that first got Maya serious about wine).

Mario Incisa della Rochetta had an iconoclastic, indeed sacrilegious, notion to turn his back on the traditional sangiovese grape of Tuscany. The resulting wine was Sassicaia ("place of stones"), made from cabernet planted near the unfashionable Bolgheri marshes down from the Chianti hills. Officialdom was outraged, and further so by the "Super Tuscan" revolution that followed (we feel sure that old Tuscan son Galileo would have kept a more open mind, but then the Chianti of his time was made predominantly from the canaiolo grape, not sangiovese—*plus ça change ...*). These wines were given the lowliest classification possible, *vino da tavola*, that is bog-ordinaire table wine. But that didn't stop them from gaining worldwide fame, and the best of them outstripping in price the most expensive traditional Tuscan wines of Chianti Classico and Brunello di Montalcino. (Furthermore, what began as a "Super" trend in Tuscany has spread to other distinguished Italian regions, including Piedmont and Veneto.)

A problem with the term *terroir* is that it has come to be used to mean so much that it's at great risk of meaning nothing at all. That would be a great shame, because the concept itself—divorced from self-interest and one-upmanship in both Worlds—possesses true beauty. So too does the related term, equally difficult to translate in its full sense and resonance, *typicité* (Italian *tipicità*)—translated with typical Anglo clunkiness as "typicality." Such a wine possesses identifiable characteristics you could consider archetypal of that variety in that region. As a term it carries less baggage and bastardization than *terroir*, and is really what the best New World wines should be aspiring to— divorced as it is from Old World place, and related only to place of its own provenance.

Claims of *terroir* are also not always what is made of them. Château Beaucastel, legendary producer of Châteauneuf du Pape, possesses a slightly feral character, described by Lawrence Osborne in *The Accidental Connoisseur*, as "a whiff of chicken coops." It has been claimed as a distinctive aspect of the wine's *terroir*. Others believed it to be due to the presence of Brettanomyces (known affectionately as "brett"), a spoiling yeast that gives the slightly animal funk. Some say that low levels can improve a wine's appeal of complexity, especially in their youth—rather like an expensive aftershave whose faintest scent contributes to a sense of worldliness, but in lashings is offensive and has the opposite to desired effect. Experiments by American wine collector Charles Collins demonstrated "significant brett infections" in the '89 and '90 vintages (don't for a moment let this put you off if you've always enjoyed Beaucastel—we love it). "Give up the myth," says Collins, "that the odd flavors are due to *terroir*—they aren't." In respects, that flavor-defining brett presence, as an interloper to the wine's other flavors, is actually working *against* the concepts of *terroir* and *typicité*.

None of this is to suggest that *terroir* doesn't exist, that it's all smoke and mirrors, or some wine-wanker shibboleth or secret handshake. When it's there, it's unquestionably there. It's just one of those things that are difficult to define but ... well, you know it when you see it or, in this case, taste it. But tradition for tradition's sake is no answer. Then again, nor is unbridled innovation severed from history.

In his classic work, *From Dawn to Decadence*, the historian Jacques Barzun makes reference to the rise and fall of the great Roman orator and writer Cicero. In an interesting parallel to what we are seeing in the wine world, Cicero's influence among Western intellectuals lasted for all of 500 years, only to fade "when physical science began to drive Latin out of the curriculum"—resulting in his replacement by figures deemed more appropriate to the time. Barzun's point being, that such icon-toppling events are the result of a "recurrent cultural need." (In the present context we might see that need as cultural market forces.) If history is a guide, the process of challenge is both inevitable and unstoppable—and very human. Barzun again—"an object or idea is rarely seen in the round. Like a mountain it presents a variety of faces. Moved by an ulterior purpose, observers take a few of these for the whole ... This partiality should not be surprising ... each individual takes only some elements of experience, and that spontaneous choice governs tastes, career, estimates of worth, and the feel of life itself." Sound familiar?

The cultural battles that inform the *terroir* debate—nature/nurture in psychology, elitism and egalitarian diversity in artistic achievement, and Old and New World philosophies of wine making—share two common threads. The first is always ideology. It is ideology that inflames emotions and encourages the passionate to remain true to their passion. But it also engenders suspicion and blinkers reason, and even when open to facts is rarely conducive to solutions. As Barzun points out, facts alone cannot settle such quarrels, for they are invariably subject to interpretation.

The hope of rapprochement lies in the second thread, fine at first but growing in strength as impasse drags on—pragmatism, a pragmatism based on standards and criteria that are as far as possible non-ideological. Devilishly difficult to achieve in the field of literature, with its academic, social and political baggage (of both persuasions). But eminently possible in the world of wine where the potential for sensible mutuality of interest is more evident.

Let us propose, then, a vinous "Canon" that combines the best of the Old and New Worlds in wine and in literature, selected by your fearless duo.

The foundation cannot but be Shakespeare. ("The difference between Shakespeare and his nearest rivals is one of both kind and degree," says Bloom. Yes, it is. But in coming not to tear down Shakespeare and his vinous equivalents, we equally intend to recognize independently the quality and contribution of styles utterly different. Just as Shaw, Synge, Beckett, and Stoppard don't have to be considered *only* in terms of Shakespeare to be appreciated in their own right.)

In the wine world the Shakespearean mantle goes to Bordeaux. This isn't to dismiss the claims of other regions, just to acknowledge the ubiquity of cabernet sauvignon (and its blending partners), and the stylistic influence of Bordeaux. Notwithstanding the fact that a hundred and fifty years ago, cabernet had nothing like the prominence in the region it enjoys today, and was in fact a minor grape variety—and also that the oldest continually producing cabernet sauvignon vineyard in the world is not in Bordeaux, but Kalimna in South Australia (producing the grapes that go into Penfolds' flagship Bin 707). But age is not the only element in pedigree. After all, even the master drew on an earlier master, Montaigne, for inspiration in his final and perhaps greatest play, *The Tempest* (at least, it's our favorite). And aside from the obvious validity of the choice, it's in the spirit to begin with a gesture of ideological impartiality.

Burgundy is next of course, and it deserves a more whimsical and idiosyncratic partner—Baudelaire, we'd say, given the duel sensualities at play in the poems and the wine, and the astonishing influence of that poet on French lit that followed.

The crystal clarity of Goethe's works makes fine canonical company to the great German rieslings—a delicate *eiswein* capturing *The Sorrows of Young Werther*, and a stately dryness in keeping with Mephistopheles' finest lines from *Faust*.

The traditional styles of Piedmont and Tuscany will appear in the company of Dante. While the modern Super Tuscans would be, what . . . Lampedusa or Pavese, or even Italo Calvino?

Spain is simple. The spirit of Cervantes flows exuberantly in the great Riojas and Ribera del Dueros.

For the modern wines of Greece we refuse the cop-out of Euripides or Aeschylus, and propose instead the modern sensibility of the sublime C. P. Cavafy.

Now the New World.

A detailed treatment would accord South American wines more than a regional place, but till then their malbec can aspire to the canonical status of Jorge Luis Borges or Gabriel Garcia Marquez.

There are American wines, we know, with reputations to rival Melville, Hawthorne, and Emily Dickinson (though it occurs to us that, stylistically, zin would have to be that master of beguiling bombast and enveloping overstatement, Edgar Allan Poe).

At the bottom of the vinous world, New Zealand wines can cement the genuine but hitherto peripheral canonical claims of Janet Frame or Keri Hulme. And let's not forget Australian shiraz (in all its variety of incarnations), which deserves its own kind of Nobel prize, like countryman Patrick White.

"All that the Western Canon can bring one is the proper use of one's own solitude," reflects Bloom, somewhat wistfully—"that solitude whose final form is one's confrontation with one's own mortality." If that is truly so (and we don't for a moment agree) then move over literature, and make way for a real contemplative pastime, one that celebrates reflection in company, and all the virtues that shared pleasure releases and inspires.

All of which begs the question (or, in fact, the questions)—Can tradition and innovation be amicably reconciled? Can Old and New World wine characteristics coincide and cohabitate? And, most importantly, *what's going to give the best drinking*?

Perhaps the rapprochement is already happening—the seemingly contradictory twin tyrannies of tradition and technology finally reconciling. You could see it as a kind of Hegelian dialectic, in which the *thesis* (Old World tradition) and *antithesis* (New World technology) find their respectively most appealing aspects equally represented in *synthesis*—the best, so to speak, of both Worlds. As wine makers travel and work in other regions and countries, compare notes and swap observations, some Old World faults are refined and rectified, and the New World aspires to a better understanding of its own kinds of *terroir*. Wine, as all drinkers well have cause to know, promotes generosity and fosters sharing. Why shouldn't that be the case at the level at which it's made—the sharing of vision and philosophy towards better wines everywhere.

Hence, observe Old World investment in the New World. French champagne houses are en masse investing in New World cool climate regions for sparkling wines. Chapoutier turns out distinctively New

World Australian shiraz-based wines with just as distinctive an Old World sensibility. And not merely one but *both* winners of the famed 1976 Judgment of Paris (of which, much more next chapter) have since been purchased by Old World interests—Montelena (producer of the event's winning chardonnay) by Saint-Estèphe "Super Second" Château Cos d'Estournal, and Stag's Leap (whose cabernet sauvignon tipped out, among others, Cos' neighbor Second Growth, Montrose) has been acquired by a venture including Italy's Tuscan powerhouse Antinori.

Old World winemakers, especially those with globetrotting experience, are frequently defenders of New World *terroir* claims. Perhaps not surprising, given their necessary streak of innovativeness, that they are more forward-looking than critics mired in old paradigms of thought. This from Alberto Antonini, whose family owns Poggiotondo estate in Tuscany, and who has also made wine in North and South Americas and Australia—"I hear people in Europe say that New World countries have no *terroir*. This is wrong, absolutely. It is nothing more than enological racism." He does, however, concede that, "The New World just hasn't been working on their *terroirs* for that long."

Was there a sting in that tail? No, we're sure he meant nothing by it. Nothing more than ... that ... than that ... How dare ... ?

It's okay folks, just a mild case of *terroir*-induced paranoia. We'll be fine by the next chapter.

Twenty-Five

Merry, Merry Meritage

"When Spurrier invited them he told them it was for a tasting of California wines; he did not say that they would be tasting both California and French wines at the same time." Ah, the consequences of a simple oversight.

We're talking, of course, of the famed (or infamous, depending on your bent) 1976 "Judgment of Paris"—the historic taste-off between chardonnays and cabernet sauvignons from California, and white Burgundies and red Bordeaux from France—described so dramatically in George M. Taber's book of the same name. Steven Spurrier, an Englishman and respected Parisian wine merchant, had for some time been impressed by what he'd heard and experienced of the developments in California wines. In those days of course, to quote one of Taber's own chapter titles, "France ruled the world." The tasting event Spurrier had organized at the InterContinental Hotel in Paris was designed to showcase selected wines from California, to allow them to strut their stuff under the collective judgment of nine experts—the cream of French wine nobility. (In sharp contrast to the original Judgment of Paris from classical myth, in which the mantle of nobility fell to the beauty candidates—the goddesses Minerva, Juno, and Venus—and the judge was Paris of Troy, a prince it's true, but still a mere mortal.) Spurrier's hope and expectation was no more (and it should be said, no less) than that the upstart New World wines would surprise and impress the tasting panel with the extent of their progress.

Seated, and discovering that the tasting would be expanded to include selected French wines, the judges now found that it was also to be blind (an obstacle not presented to Paris, who was given license to feast his eyes on his immaculate trio all disrobed, with no fear of retribution). In fact it was to be double-blind, as both Spurrier and his colleague Patricia Gallagher, whose scores were not to be counted, were also blind tasting. This last development added a further touch of formal authenticity to an event that was changing shape at each turn.

The rest, as they say, is history—and like all the best of history's titbits, has been told and retold to several different ends. Suffice to say that not only did the California wines perform better than the French might have allowed themselves to expect, they performed in short better than the French—and so won both tastings. That's to say an American wine was placed overall first in both the red and white categories, by a panel of distinguished French judges. *Quelle horreur!* (Which became *quelle horreur* squared 30 years later when, in an anniversary rematch conducted jointly in London and Napa for the red wines only, the California wines emerged even more triumphant.)

The reverberations of the 1976 Judgment of Paris are still being felt across the wine world, at both macro and micro levels. Fortunes were made almost overnight as the best-performing California wines (and their prices) went stratospheric. Wine making reputations soared, while some others suffered. New World wine producing countries besides the U.S. felt similarly vindicated and emancipated, and became more confident in their abilities and more able to chance their arms in markets previously resistant. The French were ridiculed and vilified—the result widely seen as a humiliating comeuppance for their reactions (to their own verdict), and their long history of chauvinism in all matters of the vine. *Schadenfreude* is a universal sentiment, and it was certainly the emotion of the day. Echoes of it still persist, years later.

A watershed event in the history of wine—that's what the doyen of aficionados, Robert Parker, called it. It's clearly difficult to exaggerate the significance of the events of that May afternoon. But the psychological "facts" surrounding that day are quite another matter. Interpreted by most of the wine world, certainly the New World, as a classic instance of Gallic arrogance and hubris, this story lends itself to reinterpretation. Some French judges behaved poorly, that's for sure. Others were almost gracious—a kind of grace under fire, under the circumstances. And it's these circumstances that warrant closer examination.

So why not become for a while one of those French judges, and join us while we indulge in a little psychological conjecture. A "beautiful, sunny day in Paris" and the promise of an enjoyable afternoon, that's what lies before you. A chance to demonstrate your undoubted expertise in the company of distinguished fellow professionals, and with wines offering ample scope for that most irresistible of emotional combinations—benevolent superiority. But no sooner sat, you're hit with a triple whammy—the addition of French wines to the judging, a blind tasting, and the implied rigor of a double-blind experiment.

"The nine judges seemed nervous at the beginning," writes Taber.

Any wonder. All of a sudden there's the feeling of being isolated and exposed. Even as the tasting of the whites begins, thoughts of "what if" are racing through your mind.

What if the American wines are better than I expected?

What if I rate the American wines too highly?

What if I don't know the difference—(I will, won't I?)

What if the individual scores are publicly announced?

Back to Taber's eyewitness account, "From their comments ... the judges were becoming totally confused as they tasted the white wines. The panel couldn't tell the difference." Taber could—being privy to what wines were what.

Such confusion must play on your mindset.

Mon Dieu, this is much more difficult than I imagined.

What do the others think of this wine? Those two seem to be comparing notes.

"The judges began talking to each other ... They speculated about a wine's nationality, often disagreeing." More anguished thoughts.

"They don't know either—or else they're not saying.

Finally, the tasting scores are announced. A 1973 Château Montelena Chardonnay from the Napa Valley has trumped for first place the Grand Cru and Premier Cru wines from Burgundy's famed appellations of Beaune, Meursault, and Puligny-Montrachet. In fact three of the four top spots have gone to California wines. "When he finished, Spurrier looked at the judges, whose reaction ranged from shock to horror."

Chauvinism? Patriotic mortification? Shame at this affront to the *Tricolore*? Is that what's going through your mind? Defense of the Republic? Or are you rather more self-focused—more concerned about your own possible embarrassment, the potential damage to your reputation? With who knows how much more to come—because this isn't over yet, not by a long shot, and however embarrassing the white results, well, this taste-off was always going to be defined by the reds.

Of one thing we can be certain—you and your fellow judges would have entered the day believing that the French whites were vastly superior, and would prove so in the tasting. So as you now face up to the reds your mind is grappling with the aftermath of the "disconfirmed expectancy" you've just experienced.

This is a phenomenon with a long pedigree in psychological research. Studied at length over decades, it has spawned a number of theoretical positions. But we'll take our lead from the original, seminal work by Leon Festinger in the 1950s, outlined in his book *When*

Prophecy Fails. Festinger and colleagues had managed to join the members of a sect of "true believers" awaiting the arrival of a spacecraft, prophesied to rescue them that day from a world about to be deluged and destroyed. When neither the craft nor the flood of water arrived as expected, Festinger's prediction—that the sect members would respond by becoming firmer, rather than weaker, in their belief—was put to the test. And it came through with trumps. Counterintuitively, it should be said.

Now wind the clock back, sorry forward, to Paris and 1976. When it came to the tasting of the reds, as Taber has it: "Spurrier was certain that the judges would be more careful and would not allow a California wine to come out on top again." One can well imagine the "circling of the wagons" mindset prevailing, a determination to get this *right* as a group (which interestingly enough would have increased the pressure on you, our collaborative reader, to get it right as an individual—or risk being run out of town).

Decision-time once again—"the room was hushed as Spurrier read the results." And ... it's California once again.

The 1973 Stag's Leap Cabernet Sauvignon, a neighbor of the Montelena, snatched first place ahead of the celebrated Mouton-Rothschild (only then recently elevated from Second to First Growth status—the first and only time since the official classification of 1855), leaving also in its wake the Graves First Growth Haut-Brion, and the Saint-Estèphe "Super Second" Château Montrose—all from 1970, a famously sensational Bordeaux vintage.

Expectancies were disastrously disconfirmed, yet again.

Like many powerful theories Festinger's is at once elegantly simple and disarmingly complex. Our cognitions—those thoughts, attitudes, suspicions, beliefs that form a large part of our perception of the world—comprise pieces of information that for the most part are independent of each other. Indeed they may never be connected in our minds. This is of course a salve to our sanity. As H. P. Lovecraft famously wrote in the opening line of his best-known horror story, "The Call of Cthulhu," "The most merciful thing in the world, I think, is the inability of the human mind to correlate all its contents." A greater mercy the more you think about it.

Some cognitions, however, *will* be connected. And this is where the problems arise. Conflicting cognitions, particularly about something important, provoke psychological discomfort—"dissonance" (hence the title of Festinger's theory—Cognitive Dissonance). Just like physical discomfort, this mental upset can be extremely unpleasant, so we seek to escape from or at least to lessen it. The more our significant beliefs or attitudes are out of sync, the greater the magnitude of this dissonance and the greater the motivation to reduce it. Relief can be accomplished in a number of ways—removing dissonant cognitions, adding

new consonant cognitions, reducing the importance of dissonant cognitions, or increasing the importance of consonant cognitions (to grossly
oversimplify).

So if you believe French wine to be far superior to that of the U.S.
but you've just rated the best French wines inferior to (panic-stricken-
indrawn-breath) California (and throw in the fact that your reputation
is seriously on the line and your countrymen are likely to be none too
happy with those responsible for toppling French wine from fame's
loftiest perch), all that spells dissonance—it spells it big time and in
italics. That *hurts*! Give me some options to lessen the pain! Well . . .

- You could remove the dissonant cognition (OK—this has been a charade,
  give me back my scores).

- You might add new consonant cognitions (how about—the French wines
  develop more slowly than the American, this is a mark of their distinction
  and the reason why they were in fact at a distinct disadvantage, this tasting couldn't even be called "apples and apples," and anyway they'll
  clearly surpass the usurpers given the benefits of further age).

- You could reduce the importance of the dissonant cognition (*oui, trés amu-
  sant*—these California wines are good, not as good as the French, but a
  fresh and pleasant drop). Or,

- You might increase the importance of consonant cognitions (*Vive la
  France*—French wines have always been superior, just look at the prices
  they command).

Readers of Taber's *Judgment of Paris* may recognize these stratagems.

All of us face dilemmas on a regular basis, if not usually so porten-
tous as this. We're constantly choosing between dissonance-reducing
options in our lives. (Which solution will best enable me to deal with
this unwanted mental conflict, and cause me the least distress?) But are
these *conscious* choices—and if so against what criteria are they made?
What if we get it wrong—choose an option that doesn't work? Can we
go back and start again? Our mental responses appear so immediate
it's hard to envisage that a conscious decision-making effort is occurring. Certainly we don't appear to weigh the alternatives in our mind
before settling on one.

Work by the social psychologist Elliot Aronson and colleagues suggests that our self-concept may provide the key to how we'll react to
dissonance—or, more specifically, the extent to which we need to *protect*
our self-concept. If this is of crucial importance to us then it's likely our
prioritizing of options will happen at an unconscious level, and occur as it
were automatically. And there are few professions in which the protection
of self-concept would be more important that that of wine judge.

So, now you've traveled a mile (or at least a while) in their shoes,
how much of the judges' reaction was due to chauvinism, and how

much to dissonance-reduction strategies? Did you and the others just behave with typical "French" arrogance, or did you behave like human beings?

There were losers in the Judgment of Paris—in the version of history and the version of myth. Young Paris, who chose Venus as the most beautiful over her sister goddesses, was able to take for his reward the face that launched a thousand ships and the body that went with it, Helen of Troy, née Sparta. This proved to be a dubious result for Paris (and more besides him), since it led to the Trojan War which saw his own and his homeland's ruin. A war of sorts also followed the 1976 version, an intensified struggle between Old and New World wines that continues today—in various forms and on various fronts, despite apparent truces.

Fairly or unfairly, it has to be said that the French judges were the main losers. So painful was that day for some that it's said they still refuse to discuss it.

But, winners are grinners—and losers can please themselves. The clear winners from 1976 were the California wine producers. Aside from other benefits they were freed from the tyranny of nomenclature.

When cab sav gets it together with merlot, cab franc, malbec, petit verdot ... the outcome is frequently auspicious. Such wines tended to be called *Bordeaux blends*—since Bordeaux had the fame of giving life, legend, and longevity to these wines. Imagine if you were a California producer in those days, laboring to improve your wines in the face of a status-driven bludgeoning from French producers. How galling it must have been (no pun intended) to be described in terms of your competitor? A recognition that you must remain forever in their shadow. How do you escape the cringing admission, "we cannot even define ourselves—we're defined by them"? *Them* being the Bordelais, their styles and standards, their tastes and textures, their body, breed and brawn. (Think "Kleenex," "Google," "Coke ...")

The Paris taste-off broke the shackles. With such glory coming their way, why should the Californians continue to call their prestige reds *Bordeaux blends*? (Rumors that certain parties felt the wine world should rename the wines of Bordeaux *Californian cuvees* are a little overstated.) Some years later the break became formal, with the movement to find an overarching name that would appropriately describe superior Californian blended wines. In true democratic, meritocratic American style, a competition was held, the winning suggestion selected, and that name registered with the U.S. Department of Trademarks and Patents.

And what was it? *Meritage*. A blend (how apt) of *merit* and *heritage*, with the additional distinctions of rhyme and pun and a sense that's sure to set French teeth on edge, or perhaps even set them gnashing. Whether the name eventually acquires the *cachet* of its competitor, or goes the way of Esperanto, only time will tell. According to Robert Parker the 1976 Paris event marked the democratization of the wine world. Meritage may have been its first flag.

All this of course might very easily not have been. George M. Taber, then a correspondent for *Time*, had not been singled out for attention when the publicity for the event started. He was sent a simple press release. Not for a moment expecting that the American wines would make history at the expense of the French, Spurrier and Gallagher had concentrated their promotional efforts on the Parisian wine writing press. However, and prophetically in the light of events, these had all declined. A tasting of California wines wasn't deemed newsworthy in the Paris of the day. So Patricia Gallagher pursued Taber to get him to attend, and fortuitously he did. Without his objective witness of what occurred it's doubtful if the story would have seen the light of day, certainly not in as prominent a way—and who knows how long a rematch would have taken to arrange, and under what French terms.

One of the judges in Paris is later reported to have said—"We take wine too seriously, and that makes it sad." Too seriously, we might ask, in relation to what? Art and music are taken seriously without that appearing to be sad, as are literature and dance. Politics and sport are taken seriously, and the list of course goes on. Is it "we" that are sad, because wine is taken seriously? That would be serious indeed—a serious loss of enjoyment, and reflection, and inspiration. Perhaps the "it" refers to the Paris verdict and its aftermath? If that's so, then *c'est la vie*. Or is the "it" referring to the wine itself? Why should the wine be sad? It, of all the parties, has no reason to be.

The events in Paris contained much in the way of melodrama—heroes and villains, expectation and surprise, chance and mischance, laughter and disaster. And there was no shortage of human interest angles either, with winners and the losers joined in a genuine and passionate love of wine. But there was another victor in all of this, one that passed unnoticed.

Imagine if we can, how the first flowers must have "felt" when they grasped the significance of the honeybee. Another creature, animal and alien, was joining with them in a mutually beneficial enterprise—had initiated a symbiotic relationship, without ever realizing it, or its significance (so it seemed to the flowers). The vine was a huge beneficiary of the events of Paris—as much as if the verdict had brought with it an enormous new source of pollination.

This judgment signalled the "Enlightenment" of the wine industry. By trampling on the old order it opened up the wine world to new ideas, rational and science based. New styles of wine emerged that were controversially different from the older Old World styles, and proving popular they encouraged more wine growers and greater cultivation of the grape. Even *terroir*, the official standard, the hole card of the Old World, took on a more open meaning. New World wineries could point with conviction to their own dirt and rocks and terrain and clime, their own *terroir* credentials. And all the while the symbiotic love affair continued. More vines were planted, more grapes harvested, more wine made, more pleasure taken . . .

Should you venture into a vineyard, even an Old World vineyard, late in the evening, and stand among the vines, quietly, well might you pick up their murmur on the breeze—"*Salute* to the Judgment of Paris, and to those who made it possible."

Twenty-Six

Empty Vessels

The poet H. D.—Hilda Doolittle—was ex-fiancée to fellow Imagist Ezra Pound, underwent analysis with Freud himself, and penned some of the last century's most soul-provoking phrases and lyrical pronouncements. Her poem "Wine Bowl," has an irresistible meter, a litany-like invocation of the figures from myth that populate the poem's brief, insistent lines. She will, so the poet's voice prophecies, initiate a sacrament of libation. To this end she will chisel from stone a bowl to hold the wine, both white and red. Form and phrasing together emphasize the dimension of ritual in the wine's pouring out and its ceremonial partaking. And the vessel from which the wine is drunk can't help but play its part—to an enriching extent or not—in the savoring of that wine.

The wine vessel's place in the wine-imbibing experience was recognized as far back as classical times. Following the example of Athens, Brillat-Savarin informs us, the Romans indulged in victuals and wine in a reclining position, called *lectisternium* (there were exhortations against this on moral grounds, especially when members of the opposite sex shared a couch, *tsk, tsk*). He adds that in this position "the ingestion of liquids or the action of drinking was a far more difficult matter; extreme care must have been required to avoid spilling wine from the huge cups which glittered on the tables of the great; and it was doubtless during the reign of *lectisternium* that someone coined the proverb, 'There's many a slip 'twixt cup and lip.'" Why "huge cups"?

Once again, this was in flattering imitation of the Greeks, whose wines "were examined by connoisseurs, from the mildest to the headiest; and there were meals at which the whole gamut of wines was run, and at which, contrary to the custom of our times, the glasses grew larger in proportion to the increasing goodness of the wine."

Contrary to the custom of our times? Speak for yourself, Jean-Anthelme. Things seem to have come full circle back to classical practice in our own day. Such a meal as B.-S. describes appears to be a kind of wine-matched degustation. And while our glasses might not increase in size according to quality, they do in respect of variety, style, and appropriate order. Consider a meal accompanied by ... a glass of champagne, then an aromatic white, followed by a chardonnay, a palate-cleansing rosé, bewitching pinot, and finally an almost overpowering cabernet. Such a sequence would indeed call for successively larger and differently shaped glasses (until, of course, one reverted to a sticky with dessert or cheese, or forbore on the host to break out the cognac tulips or whisky tumblers). Today, in the best restaurants with the finest stemware, one can enjoy the apex of wineglass design. Created to specifically enhance specific grape varieties, such glasses are as beautiful as they are perfectly shaped to their purpose—exemplifying in the best way the Bauhaus design axiom "form follows function." (Though before you're tempted to take up your companion's glass, just for a sip to see how its contents taste, beware the old superstition—"Two people must not drink out of the same cup ... if they do, their destinies will be linked.") While we wouldn't for a moment consent to swap our favorite crystal for a more durable alternative, still we have to wonder—how much of the perceived difference in the taste of the same wine across different glasses is *physiological*, based on the delivery of specific varieties and styles to that part of the palate most susceptible to their charms? And how much is *psychological*, given that beauty and grace of form possess an astonishingly emphatic power of suggestion?

Now let's follow the wine backwards into its primary vessel. Not so far back as old Pliny, who revealed of the wine jars of the day that they "must not be opened in mid-winter, except on a fine day when a south wind is blowing or when there is a full moon." (Though to his credit he anticipated modern knowledge in other ways—"of two wines from the same vintage, one can be superior to the other ... [surpassing] its relation because of the jar or as a result of some chance accident"— *no great wines*, remember, *only great bottles* ...) No, we're concerned instead with the modern wine bottle. Before it's even been opened the bottle has worked its influence on expectations. Sizes and shapes, utility and appearance, color, heft, punt, and label design all play to what the choice of bottle might suggest about a wine. Think of those high-shouldered, finely tapering, deep-punted Italian bottles that are a declaration of distinction. Consider the riesling bottle's upward soaring like aromatics taking flight. It's even more striking in magnum size, accentuating the resemblance to Brancusi's "Bird in Space." The claret bottle's solidity inspires confidence—what better shape for long-ageing Bordeaux, with the added edge of practicality in a shoulder design facilitating sediment-free decanting. As to the Burgundy bottle, its teasing sinuousness brings to mind the contrapposto poses of classical sculpture. *La Mitrale* of Châteauneuf du Pape, strikingly embossed with the papal headdress, is tradition's invitation back to when Avignon in Southern Rhône had—for a time at least—unseated Rome as the Papacy's seat of power. Bottles of all sizes inspire a range of attitudes—magnum, jeroboam, imperial, Methuselah ... these large formats speak of overflowing abundance, while the humble half-bottle hints at private indulgence, or perhaps an intimately shared pleasure. And while we for the most part prefer an unshowy shade of glass, a dour green or brown, the startling Mediterranean blue of a bottle of Mar de Frades albariño is a sight which cannot help but incite a raging thirst, and makes you want to pour such a glass that, if you can't actually go swimming in it, you can almost immerse your whole head.

The bottle, however, can as easily confound expectations and confuse anticipation. There's a scene from *The Godfather*—a famous one—that nicely (or maybe frustratingly) illustrates this.

You know the scene in which the Al Pacino-played Michael Corleone—as yet uncorrupted by "the family business"—prepares to gun down Virgil "The Turk" Sollozzo and the bent police captain acting as his body guard. They've taken him to Louis' Restaurant in the Bronx ("A small family place, good food, everyone minds his business ..."). The nervousness Pacino portrays is infectious. You want him to take a drink to settle his nerves ... damn it, you want a nerve-settling belt yourself. The waiter arrives, with a bottle and three glasses. It's a tall German-style bottle, though the label appears to be Italian. His hand obscures the neck of the bottle as he twists it, the corkscrew making a teasing squeaking sound as it's rotated in and his final loud pulling of the cork is, we have to say, extremely satisfying. That's where it all gets weird. From that kind of bottle, typically reserved for aromatic whites, we're expecting (and expecting, and expecting, no matter how many times we watch the scene) a cool, crisp, green-tinged white to flow as the waiter pours. A Soave perhaps. We're almost salivating at the prospect. And out instead cascades (this waiter appearing inclined to overfill glasses) ... a red! One glass that Sollozzo passes to Michael. And the shock is as palpable with the next glass poured (Sollozzo keeping this himself). It's just not right. Seeing that wine poured out that way from that bottle gives us an unshakeable feeling of disquiet every time.

One of us actually had a similar experience, just as habit-jarring. Dining in a pretty decent restaurant in Paris, he'd ordered from the list a Sancerre rouge—feeling like a pinot, though not so much that he was going to pay *that* kind of markup on a bottle of Burgundy, especially with the Euro as strong as it was at the time. They were, announced the sommelier, currently out of that wine. He suggested as the closest wine in style (having surmised my Burgundian price sensitivity and, it should be said, managing to hide the greater part of his contempt), he suggested an Alsatian pinot—the only red wine made in that region. And, by law, required to be bottled in the same tall elegant bottle as the region's riesling, gewürtz, and pinots gris and blanc. Clearly the local vignerons, as well as Karen MacNeil, share our sentiments and our bottle-shock—"Because it's surprising, if not a little unnerving, to see red wine flow from what looks like a bottle of riesling, several producers are battling the bottle law, in hopes of having the rule rescinded."

Having taken up the bottle for our consideration, one issue forces itself forward and won't be denied—the question elegantly captured by George M. Taber in the title to his book, *To Cork or Not to Cork*. We won't attempt to reinvent such a well-wrought wheel, or to cover the same ground that Taber does with such distinction—the book is part history of wine and of wine bottle closures, part history and analysis of international wine industry commerce, an examination of the science of chemical taints in wine as well as a series of riveting stories, each dealing with risk and bold experimentation, innovation, and acrimonious industry infighting. The only questions Taber's book doesn't answer are those that currently stump even the winemakers themselves. And it's an astonishing thing to think, that we have no idea—plenty of opinions, but no clear and demonstrable proof—of *what happens* in the ageing of a wine. There even exists confusion over which kind of chemical reaction is responsible for changes in the wine over the time of its maturation. Traditionally the answer had been *oxidation*—and continues to be with those supporters of cork who believe that its property of permeability allows for evenness in the wine's anticipated age-improvement. (Oxidation has long been the best-guess explanation for why larger format bottles, magnum and up, are said to age more slowly, steadily, and reliably than half bottles—stories supporting the notion abound, though evidence is decidedly anecdotal.) Others, including Emile Peynaud, cite *reduction* as the process responsible for wine's metamorphosis over time—and in so doing, rehabilitate a word that screwcap opponents have raised as that closure's greatest liability.

Anyone who has smelt the telltale taint (or, indeed, outright corruption) of a corked wine—especially an old, esteemed wine that has been hoarded for just such an occasion—knows true existential disappointment. Having said that, we've also encountered the occasionally dull, flat, slightly rubbery flavor of wine under screwcap suffering from (or so cork advocates would attest) reduction. We're not inclined to pick sides, don't remotely claim to know enough to do so—but we can't help observing the nature of the side-taking taking place. It's this element that begs some psychological speculation—the distinctly partisan aspect of the so-called "closure wars." The echo of the "culture wars" that have dominated sociocultural and political debate over the last decades is no accident. Disputes over cork versus screwcap (which is really the nub of the current situation, until plastic seals are significantly improved and glass seals receive far greater exposure), have developed all the intensity, zealotry, rancor, vehemence, and vitriol of the most contentious ideological conflicts. ("It's scary how passionate people can be on this topic," laments Brian Croser, one of Australia's most esteemed winemakers and 2004 Decanter Man of the Year, who has closely investigated the science involved. "Prejudice and extreme positions have taken over, and science has often gone out the window.") So screwcap supporters describe opponents as "flat-earthers," and "shills for the cork industry." And wines under screwcap are duplicitously positioned as being always of the cheap and nasty persuasion. Iconoclasts, and even the impartial and disinterested, have been silenced for a refusal to toe one or the other party line. Most fascinating here are the psychological phenomena at play—of choice and its motivations, of the almost evangelical fervor of both cork and screwcap advocates in attempting to proselytize others to the cause (other makers of course but, more importantly, merchants and consumers). We firmly believe that many decisions taken either way are based on a genuine concern to present wines in their best possible light, and provide that wine to consumers in its best drinking state. It's *after* that commitment is made, with its associated investment which cannot be easily or cheaply undone ... it's then that cognitive dissonance will engulf people when they're forced by new evidence to reconsider their position (or attempt to relieve their psychological tension by embracing denial).

We can't, either, ignore the experiential implications of bottle closures. No less a commentator than Hugh Johnson, who, in his extensive drinking experience must have come across more corked wines than most of us have drunk sound ones, even he can't help but observe that the screwcap is "so aesthetically unsatisfactory." There are, however, compensations for some of the flair and ceremony lost. With screwcaps increasing on better quality reds, there's a greater impetus to decant more wines more often—not merely to remove sediment from old reds but to open up youngsters—which brings with it a compensating level of ritual. Though alas, to us not even the steady *glug* of a wine decanted in the hands of an expert can compensate for what's been lost in that most satisfying of sounds—the *pop*, subtle not overbearing or bombastic, of a cork cleanly pulled from the mouth of its bottle.

And the jury remains out on how well the truly age-worthy red wines will fare under screwcaps. If, indeed, many of them even wind up bottled that way. Trial and comparison, across numerous situations, has yielded ambiguous results—from outright knockouts to split-points decisions, going both ways. Still, until further experimentation produces results more conclusive, many wine lovers, and especially lovers of distinguished wines nurtured to their most sublime state, fear the phenomenon that Taber christens Peter Pan wines—the wine, under screwcap, that never grows up. What's indisputable, in this case, is that substantial value—in the experience itself, and no less in price—will be wiped from a 25-year-old First Growth from a great vintage that pours out tasting like it's 7 years old. If and when such a thing ever happens, then exhortations from the anti-cork lobby of how much "fresher and livelier" that wine is will taste very flat indeed.

It makes you wonder whether future generations of wine drinkers will have, along with a greater propensity to decant, an entirely different sense and standard of bottle age than we have. If, that is, they're still drinking wine at all ...

Twenty-Seven

The Death of "Generation Wine"?

Looking around the assembling crowd at a classical concert you can't help but be struck by their disproportionately advanced age. Then struck even more by the scarcity of youth (with the obvious exception of ballet, where there's always a bevy of young aspiring Margot Fonteyns). Given the likely time-frame of this bunch shuffling off this mortal coil ... where, you ask, are the young enthusiasts coming through to keep the concert halls full in 10 or 20 years' time?

One of the coming young guns of international conducting has expressed just such concerns. Los Angeles-born and Berlin-based Jonathan Stockhammer has said, "Classical music is not only a closed world, it's a withering and dying world in one sense." Of traditional repertoires played in traditional ways by ensembles desperate to merely break even he asserts, "It's very, very difficult to keep these things vitalized and alive." He advocates a distinct shake up of the performance patterns of the past, calling for "all kinds of interesting collaborations, experiments, working with multimedia, working with art, working with rock artists, working with film: things that draw in the interesting audience" (interesting to see a performer passing judgment on the most desirable kind of public). And that interesting audience is, it would seem, emerging more and more in Asia, "where emerging wealth is coming to classical music without the baggage of tradition."

Could the analogy to fine wine be any starker? Isn't wine in many ways facing the same bleak prospect? Of course, that's not to say wine has no appeal to youth. Just that it has insufficient appeal to the significant majority. ("Youth" here is a relative term, and of course we're talking about drinkers of age.)

The pressing implications of generation change might, however, be ignored—or at least forestalled—in efforts to tap as-yet-untapped markets. And that's what's happening in the world of wine. Parallel to classical music, it's Asia that presents this potentially burgeoning market, driven in no small part by an unusual impetus—a comic strip (or, as younger generations might prefer to euphemize, "a graphic novel").

Kami no Shizuku (*The Drops of God*, as it's known in English, and ever-so-poetically as *Les Gouttes de Dieu*, en Français), is a Japanese manga comic devoted to a wine storyline. (We're no devotees of manga ourselves, though one of us harbors fond memories of *Astro Boy* and *Prince Planet*, and carried a preadolescent torch for the provocatively androgynous, *Princess Knight*. It's those impossibly wide manga eyes, ever-startled and startlingly captivating ...) The series follows the vinous exploits of Shizuku, son of a tyrannical wine critic who forced his offspring to experience the world, blind-folded, through his sense of smell. In (stereo-)typical youthful rebellion, Shizuku has abjured the grape for the grain—choosing to work in a brewery. The father, in response to this perceived slight to himself and the noble vine, adopts a young wine expert to be his second son. His deathbed challenge to both sons is that they seek out 13 wines of incomparable quality—12 "apostle" wines, and the pinnacle "drops of God." At stake is the vast wine cellar that is the old man's legacy. So Shizuku, with untrained palate but sharply honed senses, must compete with his wine-pro semi-sibling, aided by a love interest trainee sommelier.

The strip is penned by a brother and sister writing team, Shin and Yuko Kibayashi, wine enthusiasts who were, according to Shin, "looking for the drama behind the wines we were drinking [an admirable aspiration] ... It started with one wine, 'This wine is definitely a woman.'" To which his sister endearingly adds "with black hair." Their style of wine description is polarizing (not everyone would be drawn to drink a wine likened to Freddie Mercury)—but their influence across Asian countries is undeniable. The aforementioned Queen-compared wine, a 2001 Mont Pérat claret from the minor appellation Premières Côtes de Bordeaux, enjoyed a huge sales spike across the region after its appearance.

There's no denying the appeal of manga to subsets of the youth demographic. Could this wine-demystifying cartoon translate into a wider youth enthusiasm for wine over mixed drinks and cocktails?

It's not that the generations coming through—Gen Y, inevitably Z and ... well, do we roll back around to Gen A then, or change to letters of the Greek alphabet, perhaps numbers or even colors (Generation Mauve has a ring to it)—it's not that they can't be reached by marketing messages. No group in history has been so bombarded. The worry is subtler and more problematic than that. On the one hand, if they remain in a perpetual palate-adolescence fueled by alco-pops—who will be left to buy wine? On the other, if their imbibing preferences were to switch wholesale to the grape—what impact might this have on the very nature of wine?

This phenomenon is not restricted to the New World. In the Old World, where wine appreciation has traditionally been passed on down the generations by early exposure at meals lovingly prepared for enjoyment by the extended family—even there the future is worrying. Master of Wine Stephen Charters, professor of Champagne management at the Reims Management School, despairs that in France "wine is not seen as a fashionable subject by the young." Emphasizing the very same point, Master of Wine Matthew Stubbs observes that, "the main worry for France's wine trade is that many young consumers have not embraced the wine culture, and prefer spirit-based cocktails ... For many young French people, wine is an old person's drink."

"The Web" is the perfect image for the phenomenon that has stickily enmeshed modern culture. It has irreversibly revolutionized modern life. The changes it has brought (or should that be wrought) are, however, not wholly positive—though as Lee Siegel points out in *Against the Machine*, "criticize the Internet and you are accused of criticizing democracy." Net enthusiasts have claimed it to have made teenagers "the latest model of human being equipped with a whole lot of new features" (though these new features would seem to be of the same order as with many software upgrades—new features few want and fewer can be bothered with). In his article, "Is Google Making Us Stupid?" Nicholas Carr quotes friends and colleagues who wonder, "What if I do all my reading on the web not so much because the way I read has changed ... but because the way I THINK has changed?" This eerie query is elaborated by developmental psychologist Maryanne Wolf—"We are not only *what* we read. We are *how* we read." So we find this tool, of undeniably incomparable value, turned (especially by youth) into an amusement park and game arcade. Every aspect of it is trivialized—and so too the lives spent peering within. A small window, even on the whole world, can't help but reduce the world's sweeping scope to minutiae. (How prescient the words of T. S. Eliot in "Choruses from 'The Rock'"—"Where is the wisdom we have lost in knowledge?/ Where is the knowledge we have lost in information?")

The most famous episode in Plato's *The Republic*—perhaps the most famous episode in all of classical philosophy if not all of classical literature—is "the simile of the cave." Socrates posits a subterranean chamber in which people are imprisoned. They can only see, on one wall of the cave, a projected shadow-play. "Would they not assume that the shadows they saw were the real things?" If, however, "released from their bonds" into the wider world, they would be smartly "cured of their delusions." The prisoners of Socrates' analogy are chained against their will, so not responsible for confusing artifice and reality. Those in the modern world are under no imposed constraints—it is they who constrain their own view on the world.

This is a generation that looks at the world through the wrong end of a telescope. Instead of the scale of life's rich tapestry, everything and everyone is reduced to a scant few square centimeters on the screen of a cellphone (palm pilot, You-tube screen ... insert tech of choice). Instant access is all—quality comes a distant last. This is a generation whose primary influences come from a rigidly delineated peer group and what Toby Young describes as "the celebritariat." Refusing to engage what's beyond that (beyond their own iPod's selection, networking website cliques, the neologistic in-jargon that defines chat room dialogue, and the irksome anti-expression of smiley-face "emoticons") restricts tastes from growing, broadening ... maturing. Here's a generation that knows what it wants ... and doesn't want to know anything else. Many spend more time in chat rooms, networking sites, and virtual worlds than in the real world (we anticipate a new disorder for a future Diagnostic and Statistical Manual of Mental Disorders—a kind of identity disorder, "real self dissatisfaction disorder," defined by the chasm between online avatar appearance and the sad reality.) No value is accorded to what doesn't appeal immediately, what's not instantaneously seen as "relevant to me." In *Where Have All the Intellectuals Gone?* Frank Furedi observes that, "children tend to value what directly gives them pleasure and affirmation ... The celebration of the ordinary voice, through the idea that 'this is my story,' is not a million miles away from the emotional sentiment that cries out 'this is my toy.'" There is no yearning to learn to appreciate what's currently outside one's ken. The concept of acquired taste is, to many at least, anathema. But as pointed out by Mark Bauerlein in his book *The Dumbest Generation*—"Knowledge grows, skills improve, tastes refine, and conscience ripens only if the experiences bear a degree of unfamiliarity."

"Nothing is so singular about this generation," observed Allan Bloom in *The Closing of the American Mind*, "than its addiction to music." He was writing about Gen X but his words are even more emphatically true of the splinter generations following. "As long as they have the Walkman on," excusing the quaintness of the technological anachronism, but replacing its image with the even more ubiquitous iPod, "they cannot hear what the great tradition has to say. And, after its prolonged use, when they have taken it off, they find they are deaf." Silence seems a terrifying thing to today's youth. So it must be banished, along with the introspection and reflection that silence urges on us. In a sense, the capacity to allow thoughts to wander, in other words the skill of daydreaming, has been ... not so much lost as discarded. At what cost? "Many scientists argue that daydreaming is a crucial tool for creativity, a thought process that allows the brain to make new associations and connections," says Jonah Lehrer. He quotes Columbia neuroscientist Malia Mason—"Daydreaming builds on this fundamental capacity people have for being able to project themselves into imaginary situations, like the future ... Without that skill, we'd be pretty limited creatures." And in "The Colonization of Silence," composer Andrew Waggoner despairs at what's lost in the saturation of private and public spaces with "marauding noise"—"Reflection, discernment, a sustainable sense of tranquility, of knowing where and how to find oneself."

Reflection, hmm? Discernment, ditto. Ring any bells ... a bottle of good wine in good company? These are virtues passing out of fashion. Though if wine, fine wine particularly, demands or inspires any single virtue, it's *patience*. Not just in its making and its ageing, but in the nurturing of taste, knowledge, appreciation, and judgment. A generation reared on immediate gratification—not as an opportunity but as a "right"—is dismissive of the value of striving, application and accomplishment. (As to the merits of accomplishment, Bauerlein has the following observation—"the model is information retrieval, not knowledge formation, and the material passes from Web to homework paper without lodging in the minds of students." Some call this kind of plagiarism "digital literacy.") The great wines have taken decades, some of them centuries, to establish recognition and regard for their philosophy, style and stature. How does that sit in a culture in which appeal and cachet, fame and infamy too, have at most a half-life of weeks, not years or (heaven forbid) decades. Mark the rapidity with which designer cocktails go in and out of fashion (it's the oldies drinking the classics), or even the blink-and-you-missed-it speed with which every reality TV diva of internet-porn-proportions is rehabilitated back to the A-list.

Maybe it's an image thing. Maybe what the wine industry needs is a role model with youth access and appeal. *Sideways* aside, when was the last time you saw serious wine appreciation portrayed—on film or TV—as anything other than a peccadillo only marginally up the likeability-ladder from bestiality? (One of us once received a birthday card that showed two couples sitting at dinner. The first thing that struck you—one of the husbands is wearing a *Texas Chainsaw Massacre* Ol' Leatherface mask and tearing up the table with his power tool of choice. His wife, one eyebrow arched at her female companion, is saying, "At least my husband's not a wine geek." Only then do you notice hubby number 2, delicately holding his wineglass to the light and peering into it, fascinated.) In years gone by, beleaguered minorities would lobby Hollywood and the networks for greater representation in popular culture. Perhaps the wine industry should consider it? (We're only half kidding.)

It's the privilege of older generations to criticize their eventual usurpers, and ever the tendency of the latter to shrug at such criticism. There is, in this instance however, a distinction required between criticism and blame. Blame for the flippancies of a tech-and-celeb-obsessed youth must fall squarely on older shoulders—theirs is the failed cultural stewardship. Authority figures in wide and disparate circles have embraced everything about change for its own sake—and forsaken (in fact, conspired willingly to sacrifice) enduring qualities and values, and thereby perpetrated a fraud on their younger charges. A review of Bauerlein's book proposes that, "if teenagers and twenty-somethings appear satisfied to nurture only their own ephemeral diversions, it could be because they've never been *taught* about the events, the struggles, the art, the literature, the genius that preceded them." And, perhaps, the wines as well. This is a failure to engage emerging generations that the wine industry can't afford. There must be a concerted push, placing emphasis on cooperative efforts to educate palates and attract them to wine over competitive strategies for securing a greater share of a diminishing and increasingly carved-up market. That education must inspire as well as inform. It must train appreciation of the widest diversity in the wine world. And it must position the appreciation of wine as a lifelong endeavor of exponentially mounting pleasure and reward.

There are obstacles to this kind of education, and a number of those obstacles come directly out of developments in the industry itself. Runaway escalation of prices is one such obstacle—now impossible to roll back (and would the industry major players permit that anyway?). The ex-sommelier between us felt strongly, in his early days of palate self-education, that a great motivation and inspiration was the prospect of, even if only rarely, imbibing the acknowledged great wines of the world. What does it say to the next generation, when these are now entirely out of their price range? In the early '90s he attended a dinner with a bunch of sommeliers (self-funded, not some industry junket) at which were drunk—'67, '68, '71, and '72 Grange, '78 and '79 Second Growth Bordeaux Cos and Ducru, a lone '80 DRC Échezeaux, '76 J. J. Prüm Eiswein, and a couple of '70 Premier Cru Sauternes. Okay, we couldn't indulge in that fashion regularly, but all of those wines were then still affordable—unquestionably expensive, but still affordable—to our hospitality industry paychecks. Will subsequent generations feel that they are only ever getting second or third tier wines (for which read, in their perceptions, second and third rate wines)? What happens to the aspiration to drink—if only occasionally—true, undisputed and famed vinous excellence? Matt Kramer makes a very salient point when he distinguishes between "those wines that are merely tasted and those that are actually drunk." The former are the excessively expensive greats—dribbled out by the thimbleful to be marveled over by those fortunate enough to attend such a tasting. The latter are those wines, drunk at home or in restaurants, in which we experience the genuine sensuality of the drop, and its meaningful match to food and company. "And let's be honest," Kramer says, "tasting ain't drinking. It's a virtual wine life, not a real relationship." Virtual wine life ...? Perhaps there lies the appeal to the generations of youthful wine drinkers coming through.

Still, as it stands, we have a generation oblivious to nuance, reveling in inebriation with no taste, embracing reverie with no sacrifice to Dionysus. What kinds of wines would tempt them? (And who will fly the flag for maturing wines? Maybe the great closure debate will turn out to be moot?) Will the vast majority of wines—driven by marketing imperatives, not the quest for quality and excellence—become drink-now fruit cocktails? Or is there an even darker future in store?

The full genetic sequence of pinot noir has recently been revealed. Wine's most elusive grape stripped bare of her secrets in the laboratory. Where will it end? Will the gods of bio-manipulation be able to resist injecting at the genetic level a whole new spectrum of flavors, taste extremes we can't even conceive of now? Will winemaking—driven by a public palate addicted to novelty—become less about what's drawn out of the grape and all about what's put in? And what matters *terroir* anymore, when the lab-coats can nail its essence with no hit-and-miss? How well will tradition endure in the face of such designer wines ... or Frankenstein wines?

The future challenges to wine's ascendancy will be cultural.

Twenty-Eight

A Very Human Thing

From the fiercest struggle comes the finest wine. Hardship squeezes out the richest nectar. The spoilt and pampered, over-nurtured, over-watered vine sinks shallow roots and gives thin refreshment. Those that endure through their own hardiness reach deep into the earth and draw the hard, rewarding sustenance of eras. We have a word for this in human terms. We call it *character*. "Character cannot be developed in ease and quiet," said Helen Keller, one well qualified to judge. "Only through experience of trial and suffering can the soul be strengthened." Wine and we in parallel then, reap through our ordeals what is complex, rare and enigmatic.

"Plants are like self-willed people," declared Goethe in *Elective Affinities*, "with whom you can do anything provided you handle them properly." This was no intended slur. Goethe spoke as a scientist as well as Germany's Shakespeare. He was a natural philosopher with a deep passion for nature. He lived in a time before Darwin upended our view of nature's relationships. Still, even today most people would view the human manipulation of plants as the natural order of things.

It's a view that Michael Pollan takes to task in *The Botany of Desire*. "Did I choose to plant these potatoes, or did the potato make me do it?" he asks. (Do you sense a rhetorical ploy?) "In fact, both statements are true." Associations between humans and certain plants have developed along co-evolutionary lines—a kind of mutual exploitation. Such organisms have learned, as Pollan puts it, to participate "in the moving

game of human culture." Opportunity beckons and they respond
opportunistically, setting their sights on a human desire. Thus the tulip
responds to the desire for "beauty"—and not only survives but grows
ever more beautiful. The apple courts our hunger for "sweetness"—
and is rewarded with prosperity. "Intoxication" is well satisfied by
marijuana. And "control" has long been under the tutelage of that staple the potato.

Can we see our association with wine in such co-evolutionary
terms? In part, no doubt. There are, however, salient differences. To
start, no single desire played vamp to the grape. The number and variety of needs satisfied by wine overpower the analogy. Then there's the
individuality of response. Wine engages us all in an intensely personal
way. No one tastes the same wine in precisely the same way as anyone
else. And we can't describe a wine without describing something of
ourselves as well. Novelty, wonder, stimulation or nostalgia, the urge
to impress, to conform, to be different, to be safe, to be challenged, the
desire to remember and the desire to forget … any of these might be
found for a different person in a different glass. Dionysus or Apollo—
who can tell the god of the moment when the wine is at ease with
either?

What can we say about the grape, stripping it down to essentials? It
came to us a seductive substance, enveloping our senses, and stayed to
become the stuff of miracles and sacraments. It stirs reflection and
cedes inspiration, brings congeniality to company and wisdom to solitude. It's as companionable as a favorite book, as soaring as a symphony, and intricate as a cipher.

All that, and still the question persists—*why wine*? Other substances
can relax and excite, titillate the senses, and make us feel the better for
their enjoyment. Why shouldn't the honors that fall to wine have fallen
to one of those? Because wine connected first, and best, with the
human condition. It pushed its bond with humanity furthest. And this
couldn't have happened without a depth of possibility that mirrors our
own. What makes wine, wine? The answer lies in its psychological
roots and resonances as much as in its immediate qualities of taste,
intoxication and indulgence.

"Nature uses human imagination to lift her work of creation to even
higher levels." The words of Nobel prize–winning dramatist Luigi
Pirandello capture the essence of co-evolution. This sentiment is true of
many forms of living matter—but truest of one. The grape, through the
ages, has broken boundaries that other organisms couldn't. It has mas-
tered the mimicry of human nature, and radically changed the potential in the relationship. We reflect on a wine, only to find our thoughts
deflected to ourselves. We experience a special moment and wine cor-
rals that memory, crowding out aspects of the occasion equally deserving but unable to compete with wine's sensory advantages. So places

and people and moments and meals may participate in the recall, but not the recalling. This connection between wine and memory is a penetrating and self-perpetuating one. Who controls the past ...

We're talking here not merely of wine's flavors, but of those other less tangible properties it possesses. Yet aren't these the very ones we're inclined to *imagine*? Can these characteristics be argued to reside inside the wine, and not just in our minds? An epistemological question that deserves a philosopher's reply. These qualities, says Barry C. Smith, "exist whether we experience them or not ... Do we have to say that a wine's balance, finesse, purity, along with more descriptive characteristics like roundedness, weight, or structure consist in its having dispositions to produce different experiences in diverse populations of tasters? Why say this rather than saying these properties are in the wines?"

Isn't this how we see wine, how we talk about it and act towards it—as a sum of unique attributes and traits, many of which remind us of ourselves? We take for granted a relationship with the grape that we never could or would with music, drama, art ... with food, film or fashion, or anything else that causes wonder and brings delight. Wine—more than any other organism, entity or experience—reflects what it means to be human. Things other than wine span the palpable and the abstract, there's no doubt. But it's wine that makes the greatest demands on the senses. On all of them, and synergistically. Every sense is teased into response. Wine also engages us metaphorically, and in doing so it engages us on many levels—intellectual, emotional, aesthetic, even moral. The stream of consciousness triggered by a scent of wine, its texture on our tongue, the beckoning depth of its color or the musical clink of crystal ... this stream can be broad and turbulent and full of shoals. Going with that flow will offer quite a ride, and the longer the ride the lengthier the reflection on ourselves.

"The survival of the sweetest, the most beautiful, or the most intoxicating," claims Pollan, "proceeds according to a dialectical process ... It takes two, but it doesn't take intention, or consciousness." Okay, not what we would call consciousness in ourselves—but what of some rudimentary vegetable equivalent? Could wine, unconsciously, aspire to its own most complex development under the blueprint of nature and nurture? This is after all a living, breathing, organismic art form, existing independently of us—yet our partner economically, socially and culturally. There are a score of "human" art forms far less well credentialed, with aspirations far less noble and ennobling.

Preposterous anthropomorphic nonsense? Perhaps. Yet we're inspired, not dismayed, and nor do we smirk, when the winemaker talks of "listening to the vineyard." We applaud the intuitive realism of a concept like *terroir*, passing over the quasi-mystical connotations and Gaia-like resonances. We delight in eulogies brimful of imagery, which applied to most anything else might fairly be cause for ridicule. We're not embarrassed to attribute human characteristics to a wine, and we talk of it as if it were sentient.

We honor the grape with influence and status and an ever-expanding presence—grateful when some of the status rubs back off on us. While wine, for its part, keeps its secrets, even the knowledge of how it becomes what it can and will and wants to become—this mystery part of its compelling charm. We place it on a pedestal that it may look down on its competitors—yet there are none. Wine rules. Other physical entities and human experiences—rich and complex and satisfying as they might be—in the long term these lapse before wine's winning and rewarding ways. Barring a seismic shift in attitudes and tastes, with consequences way beyond what we drink, wine will continue its unique hold on humankind.

"For all I know every human being has as many personalities as he has interpersonal relations," said psychoanalyst Harry Stack Sullivan. This we know to be true of wine, though here there is no downside or shadow of duplicity. Diverse personalities are a part of its character and its strength and a key to its long survival and success. There's an empathetic wine for every circumstance, for every personality and pocket, every mood and moment.

And therein lies the most convincing answer to the puzzle of, *why wine*? That it presents a metaphysical reflection to the wise drinker, a speculative angle on ourselves, our situations, and surroundings. In its fluid way it rounds out the sharp edges and fills in the crevices of our self-knowledge. This emanates from deep within and it's a reassuring thing. In the opening lines of Robert Louis Stevenson's famous tale of Dr. Jekyll and Mr. Hyde, a character is caricatured as "a man of rugged countenance that was never lighted by a smile; cold, scanty and ... backward in sentiment." Yet "when the wine was to his taste, something eminently human beaconed from his eye."

And so we continue as each other's willing partners. Forging together the truth and beauty of this peerless union—the grape, the vine, the wine and our own lives.

Notes and References

(In order of appearance)

PART I: WINE, MIND AND SOUL

CHAPTER ONE—DRINKING ANTIQUITY

4 Plato, *The Laws*, Trans. Trevor J. Saunders, Harmondsworth, UK: Penguin, 2005.

4 Horace, *Epistles and Satires*, Trans. Jacob Fuchs, New York: Norton, 1977.

4 Homer, *The Odyssey*, Trans. E. V. Rieu, Revised by D. C. H. Rieu, Harmondsworth, UK: Penguin, 2003.

CHAPTER TWO—THE GOD OF WINE

5 Robert Callasso, *The Marriage of Cadmus and Harmony*, Trans. Tim Parks, London: Vintage, 1988.

6 The phenomenon of *enthousiasmas* is related in Maguelonne Taussaint-Samat, *History of Food*, Trans. Anthea Bell, Oxford: Oxford University Press, 2006.

6 Euripides, *The Bacchae and Other Plays*, Trans. John Davie, London: Penguin, 2006.

6 Norman O. Brown, *Life against Death: The Psychoanalytic Meaning of History*, Middletown, CT: Wesleyan University Press, 1985.

7 Philip Rieff, *Freud: The Mind of the Moralist*, London: Methuen, 1965.

7 Friedrich Nietzsche, "Preface from *The Birth of Tragedy*" in *The Philosophy of Nietzsche*, Trans. Oscar Levy, Ed. Geoffrey Clive, New York: Meridian, 1996.

7 Camille Paglia, *Sexual Personae: Art and Decadence from Nefertiti to Emily Dickinson*, Harmondsworth, UK: Penguin, 1991.

7   *Caravaggio*, Written and directed by Derek Jarman, Story by Nicholas Ward Jackson, British Film Institute, 1986.

7   Ovid, *Metamorphoses*, Trans. Z. Philip Ambrose, Newburyport, MA: Focus Publishing, 2004.

8   Simon Schama, *Power of Art*, London: BBC Books, 2006.

8   Ralph Waldo Emerson, "Bacchus" in *Selected Writings of Ralph Waldo Emerson*, New York: Signet Classic, 1983.

CHAPTER THREE—THE HAPPIEST OF HAPPY ACCIDENTS

9   Plato, *The Laws*.

9   Victor Hugo, *The Essential Victor Hugo*, Trans. E. H. and A. M. Blackmore, Oxford: Oxford University Press, 2004.

10–11   "The importance of alcohol … " quote, the conditions for civilization, and further fascinating reading on the invention and origins of agriculture can be found in Peter Watson, *Ideas: A History from Fire to Freud*, London: Phoenix, 2006.

10   Plato, *The Republic*, Trans. Desmond Lee, Harmondsworth, UK: Penguin, 1987.

10   Jean-Jacques Rousseau, "The Social Contract" in *The Social Contract and Discourses*, Trans. G. D. H. Cole, London: Everyman's Library, 1983.

11   Thomas Hobbes, *Leviathan*, Cambridge: Cambridge University Press, 1996.

12   Robertson Davies, *The Rebel Angels*, London: Penguin, 1987.

12   Pliny the Elder, *Natural History—A Selection*, Trans. John F. Healy, Harmondsworth, UK: Penguin, 1991.

CHAPTER FOUR—WHAT'S IN A NUMBER…?

14   James Poniewozik, "The Power of 10," *Time*, December 24, 2007.

14   Hilary Putnam, "The Meaning of 'Meaning'" in *Philosophical Papers Volume II: Mind, Language and Reality*, Cambridge: Cambridge University Press, 1975.

14   Adam Smith, *An Inquiry into the Nature and Causes of the Wealth of Nations*, Ed. Edwin Cannan, New York: Modern Library, 1937.

15   Steven Pinker, *The Language Instinct*, London: Penguin, 2008.

18   Tove Jansson, *Finn Family Moomintroll*, Trans. Elizabeth Portch, Harmondsworth, UK: Puffin, 1971.

19   Frédérick Brochet, "Chemical Object Representation in the Field of Consciousness," unpublished thesis.

20   Brendan Behan quoted in Ronan McDonald, *The Death of the Critic*, New York: Continuum, 2007.

20   Samuel T. Coleridge, *Lectures and Notes on Shakespeare and Other English Poets*, London: George Bell, 1884.

20   Rainer Maria Rilke, *Selected Letters 1902–1926*, Trans. R. F. C. Hull, with an Introduction by John Bayley, London: Quartet, 1988.

20   Karl Marx and Frederick Engels, *The German Ideology*, Ed. C. J. Arthur, London: Lawrence & Wishart, 1970.

20–21   Oscar Wilde, "The Critic as Artist" in *The Soul of Man under Socialism and Selected Critical Prose*, Harmondsworth, UK: Penguin, 2001.

21   Oscar Wilde, *The Importance of Being Earnest and Other Plays*, Harmondsworth, UK: Penguin, 1954.

22   George Orwell, *1984*, Harmondsworth, UK: Penguin, 1989.

22   Cesare Lombroso, *The Man of Genius*, London: W. Scott Publishing Co., 1894.

22   Parker and Johnson quotes from Gloria Origgi, "Wine Epistemology: The Role of Representational and Ranking Systems in the World of Wine" in Barry C. Smith (Ed.) *Questions of Taste: The Philosophy of Wine*, Oxford: Signal Books, 2007.

22   Pliny the Elder, *Natural History—A Selection*.

23   Simon Blackburn, *Truth—A Guide for the Perplexed*, London: Penguin, 2005.

23   Leon R. Kass, *The Hungry Soul*, Chicago: University of Chicago Press, 1999.

23–24   David Hume, "Of the Standard of Taste" in *Four Dissertations*, New York: Garland, 1970.

24   Ursula K. Le Guin, *A Wizard of Earthsea*, Harmondsworth, UK: Puffin, 1975.

24–25   Pierre Bourdieu, *Distinctions: A Social Critique of the Judgment of Taste*, Trans. Richard Nice, Cambridge, MA: Harvard University Press, 1984.

27   Comparisons of scores and show medals from James Halliday, "An Open and Shut Case," in "James Halliday's Top 100 Wines" supplement, *Weekend Australian*, November 8–9, 2008.

CHAPTER FIVE—THE LIFE OF THE VINE

28   T. C. Kelly and Clement Hoare quoted from A. C. Kelly, *The Vine in Australia, Its Culture and Its Management 1862*, Melbourne: Red Dog, 2008.

28   Epictetus, *Discourses (Books 1 and 2)*, Trans. P. E. Matheson, Mineola, NY: Courier Dover, 2004.

29   "Revival and resurrection . . ." quote from Northrop Frye, *Fables of Identity: Studies in Poetic Mythology*, New York: Harcourt Brace Jovanovich, 1963.

29   Samuel Beckett, *Watt*, London: John Calder, 1981.

29   "The romance is nearest of all literary forms . . ." quote from Northrop Frye, *Anatomy of Criticism, Four Essays*, Princeton, NJ: Princeton University Press, 1973.

30   Line from John Keats's "To Autumn" in *The Complete Poems*, Harmondsworth, UK: Penguin, 1985.

CHAPTER SIX—IN VINO IN MEMORIAM

31   Saint Augustine, *Confessions*, Trans. E. B. Pusey, London: Nelson, 1938.

32   William Wordsworth, *The Prelude, 1799, 1805, 1850*, New York: Norton, 1979.

33   Marcel Proust, *Remembrance of Things Past*, Volume 1, Trans. Moncrieff and Kilmartin, Harmondsworth, UK: Penguin, 1984.

33   Evelyn Waugh, *Brideshead Revisited*, Harmondsworth, UK: Penguin, 1962.

33   Jean Cocteau reference and Walter Benjamin quote taken from Walter Benjamin, "On the Image of Proust" in *Theories of Memory*, Ed. Michael Rossington and Anne Whitehead, Crawley: University of Western Australia Press, 2007.

33   Explanation of the term *bienheureux* taken from Thomas A. Lennon's excellent article "Proust and the Phenomenology of Memory," *Philosophy and Literature*, Volume 31, Number 1, April, 2007.

34   Sigmund Freud, "Screen Memories," in *The Standard Edition of the Complete Psychological Works of Sigmund Freud*, Volume 3, Trans. and Ed. James Strachey, London: Hogarth Press, 1953–1975.

34   Further information on field and observer memories can be found in Chapter 2 of Daniel L. Schacter, *Searching for Memory: The Brain, the Mind and the Past*, New York: Basic Books, 1996.

34   Further theories of memory in the writings of Plato and Aristotle can be found in William S. Sahakian, *History of Psychology*, Itasca, Illinois: Peacock Publishers, 1981.

34–35   Soren Kierkegaard, "Repetition" in *Fear and Trembling: Repetition*, Trans. and Ed. Howard V. Hong and Edna H. Hong, Princeton, NJ: Princeton University Press, 1983.

35   William James, *Principles of Psychology*, Cambridge, MA: Harvard University Press, 1983.

35–36   Daniel Gilbert, *Stumbling on Happiness*, London: HarperPress, 2006.

36   Aristotle, *Aristotle on Memory*, Trans. Richard Sorabji, London: Duckworth, 2004.

36   Jonah Lehrer, *Proust Was a Neuroscientist*, New York: Houghton Mifflin, 2007.

37–38   Gary Marcus, *Kluge: The Haphazard Construction of the Human Mind*, New York: Houghton Mifflin, 2008.

38   "Association" definition from *The New Fontana Dictionary of Modern Thought*, Third Edition, Ed. Alan Bullock and Stephen Trombley, London: Harper Collins, 2000.

38   Quoted explanations of Aristotle's and Hume's respective Laws of Association drawn from Robert I. Watson, *The Great Psychologists*, Fourth Edition, New York: J. B. Lippincott Company, 1978.

39   *Dead Ringers*, Directed by David Cronenberg, Written by David Cronenberg and Norman Snider from the book *Twins*, by Bari Wood and Jack Geasland, Mantle Clinic II Productions, 1988.

39–40   First Ian McEwan quote from "Psychopolis," second from "In Between the Sheets," both from *In Between the Sheets*, London: Picador, 1978.

40   *Sideways*, Written and Directed by Alexander Payne from the novel by Rex Pickett, Fox Searchlight Pictures, 2004.

40   Kurt Vonnegut Jr., *Breakfast of Champions*, London: Vintage, 1992.

40–41   Story of Simonides, originally told by Cicero, from Frances A. Yates classic *The Art of Memory*, London: Pimlico, 1999.

42   Further information on state-dependent and mood-congruent retrieval can be found in Daniel L. Schacter, *Searching for Memory*.

42   David Hume quoted from Immanuel Kant, *Anthropology from a Pragmatic Point of View*, Trans. and Ed. Robert B. Louden, Cambridge: Cambridge University Press, 2006.

42–43   John Keats, "Ode on Melancholy," *The Complete Poems*.

CHAPTER SEVEN—THE NATURE OF *TERROIR*

44–45   Quotes from Steven Pinker, as well as a comprehensive and exhaustive examination of the nature/nurture debate, can be found in Steven Pinker, *The Blank Slate: The Modern Denial of Human Nature*, London: Allen Lane, 2002.

45   Quote from B. F. Skinner's *Walden Two*, taken from Gorman Beauchamp "Imperfect Men in Perfect Societies: Human Nature in Utopia," *Philosophy and Literature*, Volume 31, Number 2, October 2007.

45   Riesling quote from "Riesling" entry in Jancis Robinson (Ed.), *The Oxford Companion to Wine*, Third Edition, Oxford: Oxford University Press, 2006.

45   Galileo quote taken from Sean Thackrey's "Winemaker" Web site, a compendium of wine tradition, history and esoterica at www.winemaker.net.

46   Pliny the Elder, *Natural History—A Selection*.

46   Michel Chapoutier quotes from the Chapoutier Web site, www.chapoutier.com and Stephen Spurrier, "Coming Down to Earth," *Decanter*.

46   Warren Winiarski quote (italics ours) from an address given to the Masters of Wine Institute at an International Symposium in Perth, Australia, April 15, 1997.

46   D. H. Lawrence, *Studies in Classic American Literature*, Garden City, NY: Doubleday, 1955.

CHAPTER EIGHT—WHAT YOU WON'T SEE ON THE LABEL

48   Ronald Searle, *The Illustrated WINESPEAK: Ronald Searle's Wicked World of Winetasting*, London: Souvenir Press, 1983.

CHAPTER NINE—A FLIGHT OF WINES

53   *The New Shorter Oxford English Dictionary*, Ed. Lesley Brown, Oxford: Clarendon Press, 1993.

53   Benjamin Disraeli, *Sybil, or The Two Nations*, London: Oxford University Press, 1926.

53   Lucilio Vanini discussed at length in John Owen, *Skeptics of the Italian Renaissance*, London: Sonnenschein, 1893.

54   Aristotle, *Metaphysics, Books Gamma, Delta, Epsilon*, Trans. Christopher Kirwan, Oxford: Clarendon Press, 1993.

54   Thomas Aquinas, *Commentaries on Aristotle's Metaphysics*, Trans. John P. Rowan, Dumb Ox Books, Indiana: University of Notre Dame, 1995.

54   Immanuel Kant, *Critique of Judgement*, Trans. James Creed Meredith, Revised and Edited by Nicholas Walker, Oxford: Oxford University Press, 2007.

54   T. S. Eliot, *The Use of Poetry and the Use of Criticism*, London: Faber & Faber, 1964.

CHAPTER TEN—AN UNEXAMINED LIFE, AN UNDRUNK WINE

56   Plato, "Apology" in *The Trial and Death of Socrates*, Trans. F. J. Church, London: Macmillan, 1952.

56   José Ortega y Gasset, *What Is Philosophy?* Trans. Mildred Adams, New York: Norton, 1964.

57   Lewis Carroll, *Sylvie and Bruno*, London: Macmillan and Co., 1889.

57–58   Donnell B. Stern, *Unformulated Experience—From Dissociation to Imagination in Psychoanalysis*, Hillsdale, NJ: Analytic Press, 2003.

58   Henry Ward Beecher, *Notes from the Plymouth Pulpit*, New York: Derby and Jackson, 1859.

58   Aldous Huxley, *The Olive Tree—and Other Essays*, London: Chatto and Windus, 1936.

58   Paul Torday, *The Irresistible Inheritance of Wilberforce*, London: Weidenfeld & Nicolson, 2007.

59   Russell Hoban, *The Medusa Frequency*, London: Picador, 1988.

59   Emile Peynaud, *The Taste of Wine: The Art and Taste of Wine Appreciation*, Trans. Michael Schuster, New York: John Wiley and Sons, 1996.

59   Kent Bach, "Why Talk about Wine?" from a paper given at a conference on wine and philosophy held in London, December 2004, and later included (in slightly different form) in Barry C. Smith (Ed.) *Questions of Taste: The Philosophy of Wine*.

59   Gustave Flaubert, *Madame Flaubert*, Trans. Alan Russell, Harmondsworth, UK: Penguin, 1985.

PART II: THE LANGUAGE OF WINE

CHAPTER ELEVEN—TURNING WINE INTO WORDS

63   Emile Peynaud, *The Taste of Wine*.

CHAPTER TWELVE—FLAVORS WEIRD AND WONDERFUL

67   Richard L. Gregory (Ed.), *The Oxford Companion to the Mind*, Oxford: Oxford University Press, 1987.

67   Jean-Anthelme Brillat-Savarin, *The Physiology of Taste*, Trans. Anne Drayton, Harmondsworth, UK: Penguin, 1994.

67   Pliny the Elder, *Natural History—A Selection*.

67–68   For further reading on Democritus, see John Burnet, *Greek Philosophy*, London: Macmillan, 1955.

68   Descartes quote, and "convex/concave" quote concerning Spinoza's parallelism, taken from Robert I. Watson, *The Great Psychologists*.

68   Tasting notes for the 1973 Santenay Gravieres from Jean Lenoir's *Le Nez du Vin* kit.

69   P. J. O'Rourke, *The CEO of the Sofa*, Sydney: Picador, Pan Macmillan Australia, 2001.

69–70   Miguel de Cervantes, *Don Quixote*, Trans. Charles Jarvis, Hertford-shire, UK: Wordsworth Classics, 2000.

70   David Hume, "Of the Standard of Taste."

70   Sun Tzu, *The Art of War*, London: Hodder & Stoughton, 2002.

CHAPTER THIRTEEN—"BOTTLED POETRY"

71   Lines from "The Soul of Wine" and "The Rag-and-Bone-Men's Wine" from Charles Baudelaire, *The Complete Verse*, Volume 1, Trans. Francis Scarfe, London: Anvil, 1986.

71–72   Petronius, *The Satyricon and The Fragments*, Trans. J. P. Sullivan, Harmondsworth, UK: Penguin, 1969.

72   Additional lines from Baudelaire from "The Ragpickers' Wine," Trans. C. F. MacIntyre, *The Flowers of Evil*, Marthiel and Jackson Mathews (Eds.), New York: New Directions, 1989.

72   Guy de Maupassant, *Bel-Ami*, Trans. Douglas Parmée, London: Penguin, 1975.

73   Robert Louis Stevenson, *The Novels and Tales of Robert Louis Stevenson*, New York: Charles Scribner's Sons, 1903.

73   Evelyn Waugh, *Brideshead Revisited*.

73   Matt Kramer, "How Greatness Happens," *Wine Spectator*, December 15, 2007.

74   Steven Pinker first two quotes taken from Peter Calamai, "Of Thought and Metaphor," Toronto Star, January 21, 2007.

74   Jancis Robinson quoted in Barry C. Smith, "The Objectivity of Taste and Tasting" in Barry C. Smith (Ed.), *Questions of Taste: The Philosophy of Wine*.

74   Bruce Palling, "A Legend called Lafleur," *More Intelligent Life*, November 9, 2007.

75   "Passionately entwined" reference from Frank J. Prial, "Wine Talk; Warning: Winespeak Can Often Intoxicate," *New York Times*, January 19, 1994.

75   Steven Pinker, "Block That Metaphor!" *The New Republic Online*, October, 9, 2006.

75   Ernesto Suarez-Toste, "Metaphor Inside the Wine Cellar: On the Ubiquity of Personification Schemas in Winespeak," *metaphoric.de*, December 2007.

CHAPTER FOURTEEN—WHY WINE *APPRECIATION?*

77   G. K. Chesterton quotes, "happiness doubled by wonder" in *The Collected Works of G. K. Chesterton*, Volume 20, "aim of life is appreciation" in *The Collected Works of G. K. Chesterton, The Autobiography*, Volume 16, San Francisco: Ignatius Press, 1988 and 2002.

77   Mark Steyn, "Artie Shaw (1910–2004)," *TheAtlantic.com*, March 2005.

78   Ralph Waldo Emerson, "Experience" in Ralph Waldo Emerson, *Selected Writings*.

CHAPTER FIFTEEN—THE OTHER SIDE OF APPRECIATION

79   Michel de Montaigne, *The Complete Essays*, Trans. M. A. Screech, London: Penguin, 2003.

80   The conflict between menu and wine list is well captured in Francis Percival, "Harmony Vs Gastronomy," *Decanter*, June 2008.

80   Thanks to Nick Allchurch for permission to reproduce his comments.

80   William James, *The Principles of Psychology*, Cambridge, MA: Harvard University Press, 1983.

81   Anthony Bourdain, *Anthony Bourdain Omnibus*, London: Bloomsbury, 2004.

82   Tantalus story quoted from Robert Graves, *The Greek Myths*, Volume 2, Harmondsworth, UK: Penguin, 1986.

82   Charles Darwin, *The Origin of Species*, Harmondsworth, UK: Penguin, 1985.

CHAPTER SIXTEEN—FOR BETTER OR FOR WORSE

84   Jane Austen, *Pride and Prejudice*, Harmondsworth, UK: Penguin, 1995.

84   Honoré de Balzac, *The Physiology of Marriage and Pierre Grassou*, New York: Cosimo, 2005.

85   Thomas Allsop, *Letters, Conversations and Reflections of S. T. Coleridge*, London: Frederick Farrah, 1864.

86   Evelyn Waugh, *Brideshead Revisited*.

86   Sante Lancerio reference taken from Roy Strong, *Feast—A History of Grand Eating*, London: Pimlico, 2003.

87   M. F. K. Fisher, *The Art of Eating*, Hoboken, NJ: Wiley Publishing Inc., 2004.

88–92   Sincere thanks to Pascal Tingaud and Véronique Foureur of Moët & Chandon for their generous assistance in untangling the memory of a distant visit.

CHAPTER SEVENTEEN—THE GEOMETRY OF WINE

93   Ann C. Noble quote taken from Daniel Sogg's "Striking a Balance," *Wine Spectator*, May 31, 2008—an excellent article addressing all aspects of the alcohol debate.

94   Story of Harmonia drawn from Robert Graves, *The Greek Myths*, Volumes 1 and 2, Harmondsworth, UK: Penguin: 1986.

94   Explanation of the golden mean, and reference to Luca Pacioli, taken from the "golden section" entry in *Concise Dictionary of Art and Artists*, Ian Chilvers (Ed.), Oxford: Oxford University Press, 2006.

95   Julian Baggini, *Complaint: From Minor Moans to Principled Protests*, London: Profile Books, 2008.

95–97   E. M. Forster, *Aspects of the Novel*, London: Arnold, 1949.

96   Russell Hoban, *The Medusa Frequency*.

CHAPTER EIGHTEEN—IS IT A BOY OR A GIRL?

98–99   Saintsbury quote, and her own words, from Karen MacNeil, *The Wine Bible*, New York: Workman, 2001.

99   Blonde and Brune legend recounted in Ron Herbst and Sharon Tyler Herbst, *The New Wine Lover's Companion*, New York: Barron's, 2003.

99   An excellent profile of Guigal's Côte Rôtie wines is Sally Easton's "Steeped in Tradition," *Winestate*, September/October 2008.

100   Angelo Gaja reference taken from Houn Hooke, "John Wayne meets his match," *Sydney Morning Herald—Good Living Supplement*, August 8, 2006.

100–102 8 ¹/₂, Directed by Federico Fellini, Written by Ennio Flaiano, Tullio Pinelli, Federico Fellini, & Brunello Rondi, Story by Federico Fellini & Ennio Flaiano, Cineriz, 1963.

100   Reference to Fellini's casting of Mastroianni taken from Ron Tank's obituary article of Mastroianni, *Showbiz*, December 19, 1996.

102–3   *True Grit*, Directed by Henry Hathaway, Written by Marguerite Roberts from the Charles Portis novel, Paramount 1969.

103   Howard Hawks quote and his own words from Charles Taylor, "The 'Duke' and Democracy: On John Wayne," *Dissent*, Winter, 2008.

103   Gaja *Darmagi* anecdote from Jancis Robinson, Ed., *The Oxford Companion to Wine*.

103–4   Max Lake, *Scents and Sensuality*, London: John Murray, 1989.

CHAPTER NINETEEN—THE FIFTH DIMENSION

105   Galileo quote taken from Sean Thackrey's "Winemaker" Web site www.winemaker.net.

105–6   M. A. Amerine and E. B. Roessler, *Wines—Their Sensory Evaluation*, San Francisco: W. H. Freeman & Co., 1976.

105   Lawrence Osborne, *The Accidental Connoisseur*, New York: North Point Press, 2004.

106   (The Distilled) Kingsley Amis, *Everyday Drinking*, New York: Bloomsbury, 2008.

106–7   Roald Dahl, "Taste" in *Taste and Other Tales*, Essex, UK: Longman, 1992.

107 "A glance at the label ..." quote attributed to Duimpie Bayly in Michael Green, *Around and About: Memoirs of a South African Newspaperman*, Cape Town: New Africa Books, 2004.

107 The Roald Dahl quote from *My Uncle Oswald* taken from Gert Crum, Michael Broadbent, and Phillipe Claudel, *Le Domaine de la Romanée-Conti*, Uitgeverij Lannoo Nv, 2006.

108 Peter Goldie, *On Personality*, London: Routledge, 2004.

108 Matt Kramer, "What It Really Takes," *Wine Spectator*, August 31, 2008.

108 Emile Peynaud, *The Taste of Wine*.

108–10 *Sideways*, Fox Searchlight Pictures, 2004.

PART III: HOW WINE DESCRIBES US

CHAPTER TWENTY—GAMES PEOPLE PLAY

115–16 Eric Berne, *Games People Play*, New York: Penguin, 1964.

116–17 If you're not so fortunate as to have a complete vertical collection of Château Mouton-Rothschild, labels can be viewed at www.theartistlabels.com.

117 Hugh Johnson tasting note for the Leeuwin Estate chardonnay from "Out with the Old," *Decanter*, July 2008.

117 Simone Horgan-Furlong quotes taken from Natasha Hughes' excellent article "Designs on Wine," *Decanter*, April 2008.

117 See a selection of the Leeuwin Estate Art Series labels at www.leeuwinestate.com,au.

117–18 Ronsard quote, as well as a selection of the Josmeyer Artist Label Series wines artwork can be found at www.josmeyer.com.

119 Hubert de Boüard quote taken from Stephen Brook, "A Game of Life and Death," *Decanter*, June 2008.

122 Sam Neill quotes taken from Jackie McDonald's profile "His Brilliant Career," *Selector Life Food Wine*, Winter, 2008.

CHAPTER TWENTY-ONE—"TRUTH THAT PEEPS OVER THE GLASSES' EDGE ..."

123 Tacitus quoted from Immanuel Kant, *Anthropology from a Pragmatic Point of View*.

123 Herodotus, *The Histories*, Trans. Aubrey de Sélincourt, Harmondsworth, UK: Penguin, 1996.

123 Horace, *The Complete "Odes" and "Epodes,"* Trans. David West, Oxford: Oxford World Classics, 2000.

123 Plutarch, *Moralia*, Volume 1, Oxford: Heinemann, 1927.

123 Oscar Wilde, *The Importance of Being Earnest*.

124 Pliny the Elder, *Natural History—A Selection*.

124   "Truth never hurts the teller" quote from Robert Browning, *Fifine at the Fair*, Whitefish, MT: Kessinger Publisher, 2004.

124   Immanuel Kant, *Anthropology from a Pragmatic Point of View*.

124–25 Evelyn Waugh, *Brideshead Revisited*.

125   Plato, *The Symposium*, Trans. Christopher Gill, Harmondsworth, UK: Penguin, 2003.

125   *Monty Python Live at the Hollywood Bowl*, Columbia Pictures, Directed by Terry Hughes and Ian McNaughton, Written by the Monty Python team, Columbia, 1982.

125   William Shakespeare, *As You Like It: A Comedy*, Cambridge: Cambridge University Press, 1959.

125   Terence quote taken from Maguelonne Toussant-Samat, *A History of Food*.

125   Euripides, *The Bacchae*.

125   William Shakespeare, *Macbeth*, The Challis Shakespeare, Sydney: University of Sydney Press, 1981.

126   Seneca, "On tranquility of mind," *The Stoic Philosophy of Seneca: Essays and Letters*, Trans. and Ed. Moses Hadas, New York: Norton, 1968.

126–27 Roger Scruton, "Wine and Intoxication" in Barry C Smith (Ed.) *Questions of Taste: The Philosophy of Wine*.

127–28 Robert Browning, *Browning, a Selection*, Harmondsworth, UK: Penguin, 1981.

127   G. K. Chesterton, *Robert Browning*, New York: Macmillan, 1903.

127   Ralph Waldo Emerson, "Montaigne: Or, the Skeptic" chapter in "Representative Men" in *Essays and Lectures*, New York: Library of America, 1983.

127–28 Further information on Browning and his poems can be found in Clyde de L. Ryals, *The Life of Browning*, London: Wiley-Blackwell, 1996.

128   Aldous Huxley, *Brave New World*, London: Vintage Classics, 2007.

128   Philip K. Dick, *Do Androids Dream of Electric Sheep*, New York: Ballantine, 1991.

128   Iain M. Banks "Culture" novels include *The Player of Games, Use of Weapons, Excession, Look to Windward*, London: Orbit Books.

128–29 Kingsley Amis, *Everyday Drinking*.

128–29 Franz Kafka, "The Metamorphosis" Trans. Willa and Edwin Muir, in *The Collected Short Stories of Franz Kafka*, London: Penguin, 1988.

129   George Gordon Lord Byron, "Don Juan," *Poetical Works*, Oxford: Oxford University Press, 1986.

129   Pliny the Elder, *Natural History—A Selection*.

CHAPTER TWENTY-TWO—A BEAUTIFUL WINE

131   Frederick Turner, "On Beauty" in Frederick Turner *Rebirth of Value: Meditations on Beauty, Ecology, Religion, and Education*, New York: State University of New York Press, 1991.

132   Robert Mondavi quote taken from his obituary, "A beacon to the world for Napa Valley wines," *Sydney Morning Herald*, May 20, 2008.

132   Fannie Farmer and Monroe C. Beardsley quotes drawn from epigrams to Part One of *Arguing About Art*, Third Edition, Alex Neill and Aaron Ridley (Eds.), London and New York: Routledge, 2008.

132   Thomas Aquinas and Jacques Maritain quotes taken from Deal W. Hudson, "The Ecstasy Which Is Creation: The Shape of Maritain's Aesthetics," in *Understanding Maritain: Philosopher and Friend*, Deal W. Hudson and Matthew J. Mancini (Eds.), Macon, GA: Mercer University Press, 1987.

132–33 St. Augustine, *Confessions*, Trans. R. S. Pine-Coffin, Harmondsworth, UK: Penguin, 1986.

133   Fyodor Dostoyevsky, *The Brothers Karamazov*, Trans. Ernest J. Simmons, New York: Harper, 1960.

133   Johann Wolfgang von Goethe, *Maxims and Reflections*, Trans. Elisabeth Stopp, Harmondsworth, UK: Penguin, 1998.

133   Definition of the "institutional" theory of art, and other acknowledged quotes, from Tim Crane, "Art as an Aesthetic Object" in Barry C. Smith (Ed.) *Questions of Taste: The Philosophy of Wine*.

133   Boris Groys, *Art Power*, Cambridge: MIT Press, 2008.

134   Pygmalion lines translated by John Dryden in Ovid, *Metamorphoses*, Trans. Garth, Dryden et al., New York: Garland, 1976.

134   William Butler Yeats, "Among School Children" in *The Poems*, London: Everyman, 1999.

135   Longinus, "On the Sublime" in Aristotle/Horace/Longinus, *Classical Literary Criticism*, Trans. T. S. Dorsch, Harmondsworth, UK: Penguin, 1986.

135–36 For a more comprehensive history and analysis of the sublime refer to "the sublime" entry in *A Companion to Aesthetics*, David Cooper (Ed.), Oxford: Blackwell, 1995.

135–36 Immanuel Kant quotes from Immanuel Kant, *Critique of Judgment*.

135   William Shakespeare, *Twelfth Night*, Harmondsworth, UK: Penguin, 1981.

136   Paul Guyer, *Values of Beauty: Historical Essays in Aesthetics*, Cambridge: Cambridge University Press, 2005.

136   Schopenhauer quote taken from Julian Young, *Schopenhauer*, New York: Routledge, 2005.

136   Oscar Wilde, *The Picture of Dorian Gray*, Harmondsworth, UK: Penguin, 1985.

137   Elisabeth Telfer, "Food as Art" in Alex Neill and Aaron Ridley (Eds.), *Arguing about Art*.

138   Delacroix quote taken from Jonathan Miles' riveting account of the events surrounding the shipwreck of the frigate Medusa and Gericault's efforts to capture this on canvas, *Medusa*, London: Jonathan Cape, 2007.

139   Walter Pater, *The Renaissance: Studies in Art and Poetry*, Oxford and New York: Oxford University Press, 1986.

139   Richard Wollheim, *Art and Its Objects*, Cambridge: Cambridge University Press, 1980.

139   Carolyn Korsmeyer, "The Meaning of Taste and the Taste of Meaning" in Alex Neill and Aaron Ridley (Eds.), *Arguing about Art*.

139–40   Quote purportedly made to Hegel taken from Howard G. Goldberg, "Wine Talk," *The New York Times*, January 21, 1987.

140   Georg Wilhelm Friedrich Hegel, *Hegel: On the Arts*, Trans. Henry Paolucci, New York: Frederick Ungar Publishing Co., 1979.

140   Beardsley quote "no taste symphonies" from Alex Neill and Aaron Ridley (Eds.), *Arguing about Art*.

140   Alex Ross, *The Rest Is Noise: Listening to the Twentieth Century*, New York: Farrar, Straus and Giroux, 2007.

141   Denis Dutton, seven universal signatures of art from Steven Pinker, *The Blank Slate*.

141   Marcel Duchamp quote taken from Arthur Coleman Danto, *After the End of Art: Contemporary Art and the Pale of History*, Princeton, NJ: Princeton University Press, 1998.

141   "All art is quite useless" quote from Oscar Wilde, *The Picture of Dorian Gray*.

142   Boris Pasternak, *Doctor Zhivago*, Trans. Max Hayward and Manya Harari, London: Collins and Harvell, 1966.

142   Tom Stoppard, *Artist Descending a Staircase, and, Where Are They Now? Two Plays for Radio*, London: Faber & Faber, 1973.

142   Catherine Milner, "The Tate Values Excrement More Highly Than Gold," *UK Telegraph*, June 30, 2002.

CHAPTER TWENTY-THREE—WINE AND MAMMON

143   Prominent winemaker Bill Cadman quoted by Lawrence Osborne, *The Accidental Connoisseur*.

143   Pliny the Elder, *Natural History—A Selection*.

143   Oscar Wilde, *The Picture of Dorian Gray*.

144   Thomas Harris, *Hannibal*, New York: Dell, 1999.

144–45   Steven Pinker, *The Blank Slate*.

145   James Laube, "The Untouchables," *Wine Spectator*, October 31, 2008.

145   Report of wine price versus pleasure experiments at CalTech and Stanford from Jonah Lehrer, *The Boston Globe*, February 24, 2008.

146   Eric Hebborn, *Confessions of a Master Forger*, London: Cassell, 1997.

146   Benjamin Wallace, *The Billionaire's Vinegar: The Mystery of the World's Most Expensive Bottle of Wine*, New York: Crown Publishers, 2008.

147   Details of Pétrus vertical theft from Jennifer Fiedler, "Pétrus Vertical Stolen from Restaurant," *Wine Spectator*, April 30, 2008.

147   Details of the e-tongue from Oliver Styles, "Electronic tongues set to beat human tasters," *Decanter.com*, August 6, 2008.

CHAPTER TWENTY-FOUR—THE TYRANNY OF *TERROIR*

149   *Mondovino*, Written and Directed by Jonathan Nossiter, Diaphana Films, 2004.

150   Madame Gasqueton quoted in Richard Farmer, "Wine Quality: Does Terroir Matter?" www.glug.com.au, October 14, 2005.

151–54   All Harold Bloom quotes from Harold Bloom, *The Western Canon: The Books and Schools of the Ages*, New York: Riverhead Books, 1995.

151   *Sideways*, Fox Searchlight Pictures, 2004.

152   Lawrence Osborne, *The Accidental Connoisseur*.

152   Charles Collins quote taken from the "Brettanomyces" entry on Jamie Goode's wineanorack.com site, originally published in *Harpers Wine and Spirit Weekly*, April 18, 2003.

152   Jacques Barzun, *From Dawn to Decadence: 500 Years of Western Cultural Life, 1500 to the Present*, New York: HarperCollins Publishers, 2000.

155   Antonini quote from Max Allen, "Blurring the Boundaries," *Langton's Magazine*.

CHAPTER TWENTY-FIVE—MERRY, MERRY MERITAGE

156–62   George M. Taber, *Judgment of Paris*, New York: Scribner, 2005.

158–59   Leon Festinger, Henry W. Riecken, and Stanley Schachter, *When Prophecy Fails: A Social and Psychological Study of a Modern Group That Predicted the End of the World*, Minneapolis: University of Minnesota Press, 1956.

159–60   Leon Festinger, *Theory of Cognitive Dissonance*, Stanford: Stanford University Press, 1957.

159   H. P. Lovecraft, *The Call of Cthulhu and Other Weird Stories*, Harmondsworth, UK: Penguin, 1999.

160   Eliot Aronson, "The Return of the Repressed: Dissonance Theory Makes a Comeback," *Psychological Enquiry*, 3, 4, 1992.

162   Wine judge quote taken from *Decanter*, "Primeurs," July 2008.

CHAPTER TWENTY-SIX—EMPTY VESSELS

164   H. D. (Hilda Doolittle) "Wine Bowl" in Margaret Ferguson, Mary Jo Salter, Jon Stallworthy (Eds.) *The Norton Anthology of Poetry*, Fourth Edition, New York: W. W. Norton and Company, 1996.

164–65   Jean-Anthelme Brillat-Savarin, *The Physiology of Taste*.

165   "Sharing cup" superstition from Iona Opie and Moira Tatem (Eds.), *Oxford Dictionary of Superstitions*, Oxford and New York: Oxford University Press, 1996.

165   Pliny the Elder, *Natural History—A Selection*.

166   Further information on history, design and quality charter of *La Mitrale* bottle can be found at the official Web site www.lamitrale.com.

166   *The Godfather*, Directed by Francis Ford Coppola, Screenplay by Mario Puzo and Francis Ford Coppola from Mario Puzo's novel *The Godfather*, Paramount Pictures, 1972.

167   Karen McNeil, *The Wine Bible*.

167–68   Information and quotes (including those from Brian Croser and Hugh Johnson) concerning the wine industry's debate over closure types and efficacies drawn from George M. Taber, *To Cork or Not to Cork: Tradition, Romance, Science and the Battle for the Wine Bottle*, New York: Scribner, 2007.

167   Interesting points and explanations concerning wine development in larger and smaller format bottles can be found in M. W. Beverley Blanning's, "Does Size Really Matter," *Decanter*, December 2007.

CHAPTER TWENTY-SEVEN—THE DEATH OF "GENERATION WINE"?

170   Jonathan Stockhammer quotes, and quote "where emerging wealth is coming to classical music ..." taken from Erik Jensen, "Classical music dying, says young conductor," *Sydney Morning Herald*, January 17, 2008.

171   Quotes from the creators of the *Kami No Shizuku* manga strip from Norimitsu Onishi's "Next Week, Our Hero Chooses a Médoc," *New York Times*, October 22, 2008.

171   Samples of *Kami No Shizuku* can be viewed at mangafox.com.

172   Stephen Charters MW and Matthew Stubbs MW quotes taken from Matthew Stubbs, "What do the French *really* know about wine?" *Decanter*, September 2008.

172   Douglas Rushkoff quoted from *Playing the Future: What We Can Learn from Digital Kids* in Lee Siegel, *Against The Machine: Being Human in the Age of the Electronic Mob*, New York: Spiegel and Grau, 2008.

172   Scott Karp (journalist) and psychologist Maryanne Wolf quoted from Nicholas Carr, "Is Google Making Us Stupid?" *The Atlantic*, July/August 2008.

172   Lines from "Choruses from 'The Rock'" in T. S. Eliot, *Collected Poems 1909–1962*, London: Faber & Faber, 1986.

172–73   Plato, *The Republic*.

173   Toby Young, "Lulled by the Celebritariat," *Prospect Magazine*, Issue 153, December 2008.

173   Frank Furedi, *Where Have All The Intellectuals Gone?* Second Edition, London and New York: Continuum, 2006.

173–74   Mark Bauerlein, *The Dumbest Generation: How the Digital Age Stupefies Young Americans and Jeopardizes Futures*, New York: Jeremy P. Tarcher/Penguin, 2008.

173–74   Allan Bloom, *The Closing of the American Mind*, New York: Touchstone, 1988.

174   Jonah Lehrer, "Daydream Achiever," *The Boston Globe*, August 31, 2008.

174   Andrew Waggoner, "The Colonization of Silence." *NewMusicbox.org*, August 8, 2007.

175   Liam Julian, review of Mark Bauerlein's *The Dumbest Generation*, "iPods and Nimrods," *The New Criterion*, October, 2008.

175–76   Matt Kramer, "The 21st-Century Wine Cellar," *Wine Spectator*, September 30, 2008.

176   Interesting speculations on the implications of genetically modified wines can be found in the articles "Vine Times" and "Unleash the War on Terroir," both in *The Economist*, December 19, 2007.

CHAPTER TWENTY-EIGHT—A VERY HUMAN THING

177   Helen Keller, *Helen Keller's Journal*, London: Michael Joseph, 1938.

177   Johann Wolfgang von Goethe, *Elective Affinities*, Trans. R. J. Hollingdale, Harmondsworth, UK: Penguin, 1986.

177–79   Michael Pollan, *The Botany of Desire: A Plant's-Eye View of the World*, New York: Random House, 2001.

178   Luigi Pirandello, "The Rules of the Game," Trans. William Murray, in *To Clothe the Naked and Two Other Plays*, New York: E. P. Dutton, 1962.

179   Barry C. Smith, "The Objectivity of Tastes and Tasting" in Barry C Smith (Ed.) *Questions of Taste: The Philosophy of Wine*.

179   Quote on "listening to the vineyard" an adaptation of words attributed to Elias Fernandez, winemaker at Schafer Vineyards, as given by Larry Walker in *Wines & Vines*, April 1, 2004.

180   Harry Stack Sullivan, "The illusion of personal individuality," *The Fusion of Psychiatry and Social Science*, New York: Norton, 1971.

180   Robert Louis Stevenson, *The Strange Case of Dr. Jekyll and Mr. Hyde and Other Stories*, Harmondsworth, UK: Penguin, 1979.

Index

About the Authors

EVAN MITCHELL worked for twelve years as a sommelier in fine-dining restaurants and now consults to the hospitality industry on the place of wine within the dining experience. He graduated with honors in English literature from the University of Sydney with a thesis on psychoanalytical themes in American literature.

BRIAN MITCHELL holds a PhD in psychology from the University of Sydney. After several years in clinical practice, he established his international consultancy specializing in performance management.

The Psychology of Wine is the authors' second book.